D0557011

Three Years, Eleven Months, 29 Days

But Who's Counting

Three Years, Eleven Months, 29 Days

But Who's Counting

Andrew Z. (Chet) Adkins III

Warning: This book contains three languages:
English, Navy, and military.

Some readers may find two of the languages offensive.

DEDICATION

This book is dedicated to all U.S. military:
Those who have served.
Those who are serving.
Those who will serve.

Thank you for your service to this great country of ours

Previous Books by Andrew Z. Adkins III

You Can't Get Much Closer Than This:
Combat with Company H, 317th Infantry Regiment, 80th Division

The Lawyer's Guide to Practice Management System Software

Computerized Case Management:
Choosing and Implementing the Right Software for You

CONTENTS

ACKNOWLEDGMENTS

After I wrote *You Can't Get Much Closer Than This: Combat with Company H, 317th Infantry Regiment, 80th Division*, a WWII book of my father's experiences in Europe, I was literally bitten by the writing bug.

When I started this project, I wanted to share some of my own Navy experiences, primarily with my kids. My time in the Navy was one of the most important in my life. Initially, it was a challenge to figure out which stories to describe and which to leave out. I took the easy route—I wrote down everything I could remember. Using the letters I wrote home to my mom and dad and additional research, I remembered a lot. The Kitty Hawk Veterans Association was also a goldmine of information.

I asked several friends and family to help read the initial manuscript. All volunteered their precious time and provided invaluable feedback. My good friend, Linda Kirby, who spent two years in the U.S. Coast Guard was one of the early reviewers and pointed out several things I had not thought of. My father-in-law, Dr. Rufus K. Broadaway, also reviewed and provided some insightful comments based on his experiences during WWII in the 82nd Airborne Division.

Dean Turner, my friend and work colleague helped tremendously with aircraft operations—his 26 years as a Naval Aviator provided a unique perspective I couldn't find elsewhere. My sister, Anne, also read the initial draft and helped me better understand life from the home front.

I owe an unending debt of gratitude to my loving and patient wife, Becky, who has put up with me for 30+ years telling and retelling many of these stories. She also read the initial draft and while I thought she knew everything, I often heard her chuckle, a sure sign that I was making the right points.

After I finished the first draft, I thought it would be worthwhile if I could revisit some of the old haunts during my Naval career. I asked the Navy for three things. One, visit Chicago Great Lakes to observe new recruit training. Two, spend a few days aboard an active aircraft carrier, observing flight deck operations in today's Navy. And three, to land on a carrier. The Navy granted all three requests, including a few days aboard USS Ronald Reagan, CVN-76. I got to hang out with Crash & the yellow shirts.

The older I get, the more proud I am of being a veteran. I admire and respect *all* U.S. veterans from *all* services. While world politics never cease to shift and while our own country's politics sometimes get in the way, our nation's military remains strong and committed. My dad, who fought in the ETO with the 80th Division during WWII, always said that the United States is the best country to live in and I couldn't agree more.

1 THE BIG DECISION

"Dismissed for Academic Reasons." There it was in black and white in May 1973. Now, why on earth would Florida State University want me to depart their wonderful institution? Probably it was because this was my first year away from home and my grades were not up to par. I can't believe they would kick me out because of my zero-point-seven grade point average.

My Mom and Dad are going to be pissed. What do I tell them? I've been up here for almost a year. They've paid the whole way, both for school and a "little more." I thought I was doing alright. After all, I was at the ripe old age of seventeen when I first came to FSU. Of course, it took me a few weeks to get used to being away from home. And sure, since the drinking age was eighteen, I partied a little—OK, I partied a LOT. But that is no excuse to be flunked out of college.

I was into scuba diving big time and even worked at a local scuba dive shop, North Central Florida Diving Center, owned by my friend and scuba instructor, Barry Kerley. We dove the wrecks and jetties off Panama City, but my favorite spot to dive was the St. Marks River, right off the bridge in Woodenville. I loved finding old molded glass bottles, clay pipes, and arrowheads. But then again, there was work to be done at school. The only problem was that I obviously didn't think it was *that* important.

A thousand thoughts ran through my mind. I could always join the Army and follow in my dad's footsteps. That's probably what he might want me to do, even though we were still fighting a war in Vietnam. But, after talking with my friend Ed Kelly at the dive shop and his great times and adventures in the Navy, maybe I should go and talk with them. And since I loved to scuba dive, there are probably more opportunities to dive with the Navy than with the Army.

I borrowed my roommate's bike the next day and rode down to the local Navy recruiting office in downtown Tallahassee. I can't remember the recruiter's name, but I do remember he was very cordial, informative, and seemed trustworthy. He of course saw me as one more for his monthly quota though I didn't feel that at all during the visit.

After we talked a little while, he gave me a book of Navy jobs to look through—it was pretty thick. So much to read with so little time, and since I didn't have a long attention span, it did not take me long to point to the job I wanted. It was almost like spinning a globe and stopping it with your finger saying, "here's where I want to go."

Actually, my thought process was very logical. I loved scuba diving, so that brought me to the Navy. I loved being outdoors and I had always been interested in airplanes. As a kid, I probably assembled about every model airplane there was and I was *truly* fascinated with airplanes. So the Navy job I picked was an Aviation Boatswain's Mate Handler. "No problem," the recruiter said. "The Navy needs ABHs and you will probably be able to go anywhere in the world you want." He probably said that to *everyone* that walked through his door.

Since I was eighteen I could legally sign documents. "Sign on the dotted line. Press hard, the third copy's yours." And that was it. Many people have asked over the years if I signed up for the Navy to really join ("it's not just a job, it's an adventure") or if was I worried about being drafted into the Army. It was 1973 and even though the Vietnam War was winding down, there was still a draft. Honestly, I wanted to join the Navy. I don't think the thought of being drafted ever crossed my mind.

The recruiter did tell me that when I reported to the Armed Forces Induction Center in Jacksonville, where all newly recruited young men and women headed to the military in Florida check in, it would be a long day of waiting and processing. "No problem," I said. "I've made it through three quarters of college at FSU; I can handle it."

A few days later, I was working at the dive shop when my mom and dad called me. My dad said, "Son, we just got your report card and wanted to talk with you about your grades." "Yeah, I know. I didn't do as well as I should have." Before my dad or mom could say another thing I blurted out, "I joined the Navy." There was a silence—a *long* deafening silence. I think I heard a collective gasp from the other end of the phone. My mom said, "What?" I told them again.

I forgot whatever else was said during that phone call, but my mom told me years later that she and my dad were very proud of me at that moment. They said that I had made one of the most important decisions in my life. More importantly, I stuck with it, all *three years, eleven months, and 29 days.*

2 CHECKING IN
Welcome To Hell

My sister Anne lived in St. Augustine, Florida and I wanted to visit her one more time before going into the Navy. I borrowed my mom's '72 blue Oldsmobile Cutlass Supreme and headed to St. Augustine. I drove by our place at Kingsley Lake, again another thing to check off the list before going into the Navy. From there, I drove down Highway 16 through a small town called Penney Farms, named for one of its most famous residents, Mr. Penney, as in J.C. Penney.

Coming into the town, the posted speed limit was 55 mph and there was no sign warning of the change of speed to 45 mph—it just sort of sneaks up on you. Even though I had driven through this small podunk town dozens of times, this was the first time I ever saw a cop. Unfortunately, he saw me, too, cruising about sixty miles per hour.

"What's the hurry, son?" the trooper asked. "I'm on the way to visit my sister in St. Augustine, sir." My dad always demanded that my sister and I say "sir" and "ma'am" to others. "I just joined the Navy and I wanted to visit her and say goodbye before I ship out." I figured what the hell; I'd try to impress the cop. It didn't work. I got a speeding ticket.

A few days later, I was checking into the Armed Forces Induction Center and the personnel officer asked me if I had any outstanding traffic tickets. I was not going to lie, so I told him that I did, but I should be able to take care of it at a later time. He informed me that I could not enlist until I cleared my record and took care of the speeding ticket. Well, that was my first disappointment. I couldn't join the Navy... not yet.

It did not take long to take care of the speeding ticket. My dad was a lawyer in Gainesville and he called the local judge in Green Cove Springs, the county seat where Penney Farms was located. The judge told my dad to tell

3

me to drive over to the Green Cove Springs courthouse to meet with him and to make sure to obey the posted speed limit.

The judge and I had a nice chat and because I was joining the Navy, I think he was a little more lenient with me than he would have been with some other half-cocked, young kid who was speeding in his county. He realized I could not enlist in the Navy until I paid the fine. "Fifty bucks and make the check payable to Green Cove Springs."

I was cleared to join the Navy. I called the recruiter and he told me to show up at the Induction Center the following Tuesday morning, July 10, 1973 at seven a.m. sharp. They even made arrangements for us to stay at the Heart of Jacksonville Hotel the night before, as well as breakfast and a free bus ride. I got in a little early the day before and had made arrangements to have dinner with Elaine Harris, an old friend of mine from Kingsley Lake.

The next morning at five a.m., all of us potential recruits received a wakeup call, herded down to breakfast at the hotel, checked out, and ushered onto the bus that would take us to the Induction Center and be our last ride as free men.

I don't remember the total number of young men at the Induction Center, but I do remember that five of us ended up being assigned to the Orlando Naval Training Center, otherwise known as boot camp. I was placed in charge of our little group because I had a full year of college (did they know I "graduated" with a 0.7 GPA?). I was also assigned an E-2 rank, Seaman Apprentice. All the other low-lifes were ranked as E-1s, Seaman Recruits.

The Tallahassee recruiter was right; it *was* a long day at the Induction Center. I don't remember all the wonderful things we did during the day other than waiting around, talking with Navy personnel in their shiny white summer uniforms, filling out paperwork, and properly answering the question, "Are you a homosexual?"

This is where I first learned the phrase, "Hurry up and wait," something I would repeat many times during my short career in the Navy. I do remember being stretched out across a row of chairs napping when some big lug in a white Navy uniform kicked my feet and ordered me to sit up straight. I did not know what to think and since this was the start of a new adventure in my life, I figured I would do what he said. I did not want to screw up a good thing before it started.

Has anyone ever told you to "Turn your head and cough?" Well, you hear it a lot in the Induction Center. Basically, you stand in your underwear along with a couple of dozen other recruits-to-be. All are facing forward. The doctor comes in with a Navy hospital corpsman following close behind. The corpsman carries a box of latex gloves—this does not look good.

"You men on the right, turn your head to the right; you men on the left, turn your head to the left. Now drop your shorts." The doc walks down the line of men, grabs your nuts and tells you to "turn your head and cough." I guess he was checking to see if you can do two things at one time (like chew gum and walk). Once he was done with you, he yanked off the latex glove, grabbed another one from the corpsman, and proceeded to the next man. I thought to myself, "What does this guy do on vacation for fun?"

Just when you think you've been humiliated enough, the doc orders "men on the left, turn to the left; men on the right, turn to the right. Now, drop your shorts and bend over, reach behind, and spread your cheeks." Oh no, what's happening now? Well, the doc goes down the line of men looking at butt holes, all twenty-four of them. God only knows what he was looking for. I certainly was not hiding anything. I passed that test, too. Geez, can we get a little more humiliated? I didn't ask that out loud, but I bet every one of the new recruits in that room at that time was wondering the exact same thing.

After losing all sense of privacy, those of us who passed the physical exams (I often wondered who couldn't pass those) were sworn in. While it was a pronounced speech, I felt that I had taken a major step in my life—I was now enlisted in the United States Navy.

We left the Induction Center on a Trailways bus heading south to Orlando, about a three hour drive, arriving at the Orlando Naval Training Center around midnight. We were met by a big, burly guy dressed in Navy whites.

We were placed in a temporary holding company for a few days, awaiting more recruits until we had enough to build a company of eighty men. There were all sorts of us: guys who had nowhere else to go, guys who had the choice between going to jail or joining Uncle Sam's Sailing Club, and guys like me who wanted to become a man. That is, we didn't have a clue what we wanted to do with our lives.

The first morning we woke to the sound of a fifty-gallon metal garbage can being kicked down the middle of the barracks and some asshole shouting, "Get the fuck up. Drop your cocks and grab your socks. You've got fifteen minutes to shit, shower, and shave." Welcome to the United States Navy— it's 0400 (pronounced "O four hundred"). That's four o'clock in the frigging morning. Before heading to the bathroom, we first had to stand in front of our bunks to be counted to make sure no one had jumped the fence to go AWOL (Absent without Leave).

Chow was served starting at 0600 (6:00 a.m.). How they determined which company went when was a mystery to me. Chow lines were long, but they moved fast. Here I was introduced to one of the most beloved meals in the Navy: Shit on a Shingle, which is chipped beef in white gravy on toast. It wasn't half bad, especially if you added enough salt and pepper. But I was wondering, where were the bacon and eggs? Where were the biscuits like my mom used to make? My God, how can anyone eat this crap?

The first couple of days we were lined up for all sorts of fun activities, starting with haircuts. By lined up, I mean we were nice and tight, or as you get more used to it, the Navy term is "Nut to Butt." It was funny because for those of us who grew up in the seventies, long hair was in. Most new recruits had long hair.

We were all lined up standing at attention outside the barber shop. There were about five or six barber chairs in the place. There was also about two feet of hair on the floor, almost like walking through a field of wheat. I got into the chair and while my hair was not that long, I asked the guy to "take a little off the top." Well, after thirty seconds (the barbers had a contest to see who could shave a new recruit's hair off in the shortest amount of time, sort of like shaving wool off a sheep), he was done with me and said, "How's that smartass? Now, get the fuck out of my chair." Welcome to the United States Navy.

Once done with our new crew cuts, we gathered outside in a straight line, again standing at attention. Funny thing though; I did not recognize anyone since we had all had our locks trimmed. "Is that you, Smith?" I asked someone that looked a little familiar. I'm sure I looked as funny to everyone else as they did to me.

Besides being woken up at 0400 with some asshole kicking a garbage can down the middle of the barracks and screaming at the top of his lungs some vulgar obscenities, we got into a somewhat regular routine those first few days: early morning calisthenics, three meals a day, and cleaning our barracks. I thought to myself, this isn't so bad. Was I in for a surprise.

3 BOOT CAMP
Company 163

The Orlando Naval Training Center (NTC) was first commissioned on July 1, 1968. It "was established to enhance the manpower training capabilities of the United States Navy." Navy boot camp is different than the other military branches because you are trained with the goal of serving on a ship, so you don't have all the field and weapons training as in the U.S. Army or U.S. Marine Corps. In the same sense, they were not taught to tie knots, moor ships, or put out fires in a compartment.

Orlando NTC was the final of three active training facilities for Navy recruits, the others being Great Lakes Naval Training Center Illinois and San Diego Naval Training Center. I later learned there were about 3,500 to 4,000 recruits at Orlando NTC at any one time. There were five barracks, each housing twelve recruit companies of about eighty men.

The central dining area, also known as the mess hall, could feed up to 4,600 recruits at one time. There was also a Chapel, a Community Center, a large, Olympic-sized swimming pool, an outside obstacle course, and the omnipresent Grinder—a four-acre concrete slab where we held daily and frequent Physical Training (PT). There was even a mock ship on the site, called the *Blue Jacket*.

Boot camp is normally eight weeks of mental and physical training, both rigorous and demanding. Training is broken out by weeks, each week building upon the previous week. If you screwed up, then you could be sent back a week or more, depending upon how bad you screwed up. Typical incidents that would send a recruit back a week included smoking without authorization, failure to follow orders, and fraternizing with the wrong people at the wrong time. We probably lost eight to ten recruits during my time in boot camp, the worst being sent back two weeks for smoking in the wrong place at the wrong time with the wrong person.

Three days after arriving at Orlando NTC, we had enough men to form a real company, at least a company of young recruits. Our temporary drill instructor herded us into an auditorium and we were introduced to Aviation Machinist's Mate-Jet, First Class (ADJ-1) Louis Wright, our Company Commander (CC). They are called Recruit Division Commanders (RDC) now. Companies were formed in sequential number order. From now on, our company would be known as Company 163. Petty Officer Wright seemed like a nice enough guy, but I was about to get another surprise over the next few weeks. He would be our mother and father, our judge and jury, and in some cases, we would think he was the devil's right-hand man.

Boot camp was supposed to be eight weeks. For some reason unbeknownst to us, we would complete recruit training in six weeks. To this day, I still don't know why it was cut to six weeks, but at the time, six was fine with us.

Once formed into a company, the first week in boot camp was Processing Week or P-week where we were issued clothing and our dog tags, got medical and dental checkups and our shots, and began to learn how to become a sailor in today's Navy. We called it Hell Week because (as I learned years later) the main job of the company commander, drill instructor, or whatever they wanted to be called, was to break down each recruit individually and build the company back up as a team. In fact, the first letter I wrote home to my mom and dad from boot camp began, "Dear Mom & Pop: This place is a hell hole!" and it went downhill from that.

Of course, I did not realize that at the time. I just thought PO Wright was the meanest son-of-a-bitch I had ever met. He also had a mean look about him, too; the kind of look that made you not want to piss him off. He would yell at anyone and everyone for everything and anything. He would single out a recruit and yell at him. If one person did not answer him loud enough, he would have everyone on the floor in pushup position.

Each CC selected four recruits for leadership roles in the company. This included a Recruit Chief Petty Officer (RCPO), a Master-at-Arms (MAA), a Yeoman, and an Education Training Officer (ETO). I was selected to be the Yeoman of the company since I was dumb enough to raise my hand when the CC asked if anyone could type.

I did not realize it at the time, but the Yeoman's job involved a lot of paperwork: mostly morning reports of who was present, who was missing, who was in Sickbay, inspection reports, and so forth. In the Army, they called this position the Company Clerk. It was not much of a glamour job, but because of that position, I got the bottom rack closest to the bathroom (or was that because my last name started with an A?) I also got out of many of the cleaning details, so I was OK with that.

The first day in our new company after morning chow we marched over to the Quartermaster's building to be issued clothing. Our class (there were several companies in our class that would graduate on the same day) was the first to get the new Navy uniforms which we all thought sucked, but then nobody asked us for our opinion. Everyone was issued three sets of uniforms. Instead of the sharp-looking denim blue jeans with bell bottoms and button-down denim shirts, we got the new navy-blue utility pants, pull-over blue utility shirts, and a navy-blue ball cap, now called a "cover."

We were measured for "whites" which was the summer dress uniform that consisted of a pair of white-zippered trousers and a short-sleeve white button-down shirt, not the white long-sleeve jumpers we had seen on the Navy recruiting posters. We also got fitted for the new Navy dress blues which were called CPO jackets, a double-breasted button coat, instead of the Navy Cracker Jacks which were blue wool jumpers worn in the winter.

Instead of the traditional Dixie Cup, a white canvas cap worn with dress blues and dress whites, we were issued white combination covers or hats. We looked like really bad examples of wannabe Wall Street executives—all the same clothes with that useless, clueless look on our faces. A year after I was discharged, the Navy went back to the old style jumper uniforms.

We also had to mail all of our civilian clothes back home. Everything was shipped back, even our 70s tie-dyed underwear. Nothing, including jewelry, would be allowed to stay unless it was for religious beliefs.

Everybody got the same uniforms, the same amount, and the same luggage—an olive green seabag. It is called a duffle bag in the Army and Marine Corps. And yes, there is a proper way to pack and stow your seabag and you learn very quickly how to pack it. We even had several inspections during our stay at NTC on how to properly pack a seabag.

We were also tested for classification purposes. I think we sat through a dozen aptitude type tests that were supposed to help the Navy figure out just how dumb we were. Well, I can tell you from experience after a few weeks of boot camp that N.A.V.Y stands for "Never Again Volunteer Yourself." They didn't ask that on the test though.

One thing every recruit learned on his own and was tested on again and again, before, during, and after boot camp was the "11 General Orders for a Sentry." If you're bored, look it up in the standard issue Navy Bluejacket's Manual. I still remember some of them today, even thirty-five years after boot camp.

CC Wright taught us many of the basics of recruit life during the first week. "Here's the floor—get used to it because you are going to spend a lot of time on it." We learned how to properly fold our clothes and I'm happy to say, I still follow many of these same clothes folding techniques even today. I even taught my kids how to fold their laundry the Navy way, but I'm convinced that they did it just to amuse me.

We not only learned how to fold clothes the Navy way, we also learned how to properly store them neatly into our stainless steel lockers which were in front of our bunks, one stacked on top of another. They had no doors and only one drawer that locked which is where we put our personal valuables, such as money, writing paper, and stamps. At a glance, the CC could quickly inspect the neatness, or lack thereof, of all our lockers and clothes.

We learned how to fold and stack clothes quickly, because if everything was not ship-shape, CC Wright would go through the entire barracks and yank every recruit's uniforms out of their lockers and scatter them all around. It looked like a tornado had hit the inside of the barracks. If any one of us failed inspection, we all failed as a company and that meant a deck party.

We learned close order drills, including the proper way to "left face, right face, and about face." There is only one way to do it properly and that was always the way the CC wanted it done, *not* the way we did it. It must have looked like a three-ring circus when we first started. You wonder where they get some of these guys from, those who do not know their right (or as it was now called, Starboard) from their left (Port). If any one of us failed, the entire company failed—deck party.

Floors are not floors, they're decks. Walls are not walls, they're bulkheads. Hats are not hats, they're covers. Bathrooms are heads. Toilet paper is non-skid. Underwear is now called skivvies. The water fountain is a scuttlebutt. I always wanted to learn a second language and here I was right in the middle of it. I've even passed along some of this colorful language to my wife and kids.

In a company of this size, we had bunk beds called racks in the Navy. Nothing fancy, they were all stainless steel, but with fairly comfortable mattresses. They were all lined up, just like you see in the movies. The only difference was that these racks were lined up perfectly, twenty sets on each side of the barracks. By perfectly, I *mean* perfectly. We had a yard stick that you would place at both the head and the foot of the rack. Thirty-six inches between racks—*exactly* thirty-six inches.

And if that isn't enough for you, we would run a string along the top of the racks from rack #1 to rack #20 and shift each rack ever so slightly to make sure that the two posts at the foot of each rack just barely touched the string. You could stand at one end of the barracks and look over the posts and they would all be *perfectly* lined up. The CC had a keen eye because if one rack was out of place by so much as a nose hair, the whole company would pay the price—a deck party.

We also learned how to properly make up a Navy rack. Everything was tucked in tight. You should be able to bounce a quarter off your rack. We learned not to sleep under the sheets but only under the wool blanket which was folded and placed on top of the sheets at the foot of the rack. That way, when you woke up you did not really have to make your rack, just straighten and tighten the sheets and fold your blanket. No muss, no fuss. And yes, almost every morning the CC would walk down the line, inspecting everyone's rack and even bounced a quarter off several of them to make sure they were nice and tight. If any of the racks did not bounce the quarter, we would get dinged as a company—deck party.

Did I mention deck parties? Oh yeah, lots of deck parties. Whenever anyone screwed up which usually happened several times a day, the whole company was called to attention in front of their racks. A deck party is, by definition, a party on the deck. Remember, there are no floors in the Navy only decks. Eighty guys would be on the deck in front of their racks at one time doing whatever the hell the CC told us to do. Push-ups, sit-ups, and my favorite, Hello Dollys.

Hello Dollys are really simple, but they suck the strength right out of you. Today's extreme core exercises can't even compare to Hello Dollys. You lie on your back face up with your legs stretched out in front of you, nice and relaxed. The CC tells you to lift your legs off the floor six inches, keeping them straight, and hold them steady. And yes, he had a ruler in his pocket to measure the distance off the floor. No cheating now, you can't place your hands under the small of your back, you lay them flat on the deck by your sides. Wait ten seconds or so—not too bad. Then raise your legs up another six inches.

After another ten seconds or so, the burning pain in your thighs starts to remind you that it's another fine day in the Navy. Then raise your legs up another six inches, more burning, more moaning. Then when you think you'll get a break, you spread your legs as wide as you can and yell at the top of your voice, "Hello Dolly." Yeah, you get the picture. It doesn't take too many of those babies to help get your body in shape.

Anytime we left the barracks, we would either march in formation or we would have to double-time it. We would march to chow, we would march to class, we would march to the Grinder for morning PT, and we would march just to march. We always marched in a four-man wide formation. Marching was easy and because I was the Yeoman, I got to be the last guy in line on the far right column. The RCPO marched along on the left side of the company.

It took us a while to catch on, but after a couple of weeks, we started marching like a real company. We would pass another company marching the opposite way and you would hear whispers, "Anyone from Texas? Anyone from New York? Anyone from Mississippi?" It was funny because if someone would say, "Yeah, I'm from New York," it really didn't matter because our company would continue marching as did the other company and you would never see that person again. But, it did boost your morale a little to know that somebody from your state was also in boot camp suffering the same as you at the same time.

We had been issued standard Navy boondockers, a steel-toed half boot which was pretty comfortable. Everywhere we marched, we dug in the right heel every fourth step. "MARCH, two, three, four. HEEL, two, three, four." The idea was that this would help us keep cadence and after a while, we got to where most of us hit the heel step at the same time. The only problem was, the boondockers had rubber heels and doing this on cement did not produce a lot of noise.

We also learned to call cadence. Someone in the back, including me, would call cadence to the march:

"I don't know what I've been told;" (echoed by the rest of the company: *"I don't know what I've been told"*).
    "163's got a whole lot 'a soul;" (echoed: *"163's got a whole lot 'a soul"*).
    "Sound off;" (echoed: *"1, 2"*).
    "Sound off;" (echoed: *"3, 4"*).
    "Bring it on down now."
    Echoed: *"One, two, three, four, one-two; THREE-FOUR!"*

Some guys got a little more clever with their cadence calls and the black guys always seemed to have more rhythm.

Anytime you were outside by yourself, you were supposed to double-time it. If not, any officer or CC could and would stop you and yell at the top of his voice "Drop down and give me twenty!" At which point, you would give an "Aye, aye, sir!", drop down to the ground, and give the guy twenty quick and perfect pushups. The last thing you wanted to do was to be put on report with the possibility of being sent back a week in training.

Running was not a problem for me either. Every time you passed an officer or a CC outside, you would have to stop, salute, and say, "Good morning (or afternoon), sir!" You would wait for him to return the salute and then be on your merry way, double-timing it. Our barracks was located at the end of the compound about a quarter mile to and from the chow hall. So, I ran quite a bit.

For breakfast, besides SOS, the mess hall would serve us scrambled eggs and link sausage though the eggs were powdered eggs. I heard rumors that the cooks put saltpeter in the eggs, supposedly to keep your libido down. That means you're not supposed to get an erection.

We got our first paycheck at the end of the first week with the company. At that time, the Navy issued you a check and then you would line up (hurry up and wait!) to cash it in if you wanted to. CC Wright marched us down to the Post Exchange (PX) after our first payday. We had a shopping list for the company. This included Navy stationary since we were going to write letters home and personal hygiene stuff like shaving cream and deodorant. He also told us to buy Zest soap. He said it was the only soap that did not leave a soap film on the shower walls. And since we had to clean the barracks every day including the bathrooms and showers, this would be a good thing—one less wall to scrub down.

When we got back to the barracks, the CC told us all to write letters home to our parents. No problem since I wanted to let my mom and dad know I was enjoying the good Navy life. We had been in boot camp for a full week before I could write my parents. I think I remember in this first letter that I asked my mom to keep all the letters I would write home during my time in the Navy. When my dad was in the Army during WWII, his mom and dad kept all his letters that he had written. I still have his letters even today in the original envelopes and I hope to pass those as well as the ones I wrote home during my time in the Navy along to my kids.

We no longer woke up to the sound of a fifty-gallon garbage can being kicked down the middle of the barracks. Instead, the sound of *Reveille* was piped over the barracks loud speakers. We still got up early, about 0430, and learned to take a three-minute Navy shower. Since there were more men in the company than there were showers, we had to be quick. The three-minute shower would come in handy when I got to the ship.

We did not have individual shower stalls in the barracks. The showers were two posts with about six showerheads each. So, besides being in the same shower with a bunch of other naked guys, we learned about the old "soap on a rope" trick. You did not want to drop the soap and bend over to pick it up; not with a bunch of naked guys who hadn't seen a woman in several weeks. You learned to be very careful in these precarious situations.

During personnel inspections which we seemed to have every day, the CC would look us over top to bottom. While the uniform was clean the body must also be clean. The CC would look so closely at you that you thought he was going to plant a big one on you. All the while you were supposed to stare over his head about six inches without blinking. He was actually looking at nose hairs and the shaving job you had just done that morning. Personnel inspections were usually held in the early morning hours where the sun was just peaking over the trees. If you looked at someone from the side, the sun would highlight any nose hairs or any facial hair you might have missed when you shaved. It did not take long for us to learn how to dry shave since water and shaving cream dampens the stubble and when you shave, you do not really shave down to the skin like a dry shave.

The barracks were always kept clean by everyone. We would swab the decks (mop the floor) and we would have to make sure the bathrooms were sparkling. Most of all, we would make sure there were no "ghost turds" lying around—those are the small, nearly invisible dust balls that seem to appear out of nowhere. They were the hardest to spot but somehow the CC could find them. I swear that PO Wright had eyes that could spot a fly taking a dump at two hundred paces.

Life in boot camp was becoming fairly routine: eat, sleep, exercise, train, then do it all over again. We did get specialized training in how to tie knots, called marlinspike, how to fight fires, and basic first aid. You have to realize that most Navy men, and now women, would be stationed aboard a ship at one time or another in their Navy career, brief as it may be. This floating city would be self-contained and we needed to know these things in case of any emergency. It's not like you would call the fire department to come put out the fire while you evacuated—you *were* the fire department.

There is not really much free time in boot camp, but after the first three weeks, we seemed to have a little more each week. We would spend time shooting the bull, writing letters, and shining our boondockers. Everyone had to have shiny boots, even the Yeoman. I learned how to spit shine my boondockers and while it did take some time, I found it somewhat relaxing.

After you put a shine on your boots the regular way using standard Navy issue shoe polish, a brush, and a shoe shine rag, you would find some cotton balls and with a little spit and polish, shine them up a little more. We even had contests in our company as to who had the shiniest boots.

Did I mention inspections? There were uniform inspections, there were personnel inspections, there were barracks inspections, there were locker inspections, and there were inspections of inspections. This was also in the middle of summer, so we spent a lot of time outside. Let me tell you the summer of 1973 in Orlando, Florida was hot and humid. Actually, *every* summer in Orlando, Florida is hot and humid. Every company was also in competition with every other company for the best inspection record. If a company scored perfect on an inspection, that company received a banner to put alongside their company flag.

During one of our whites uniform inspections, the CC got all the way down the last row (remember, I was the last one), when he stopped in front of the guy next to me. His uniform, as everyone else's, was impeccable, except that he had put his military ID card backwards in his white shirt pocket. I got chewed out for it too, because I should have inspected my buddy before the inspection. We flunked, just when we thought we would get our first perfect uniform inspection. After the inspection we did let that young recruit know he disappointed us.

There was this one episode, I dare tell, where I learned the hard way about patience. As Yeoman, I was supposed to know where everyone in our company was at all times of the day. One day we had a substitute CC; he was all over me like white on rice. I don't know why, but he had it in for me from the time he walked into the barracks. For some reason, one of our guys was missing and I could not account for him. It turned out he had gone to Sickbay and while he did tell someone, that someone did not inform me. So, I was up the proverbial creek without a paddle.

This substitute CC led me outside the barracks and I knew it was not going to be a pep talk. There were two other guys there, too. They had screwed up and were joining me in this little exercise. First, this *CC-de-Sade* had us do ten pushups against a wall then ten pushups on the ground—that wasn't too bad. Then we did nine pushups against the wall then nine on the ground; then eight and eight. When we got down to one pushup against the wall, none of us could hold our arms up to do it. Think I'm kidding? Try it.

Next, he had us lie face down at attention in the dirt. For two straight hours we lay there face down while this lifer prick lectured us about some bullshit Navy ideals of leadership. Frankly, I could care less what he was talking about, but I am proud to say that I lay at perfect attention for two solid hours, even with bugs crawling in and out of my nose. I've heard of communing with nature, but this was not what I had in mind.

I made it through that little ordeal as did the other two guys. It was reported to CC Wright and he asked me about it. By that time, I had found out that the recruit had reported to Sickbay and the dumbass that forgot to tell me fessed up. CC Wright wasn't too pissed at me. In fact, I think he got kind of pissed at the substitute CC. This was about the third week in boot camp and I believe CC Wright was starting to feel protective of all of us.

In fact, about half way through boot camp, CC Wright asked us to come up with a nickname for the company and he would have his wife sew a company flag for us. We came up with "Wright's Raiders" which seemed fitting to us. It was a proud moment because we had come a long way from a bunch of candyass recruits and had been molded into a *lean, mean, fighting machine*. Well, maybe that's carrying it a little too far, but we were starting to shape up as a company.

One of the training exercises in boot camp is to send everyone in the company out to different jobs around the NTC for a full week. One group goes to the galley (kitchen), one group goes to the scullery (dishwashing), another group goes to administration, another goes to help out with the newly arriving recruits, another goes to help out with classroom training, and a few guys get to stay for barracks detail. Groups would split out at different times in the morning and come back to the company barracks at night when their shift was over.

This was called Service Week and it was designed to see if the company could still hold together even though everyone went in different directions throughout the day. Since I was the Yeoman of the company, it was up to me to assign the recruits to various jobs. Here, I learned the term wielding power. If I didn't like a guy, I would send him to a crap job. If I did, I would send him to a skate job. Plain and simple. I didn't *abuse* my position, I *used* it.

It was not uncommon to hear, "Make a hole, Service Week," which meant that someone was in a hurry to do their job and you needed to get out of the way in order for them to do it. Even today, I find myself saying "Make a hole,

Service Week," usually when I'm in a crowd of people. It is funny to see them look at me when I say that, but they part like the Red Sea and I get through.

As the company Yeoman, I stayed at the company barracks during Service Week and was in charge of the crew that kept the barracks clean. Big whoop tee-do. About the third day into Service Week, I got really bored so I decided I would check on the guys in other areas. I ended up heading to the mess hall and caught up with my guys who were in the scullery. There were about nine of them and they were sweaty and stinky with food all over their not-so-white T-shirts.

I joked around with them a little and then one of the little bastards invited me to join them. I stripped off my utility shirt to *my* soon to be not-so-white T-shirt and dove right in, helping them wash dishes. I probably did that for a couple of hours, laughing and joking with them. It was actually kind of fun and certainly helped to pass the time of day.

This was one of those firsts I learned in life that in order to understand what other people go through, you sometimes need to walk in their shoes. That lesson has helped me in many ways throughout my life and my careers.

Today's new recruits don't go through Service Week during boot camp. There are probably several reasons for this, but my guess is that the Navy decided that by eliminating Service Week and privatizing mess hall duties, it could shorten recruit training by a week and therefore save money and get recruits out to the real Navy in a timely fashion. But these new recruits don't know what they are missing—I mean, come on. How many times in your life will you have the opportunity to wash dishes for twelve hours a day, seven days a week?

The Navy has ships and ships are almost always in the water somewhere around the world. The Navy also thinks it is very important for sailors to know how to swim. I did not have any problem with that—my mom always told me I had learned to swim before I learned to walk. At the NTC pool, we were taught how to survive in the water, should our ship sink or if we got blown (or thrown) overboard. They taught us that if we tied the legs of our pants into knots at the ankle, we could inflate them by filling them with air at the waist and use this technique to float in the water. What a cool concept; it actually worked. Thank goodness that during my entire Navy career the ship I was on never sank, I was never blown overboard, and no one threw me over the side.

One night, the RCPO was having a fireside chat in our barracks. Nothing heavy but just a good pep talk. The DPO (Duty Petty Officer) walked in on us and we jumped to attention, "Attention on Deck!" This guy was looking for someone to mess with and found one of the guys out of uniform. He told this guy to "get down and give him fifty." After the first pushup, the rest of the entire company got down and gave this DPO fifty of the best. We sure showed him. He didn't know what was going on. I think that was the first time we all realized that we had become a real company, a real team. We were watching out for each other.

The DPO told us to shape up the barracks and that he would be back in fifteen minutes to inspect and if the barracks were not ship shape, we would have an all-night deck party. We all rushed around getting everything as spotless as possible, lining up the racks, and checking our lockers. In less than fifteen minutes, we were ready for anything. The DPO never showed up. I guess *he* showed us.

We were starting to wind down with only a couple of weeks left to go in boot camp. One of my favorite activities in boot camp was the obstacle course. It was a typical obstacle course like you see in the movies, complete with ropes that swung over a water filled ditch, crawling over eight foot wooden fences, straddling and running over a log, and crawling through a pipe. I was pretty good at it and had one of the fastest times in the company. I loved to run outdoors and the obstacle course was a good challenge for me.

Sometime during the last week, the guys in the company were starting to get punchy. I guess after five weeks of hell and the fact that we could see the diminutive light at the end of the tunnel, testosterone levels were probably peeking. I was joshing around with some of the guys and I guess they thought they might try to wrangle me down and throw me in the shower. I found myself surrounded by about eight recruits. Half of them looked like they were serious.

Well, I'd show them I'm not one to mess with. I stepped back and put my elbow into one guy's chest, sending him to the ground. I took a strong hard karate stance and in a very confident voice, I told them that I had been trained in karate. What I didn't tell them was I had exactly two weeks of karate training while at FSU and *Kung Fu* was one of my favorite TV shows. Whatever I did or whatever I said seemed to cool their jets. They backed down. I must admit though, I was beginning to worry.

A few days before graduation, we were lined up ready to march back to the barracks after noon chow. It was a typical hot and humid Florida August day. We had always been told not to lock our knees when standing at attention. I guess this particular day and particular time I locked my knees because I fainted, right then and there on the concrete. I don't know how long I was out, but apparently only a few minutes.

The CC had me go over to Sickbay to be checked out. The doctor told me that I had a head cold. It must have been because we would sweat so much outside then head into the barracks which was as cold as a meat locker. It turns out that when I graduated from boot camp and got home, I went to my regular doctor who told me I had pneumonia. So much for the Navy doc's diagnosis.

The night before graduation, we were all bunked down and lights out. I was thinking about where I had been over the last year and how much I had grown since joining the Navy. We had been in boot camp for only six weeks, but it had gone by fast. I was proud of myself. We had come such a long way as a company and had only lost a few guys who had been sent back a week to another company because of disciplinary problems.

I had been raised a Methodist and while I did regularly attend church and Sunday school when I was in elementary and junior high school, I dropped out of that scene when I reached high school. I was so full of myself that night and I felt so moved that I got out of my rack, walked to the middle of the barracks, and started praying out loud.

"Dear Lord, thank you for getting us through these six weeks of boot camp. We don't know where we'll be heading after this, but we know that you will be with us. We've come a long way and we know your strength has kept us together as a company." I then started reciting the Lord's Prayer and I swear I think I even heard some of the Jewish guys praying with us.

I graduated August 31, 1973 with Company 163 from Orlando Naval Training Center. I was even honored by a letter from the NTC Commander noting what an exemplary young recruit I had been. I was named "Outstanding Recruit" from my company. For all I know, he sent the same letter to everyone who graduated.

Unfortunately, I did not march on the parade grounds during graduation. My cold had gotten so bad the CC did not want me to faint during the parade exercise, so I sat out of the graduation though I was able to sit in the bleachers and watch. It was quite a fanfare and even though my mom, dad, and sister were there, they did not know I was on the sidelines until later. I'm sure they kept looking for me on the parade field.

After the parade grounds, we headed back to the barracks to pack our gear into our seabags and say our goodbyes. No, it wasn't like everyone was telling CC Wright that "I wouldn't have made it without you." But I think we were all glad to have been part of something real. He turned out to be a decent guy and though I never ran into him again during my brief Navy career, I often thought about him and how he really did bring us all through a tough start in the Navy.

So what did I learn in boot camp? I came away with a new level of self-respect and self-confidence. I certainly learned a new language; some words were a little more colorful than others. And most importantly, I learned I could put up with a whole bunch of crap and get what I wanted out of life. That was something that would help me through my entire life.

I also learned that I was becoming part of something much bigger than me. I did not quite have a handle on what that was, but at every step in my Navy career, I would learn that you could get a lot more done working as a team rather than by yourself.

Did all those pushups, sit ups, and Hello Dollys help? You betcha! While I didn't have a six-pack, I was in the best physical condition I had been in my entire eighteen years. I would find out later that I could run a mile and a half in less than ten minutes (a qualification test for the EOD, or Explosive Ordnance Disposal program). I had toned up my muscles to the point where I looked kinda buff, if I say so myself. I was a slim and trim 185 pounds at six-foot four inches and I had blonde hair, although somewhat shorter than when I first arrived.

I had my orders, as did the other recruits. Since I had signed up to be an Aviation Boatswain's Mate Handler, I was headed to training. I could take up to fourteen days leave before my next stop: ABH "A" School located at Naval Air Station (NAS) Lakehurst, New Jersey.

# # #

In 1993, many military installations across the country were ordered to close by the 1993 Base Realignment and Closure (BRAC) Commission. Orlando NTC graduated its last class of 459 recruits on December 2, 1994. The command officially closed March 31, 1995. More than 625,000 Navy recruits graduated from Orlando NTC during its twenty-six years in business.

Now, there is only one Navy boot camp—Great Lakes RTC, Illinois which processes more than 54,000 recruits through Navy boot camp every year. It is located about halfway between Chicago and Milwaukee on the western shore of Lake Michigan. Why they chose frozen Illinois over sunny Orlando or San Diego, I'll never know. But then, no one asked my opinion.

In 1973, the year I joined, Orlando NTC became the sole site of recruit training for enlisted women. Prior to this, women sailors were trained in Bainbridge, Maryland. While there were women at Orlando NTC when I was there, we were obviously segregated. I can't understand why. It was the early seventies. Even FSU has co-ed dorms though the girls were on one floor and the boys were on another (like *that* would stop us). It wasn't until February 1992 that the Navy decided to have co-ed recruit companies in training. The pilot program included nearly nine hundred recruits. That must have been some transition.

4 ABH "A" SCHOOL

Most Navy recruits are sent to a training school after boot camp where they learn their craft for their naval career. Keep in mind that most of the time you chose your job at the recruiter's office where you had very little time or knowledge for what you were about to volunteer. "A" School, as opposed to "B" or "C" School, is typically only a basic introduction to your new job and usually lasts anywhere from four to six weeks. As an ABH, there was only an A School. Recruits who chose a more technical rate, such as an electronics technician or a hospital corpsman, would go on to B or C schools since those jobs were more detailed and technical and lasted up to a year.

The Boatswain's Mate (BM) is one of the Navy's oldest rates—their main job is to take care of the ship. Navy aircraft weren't introduced into the service until World War II and the Navy needed a rate specifically trained to take care of aircraft on the ship as well as on the ground. Hence, the *Aviation* Boatswain's Mate.

The Aviation Boatswain's Mate rating was first established in September 1944. There are three different AB ratings: ABE—Aviation Boatswain's Mate-Equipment; ABF—Aviation Boatswain's Mate-Fuel; and ABH—Aviation Boatswain's Mate-Handler.

ABEs operate, maintain, and perform organizational maintenance on catapults, arresting gear, barricades, and associated flight deck launching and recovery equipment on an aircraft carrier.

ABFs operate, maintain, and repair aviation fueling, defueling, lubricating oil, and inert gas systems.

ABHs operate and service aircraft ground-handling equipment and machinery, operate and service aircraft crash, firefighting, and rescue equipment, handle aircraft afloat and ashore, and perform crash rescue, crash removal, and damage control duties. Basically, ABHs move aircraft and fight aircraft fires.

At least that's what the standard Navy issue ABH manual states. In reality, we do whatever the hell we are told to do in whatever situation we find ourselves in and by anyone who is of higher rank—just like any other enlisted sailor.

The original training facility for ABHs was located in Philadelphia, Pennsylvania. In 1966, it was moved to Lakehurst, New Jersey. Lakehurst is probably best known as the site of the famous blimp Hindenburg disaster when on May 6, 1937 the German zeppelin *Hindenburg* caught fire at Naval Air Station Lakehurst. That's where I was headed. The ABH A School moved to Pensacola, Florida in October 1996. That's where all ABHs are now trained.

I arrived at ABH A School in Lakehurst on September 6, 1973, about 1830 (6:30 p.m.). Things were a lot different here than boot camp, but checking in, I didn't know what to expect so I acted like I was still in boot camp. I saluted everybody—no sense taking any chances—and I called everybody "Sir." I slapped the door three times instead of knocking and I stood at attention when I was in an office.

It did not take me long to figure out I didn't have to do half that crap anymore. I did not have to march, I did not have to double-time it, and I could sleep and eat pretty much whenever I wanted. We could even watch TV in the barracks—what a change. I could get used to this. The best? There was an Enlisted Men's Club nearby.

When I first got to Lakehurst there weren't enough men to put into a full training class. Similar to boot camp, I was assigned to a temporary outfit. There were about a dozen barracks at NAS Lakehurst, but only about half were renovated enough to live in. During the first couple of weeks, those of us in temporary companies were assigned to help renovate the barracks. My job was hanging ceilings. There were four of us working diligently as a team on this particular complicated task.

Like most modern day buildings, a hanging ceiling consists of a framework of metal strips spaced two feet by four feet apart, suspended from the ceiling using stiff wire. These are the size of the ceiling panels (if you don't believe me, look up). Metal strips were first attached to the walls with screws. They were *supposed* to be level all around the room, but let's just say that some were a little more level than others, depending upon how long I had stayed at the Enlisted Men's Club the night before.

A couple of blocks away and up the hill was our Paradise—the Enlisted Men's Club. I was only eighteen at the time and the drinking age in New Jersey was, well, eighteen. I had never visited liquor stores or bars when I was growing up; my parents were fairly strict about that as they should have been.

So I was experiencing something new. I liked Coca Cola so I had bourbon and cokes. I liked Seven Up so I had seven and sevens. I didn't drink much beer at the time, but I don't know if it was the taste or because of an incident that happened when I was at FSU where I downed two pitchers of beer back-to-back on a dare. It didn't matter, bourbon and cokes and seven and sevens were my drinks. Besides, they were cheap—only a dollar each.

Back then, you could stack drinks, meaning you could order and order and order again without finishing up the first one. One night, I had in front of me about seven bourbon and cokes and I was drinking casually. The fellas were egging me on so I ended up finishing them all (I think). It was a good thing that the barracks were located downhill. I figured if I fell, I could just roll down hill and end up somewhere close to my barracks. I left the club that night after midnight with one of my buddies, but I swear I don't remember a thing. I don't remember getting back to the barracks, climbing into my rack (I was in the upper rack) or anything, other than waking up with a standard Navy issue headache the next morning.

I saw my buddy Jim the next morning, who had left the club with me. His face was all bruised up and he had a black eye. He asked me, "Did you see the guys who jumped us?" I had no idea what he was talking about. "What guys?" I asked. "We got jumped last night on the way back to the barracks. Don't you remember?"

For the life of me, I could not remember what, if anything, happened. Jim was obviously banged up, but I didn't have a scratch on my face though my hand was a little swollen like I had punched something or someone. Anyway, neither of us was hurt too much, so I didn't make a big deal out of it. We never did find out who jumped us, but it would not have mattered since *one* of us could not remember a thing.

That did teach me a lesson though. Since that time thirty-eight years ago, while I may have had a drink here and there and maybe one or two too many, I have never been drunk enough to *not* remember what happened. I also learned that if you drink you should also eat. I've shared this story with my kids many times over the years. I've tried to convey to them that while it is OK to drink every now and then, never put yourself in a position where someone can take advantage of you. I think (I hope) that stuck.

The Enlisted Men's Club also served lunch and I found out after a few days that during lunch, they often had a dancer. The lunch wasn't bad and I usually ordered a hamburger and fries with a coke (no bourbon or rum though). The dancer was usually a nice looking babe in a bikini that danced around the floor and occasionally close to the men sitting at the tables surrounding the dance floor.

Keep in mind this was the mid-seventies and bikinis back then were nothing like they are now (remember Goldie Hawn in *Laugh In*?) Every now and then one of the guys would try to cop a feel on one or more body parts which was unequivocally slapped away, but always with a smile and the ol' "don't do that again" look. But a few minutes later, she would be dancing close to some other guy. When will they ever learn?

Finally after two weeks, we got enough guys in for a real ABH class. Since this was in the seventies, ABHs were rates, or billets, for men and not women. That changed though, even while I was still in the Navy though we did not have women on ships at the time either. Most of our class work consisted of book learning, which was pretty boring, and practical exercises for ABHs. I did fairly well in most of the class work, scoring high on most of the tests. After all, I did leave FSU after a year with a 0.7 GPA. But, I really liked the practical exercises, especially the firefighting. I don't know why, but it seemed natural to me.

The instructors started us out slowly on the fire fighting for obvious reasons. It was awesome when you got to fight a big one. Initially, they would pour about fifty to a hundred gallons of gasoline on an old jet and light it. Our job was to put out the fire. Every now and then, they would hide a 150 pound dummy, affectionately named Oscar, and we would have to find him and pull him out without damaging him. You can bet he had seen better days. We wore asbestos proximity suits, the silvery kind with the big hood you often see in the movies. I loved walking directly into a wall of flame in that suit—it made me feel invincible.

Did it get hot in the fire? Not really; there was a liner inside the suit which helped keep the heat out. The outside silver asbestos lining reflected the heat, too. The helmet also had an asbestos hood with a faceplate that was coated with gold flake of some sort. The gold was there to reflect the heat, so while you could walk directly through fire, the faceplate would help reflect the heat from your face. After a few minutes though, the suit did start to heat up, but the idea is that while you *could* walk through direct fire, you *shouldn't* stand around in it toasting your tidbits. We had a job to do—put out the fire and rescue people.

It all boiled down to the teamwork of the fire crew and at the school, performance was graded as a team. There were five of us in the crash truck: the driver, the turret man, the hose man, and two rescue men. The driver was actually one of the instructors since none of us had learned to drive the fire trucks. Another instructor was also suited up, directing us how to fight the fire. On top of the truck was a turret about four feet long and looked almost like a large silver ray gun. It sprayed out a lot of firefighting foam in a short amount of time. The turret man stood on a metal platform inside the cab of the truck and poked the upper part of his body through a hinged opening in the roof of the cab to operate the turret. On the front of the truck was a smaller hand line on a reel which was about seventy-five feet long and also sprayed out foam.

In the Oshkosh firefighting trucks we drove in Lakehurst as well as the ones at NAS Agana Guam and aboard Kitty Hawk, the engine was also used to provide power to the firefighting pump. The transmission had to be in neutral and the driver would engage the pump and then rev the engine up to a prescribed RPM. When the truck approached the fire and was placed in neutral, the driver slapped the turret man on the leg who then engaged the turret spewing out the firefighting foam. He had about five seconds to swing the turret back and forth knocking down as much of the fire as he could, all the while trying to make a path for the rescue men to get to the aircraft. The truck only carried about five hundred gallons of water and firefighting agent, so it was disbursed quickly.

While he was doing that, the hose man got out of the truck as well as the two rescue men. When the hose man was ready to go in with the rescue men, the driver tapped the turret man on the leg again indicating he was to stop spraying the fire and standby in case he needed to reactivate the turret. The hose man led the way fighting back the fire while the other two men went in and rescued people. The hose man then tried to put out the rest of the fire. Pretty simple but it did take teamwork. The whole process, if done properly and depending upon the actual situation, took about three to four minutes during the fire drills. Keep in mind though, that these were only small fires in a very controlled situation.

When I was at FSU I took the opportunity to learn how to skydive. My parents were very protective during my childhood and at the time I felt like I was the only kid on earth that couldn't do this or couldn't do that. They would not let me scuba dive, though during high school I managed to sneak a dive in with my sister's boyfriend every now and then. They would not let me ride a motorcycle, though I had a friend who showed me how and I borrowed his bike a few times. With all that parental protection when I was growing up, I figured it was time to test the waters now that I was out on my own. So, I tried sky diving. I made two jumps while at FSU and thought it was the next best thing to sex, though I wasn't that experienced at either.

It just so happened that there was a skydiving club at NAS Lakehurst. I got in with the guys and made three more jumps including my first Dummy Rip Cord Pull, or DRCP, where you simulate pulling your own rip cord even though you are still jumping with a line connected to the plane that automatically pulled your parachute cord. I thought that if I got good at jumping, I might be able to do more jumps in the Navy.

Now why would anyone jump out of a perfectly good airplane? It is hard to explain, but once you do it, it is exhilarating. On my skydiving adventures, we were in a very small airplane cockpit with passenger room about the size of a Honda Accord that holds five people. There is only one seat in the plane for the pilot. Everyone else is crammed in the cockpit, sitting on the flat wooden floor with both a main parachute on your back as well as a reserve chute on your chest. The plane flies about three thousand feet above the ground when the pilot cuts the engine and the plane begins to glide.

The skydiving instructor, or Jump Master, is up front and opens the starboard door which on this particular skydiving plane swung up and locked into position under the plane's overhead wing. He tells you to grab the wing strut and step out onto the platform. You look down and ask, "What platform?" There is only an 8-inch by 8-inch step down there—that's the one. You grab the wing strut while still sitting on the floor of the plane and swing your legs out.

The plane is gliding and the wind speed is about seventy miles per hour so your legs get swept aside and you struggle to bring them back to that little itty-bitty platform. It's almost like when you're driving down the highway at seventy miles per hour and you stick your arm out—lots of wind resistance. Once you have a hold of the wing strut and your feet are firmly planted on that little teeny step, you then swing out and put your full weight on the step. You are now outside the plane.

The next part is easy—the instructor looks directly at you and yells, "Go!" You look directly at him and ask, "Who, me?" like there's someone else out there with you. You're taught to first jump a little to get off the step then let go of the wing strut all the while trying to remain spread eagled. Fortunately, other than letting go, there is no thought process other than the occasional "Oh shit!" or "Geronimo!" depending on whether or not you had your Wheaties that morning.

Your parachute cord is attached directly to the airplane with about a twenty foot strap called a static line. When you jump, the static line is fully pulled out which then pulls the main parachute open so you don't have to worry about anything—unless of course you find yourself hosting a "Mae West" which in itself is another "Oh shit!" moment. A Mae West is when one of the parachute cords is looped over the top of the parachute, making two smaller billows, similar to what some would consider Mae West's bra. But that rarely happens and if it does, that's what your reserve chute is for.

I did not know it at the time, but that would be my last parachute jump ever. I have never regretted jumping nor do I feel like I need to do it again. I guess it is just one of those things you want to prove to yourself and I could add it to my growing Been There, Done That list.

We all got our orders for our next duty station in mid-October. When I first got to A School, we filled out paperwork called a "dream sheet." The idea is that *you* would tell the Navy where you wanted to go for your next assignment and then *they* would send you wherever they wanted you to go. I filled out the West Coast for ship duty and the Philippines for shore duty.

Not that I wanted to get that far away from home, but because I had heard the west coast had the better cruises. My orders read, "Report to Naval Air Station Agana, Guam." I guess I couldn't get too much farther away from home now, could I? I was into scuba diving so this new duty station would probably be a diver's dream. Now if I could just figure out where in the hell Guam was.

I graduated from ABH A School on Halloween, October 31, 1973, and had a few weeks leave before I left for Guam. At the time, I did not know how long I would be stationed on Guam, so these few weeks were extra special spent with family and friends. One of the things I missed most was my Mom's home cooking, so she made me all my favorite things—such a good Mom.

So what did I learn in A School? I learned how to fight fires, something I would do again in civilian life. I learned how to drink and more importantly, how *not* to drink. But I think I came away with a greater sense of self-respect and it certainly boosted my confidence. Not too many people in this world dare to get close to a big fire, let alone walk through it. Most of the time when there's a fire, people run away from it, as well they should. Firefighters run *toward* it.

5 NAS AGANA GUAM
Welcome To Paradise

Do you have any idea how long it takes to get from Gainesville, Florida to Guam? I didn't either, but near as I could figure it took me about thirty-five hours of traveling from Gainesville to Atlanta to San Francisco via commercial airlines. After an overnighter in San Francisco, I transferred over to Travis Air Force Base where we boarded a chartered commercial airliner that took us to Hickum Air Force Base in Hawaii in about three and a half hours. We were only able to relax for an hour before boarding another commercial airliner, Pan Am. It took another seven and a half hours to get from Hawaii to Guam. I was tired, but fortunately, no marching, no double-timing, and nobody yelling at me. Best of all, no security checkpoints like they have in place today. I was tired after such a long trip. It was Monday, November 26, 1973, when I stepped off the plane onto a beautiful island that would be home for the next fifteen months.

Guam is located in the western Pacific and part of what is known as the Mariana Islands. It is a United States territory with its own civilian government. The capital of Guam is Hagåtña, but at the time when I was there, it was called Agana.

During World War II, Guam had been occupied by the Japanese in December 1941 and was subject to fierce fighting when American troops recaptured the island three years later in July 1944. During my tour at NAS Agana Guam, one *really* old Japanese soldier came out from hiding on the island. Supposedly, he had no idea that World War II was over and had been living off the land with no human contact for thirty years—amazing.

The older Guamanians loved Americans. I guess it was because Americans helped liberate Guam from the Japanese. The younger generation Guamanians did not think much of Americans and I guess it may have been because most Americans on Guam were servicemen and there were probably a lot of incidents involving servicemen and younger Guamanians. I never had any problems, but I could sense there were some tensions. I tried to stay away from groups of younger Guamanians, mainly because I did not want to get into any fights.

Guam is about thirty miles long and anywhere from four to twelve miles wide, depending upon where you stand. That may not seem that big to you, but for me—a FNG (Fucking New Guy) to the island—it was to be my home for the next fifteen months.

At that time, there were four military installations on Guam: the U.S. Naval Station, located midway on the west coast; Anderson Air Force Base, located on the northern part of the island; Naval Communication Station, located toward the northern part; and my duty station, NAS Agana Guam, located in the middle of the island about a mile from the western coast.

After I checked into the base headquarters with my new orders, "Airman Apprentice Andrew Zenas Adkins III reporting for duty, Sir!", I was escorted to my new home. We were placed in an older, one story, open barracks that had built-in wooden dividers similar to cubicles you see in today's modern offices. Our space was about twelve feet by fourteen feet with three bunks and a total of six lockers. It was hot and humid and we were right smack dab in the middle of the rainy season. After spending six weeks in a hell hole called boot camp and another six weeks in A School, life was beginning to look pretty good, especially in this island paradise. Over the next fifteen months, I would not be disappointed.

You probably already figured out that a Naval Air Station has runways. At NAS Agana Guam there were two parallel runways: runway 6 Left/24 Right (6L/24R) and 6R/24L. Runway numbers are based on the compass direction. That means the runways are northeast to southwest (or vice-versa). The Guam International Airport also shared the same runways as the Navy. I was about to become an expert in airports and aviation over the next year and a half.

I was assigned to the Crash and Rescue Division. I was excited because I loved to fight fires from the experience I had in A School. We were short-handed, at least that's what they told us, so we worked two shifts, Port and Starboard, twenty-four hours on and twenty-four hours off. I was assigned to the Port section. Initially, we changed shifts at 1130. That was good if you liked to sleep in, but bad because you lost half a day of daylight.

There were six crash trucks at the Crash Barn (fire station) and each truck had four- or five-man crews. I was initially assigned to Unit #6, an Oshkosh MB-1. Like all new FNGs or "boots," my initial job on the crash truck was to man one of the two turrets. Unit #6 held five men: the driver/crew chief, two rescue men, and two turret men. All but the driver wore the silver proximity asbestos suits. Fortunately, we did not have to wear them all the time, only when we would have a drill or during an emergency. The five of us were crammed into the cab of the fire truck which was not that uncomfortable. The driver/crew chief and lead rescue man sat in cushioned seats up front while the rest of us sat in the back on folded down metal seats.

At a Naval Air Station with an active runway, one crash truck is always stationed out on the field parked strategically somewhere between the runways. This was done because if a plane ever crashed, this truck would be the first on the scene within a few seconds (assuming the plane didn't crash into the crash truck sitting in the middle of the airfield). All the other crash trucks would subsequently be called out to help fight the fire. This location was called the Alert Spot and we would have three- to four-hour shifts out there in the truck. During our 24-hour duty at the crash barn, if we had the 0800-1200 morning shift, we also had the 2000-2400 shift (8:00 p.m. to midnight).

While it was usually hot, there was always a good breeze blowing across the island so most of the time it was bearable. We did not have to sit in the truck all the time when out on the alert spot either. We could get out and stretch our legs if we wanted to. If we were lucky to be out on the alert spot during dawn or dusk, there were some spectacular sunrises and sunsets on Guam.

I learned early on in the Navy to always listen and always, without question, do what I was told to do. I'm a laid-back kind of guy and I think I made friends quite easily. You get to know the guys around you fairly well when you're stuck in a crash truck for hours at a time.

Our driver and crew chief was Gary Borne. He was an ABHAA (ABH Airman Apprentice) like me and hailed from Hagerstown, Maryland. He had already been on Guam for several months. Borne was a big guy and a chain smoker. "Can't beat ten bucks for a carton of Marlboros," he would say when I commented about his smoking. He would be with me on Kitty Hawk, too.

John Melcher was one of the rescue guys. He was a decent guy, too and also a chain smoker. One day he came on duty with a bad burn on his left forearm. "What happened?" I asked. "I won a bet," Melcher told me. "Sitting at the bar last night, this guy bet me that I would move before he did when he placed a burning cigarette between our arms. It took about ten minutes to burn down, but I didn't flinch, he did. So, I won the bet." What an ass! I could not believe what I was hearing, but I would be surprised many years later when my eighteen year old son came home from college one weekend with a similar burn. Dare I ask what happened?

Melcher gave me my nickname in the Navy: "Chet" Adkins. I grew up listening to country music and since I played guitar, sang country music, and my last name was Adkins, Melcher started calling me Chet. It stuck with me and for the rest of my time in the Navy, my name was Chet Adkins. The *real* Chet Atkins was a phenomenal guitarist and record producer in Nashville.

Gary Cuzner was a cute kid from Boston. He was short and always happy. I think he was high most of the time, but that didn't keep him off the truck. We lost Gary toward the end of my tour of duty on Guam. He had taken six days R&R (Rest & Relaxation) in Hong Kong. Unfortunately, it was reported that he died one night after drinking too much rice wine and he literally drowned in his own vomit. Such a waste—he was such a nice guy. Everybody liked him. I know his family was devastated. Bill Riggs, one of the guys in our section, flew back home accompanying his casket to present the American flag to his family. We had a memorial service at the base chapel for him on January 7, 1975 and everyone in our division attended.

The last guy in our truck, who turned out to be my very best friend in the Navy, was a big black guy named Glenn Law. He was from Council Bluff, Kansas and was built like a linebacker. He had the funniest laugh and a great big, bright smile. Everybody liked him and we ended up being roommates when we moved a few months later to the new barracks. After our tour was up in Guam, Glenn and I flew out on the same freedom flight back to the states. We would serve together again on Kitty Hawk.

We didn't always have the same guys in the crash truck crew. We often switched around, working different trucks, so that everyone became familiar with all the trucks and how they operated. Most of the time, we had full crews, either four or five to a truck, and I got to know all the guys fairly well. Some I liked better than others. I guess when you work twenty-four hours a day, every other day with the same guys, you become pretty good buddies after a few shifts.

6 NAS AGANA GUAM
On Duty

So what does a firefighter do all day when on duty at a Crash Barn? When I arrived in November 1973, we started duty at 1130, meaning we all had to muster for quarters at the Crash Barn. We would all stand at attention in formation in the Crash Barn, Port section on the left and Starboard section on the right. The Division Section Petty Officers would make sure everyone was present and accounted for and report to the Division Officer. I would usually be up by 1000, so chowing down and getting ready for duty was not a problem for me.

After being briefed on the day's events and mail call, we would relieve the Starboard section. About 1145, the first truck on our shift headed out to relieve the truck from the Starboard section on the alert spot. While the alert truck was out on the spot everyone else performed Planned Maintenance System (PMS) on the crash trucks which meant we checked the engine oil, the air in the tires, topped off the water and firefighting agent tanks, and we would wash and dry the truck if needed.

The system was so organized, we had checklists and clipboards for every crash truck and the crew chief would check off each item and sign the daily PMS sheet. We would then turn to, cleaning up the Crash Barn if needed, including making our racks—each truck crew shared their own room with bunk beds. The Navy issued us white sheets, but it was up to us to wash and dry our own. All the barracks had washers and dryers in a central location though the Crash Barn did not. We would also periodically train (hot drills) and have aircraft checkouts.

About 1600 (4:00 p.m.), we started holiday routine, meaning we could do about anything we wanted to do as long as we remained at the Crash Barn. Most of the time, we would play cards because there was only one TV station

31

on Guam and it broadcast mostly soap operas. The Crash Barn did have a pool table and ping pong table. I had grown up with both a pool table and a ping pong table in my house so I was pretty good at both. I even made a few bucks along the way. Poker on the other hand, was *not* my game. I didn't get into it as much as some of the other guys. Looking back, I probably came out about even—I didn't win a lot of money and I didn't lose a lot.

Sometimes we would play touch football out in front of the Crash Barn on the tarmac. I'm sure we provided some comic relief to the Air Traffic Control (ATC) tower which was only about a hundred yards away from the Crash Barn, watching a shirts and skins game around dusk. We might have been out of our minds playing football on concrete, but we enjoyed it and nobody ever got hurt. After all, we were Navy men and what's more, we were Crash and Rescue—we were invincible.

We did not have a galley at the Crash Barn. We got our meals on wheels, so to speak. Since we changed shifts at 1130, we were expected to grab chow before coming on duty. When the shift changed over from the Starboard section to the Port section and we were officially on duty, there was a signup sheet listing what was available for dinner which someone on our shift would retrieve from the base mess hall. We could not drive the crash trucks over to the mess hall because it was too far away from the airfield.

Usually there were a couple of different meats as well as a couple of different starches available. The vegetable of the day came with the meals, we did not have any choice in that, but you could always count on something from a large standard Navy issue tin can. Someone later in the day would take the utility pickup truck and run the chow sheet over to the mess hall on the main base and put in our orders. About 1800 (6:00 p.m.), one of the guys would take a pickup truck over to the mess hall and load up our chow. Hopefully, he didn't hit any potholes on the way back and chow would be delivered to us in stainless steel serving dishes.

We would have our standard Navy issue metal trays and load up on chow. There was always more than enough food for us to eat and most of the time it was warm. I don't ever recall going hungry during my time in the Navy. Now, whether the food was edible or not was another story, but for the most part, it was chow and it tasted good. After chow, we dumped whatever was left over in the standard Navy issue shit can (trash can), rinsed and stacked the trays. Someone would later run the serving dishes back to the main mess hall scullery to be washed.

We would also fill out a chow sheet for breakfast the next morning. Usually you could ask for whatever you wanted. Eggs, pancakes, sausage, bacon, toast, SOS (a.k.a. "creamed foreskins"), and cereal were standard. Again, someone from the Crash Barn would head over about 0630 in the morning to pick up chow and bring it back to us with the same routine as dinner. I learned that if I ordered eggs, they were usually either really runny or really hard; the only thing I could count on is that they would be stone cold. Back then, microwave ovens had not been invented. I got used to it though.

There were times though, that either we screwed up on the chow sheet or the mess hall decided they would screw us big time. More than once, they sent over a bunch of bologna sandwiches which we fondly called horsecock sandwiches.

During a normal work day, reveille was at 0600. We did not have a musical reveille (like a trumpet call). Actually, the person on watch duty in the Crash Barn's central Phone Office would get on the 1MC (the loud speaker system) and announce, "Reveille, reveille, all hands on deck. Reveille, reveille, all hands turn to." Sometimes the watch would sprinkle in a few more colorful Navy words like in boot camp, but that was discouraged.

We had showers with stalls so you did have privacy. Not everyone got up at the same time. Some guys got up quicker than others; some you had to literally drag out of their racks. I was usually one of the first ones up. We had chow about 0700, and then spent the rest of the morning either training or cleaning the Crash Barn. Sometimes, if one of us screwed up for some reason, the section chief would hold a field day where we scrubbed the Crash Barn top to bottom. He would tell us, "I want to see assholes and elbows." That wasn't much fun after the first two or three times.

That was pretty much a daily routine at the Crash Barn.

When I first got to the Crash and Rescue Division, the shift rotation started at 1130. I was new so I didn't know any better. But as time went by, I realized that we actually lost a good half day. Several of us lobbied to have the shift changed to earlier in the morning and in August 1974, the Division Officer changed the start of the shifts from 1130 to 0730. This was a good thing to me since it gave us the whole day off. I also realized I would not be able to sleep in since we had to get up early enough to shit, shower and shave, get some chow, and get to the Crash Barn for muster by 0730. But I was ready for it as were most of the guys since for ten months we had been losing a half day's fun in the sun.

About a month into my tour I was told I would learn how to drive the crash trucks. I was stoked. I had just turned nineteen years old and while I was only an E-2 (ABHAA), I guess I was keeping out of trouble and proving myself to the division. I always did what I was told and never asked questions. I would soon find out that driving the crash trucks was the most exciting part of the job.

We had six crash trucks in the division: Units #1 and #6 were Oshkosh MB-1s that took a five-man crew. These were state-of-the-art crash trucks with an automatic transmission and each of the two firefighting turrets had its own engine to power the pumps. Each of these trucks held one thousand gallons of water and two hundred and fifty gallons of firefighting agent. All five crew members sat in the cab of the truck.

Units #2, #3, and #4 were smaller Oshkosh MB-5s that held a four-man crew. They only carried about four hundred gallons of water and one hundred gallons of firefighting agent. They had automatic transmissions, too, but the one turret pump was powered by the truck engine which meant the driver had to put the transmission into neutral before engaging the pump and use the accelerator to rev up the engine to power the pump. Like the MB-1s, all crew members fit into the cab of the MB-5. I would drive this type of crash truck again on the flight deck of Kitty Hawk.

Most of us who drove the MB-5s learned to downshift to neutral while still rolling up to the fire. The only problem was that reverse was the next gear below neutral on the gear shift. It only took one or two times of accidentally shifting into reverse while still moving forward to learn the trick. The crew, especially the turret man standing up in the truck with his head through the roof hatch, got quite a jolt if the driver accidentally shifted into reverse while still rolling forward.

My favorite truck though was Unit #5. It was an American LaFrance crash truck and the oldest in the Crash Barn. It had a 5-speed manual transmission. I grew up driving a '54 Willys Jeep which had a 3-speed manual transmission and a top speed of 45 mph. The cab of Unit #5 only held the driver/crew chief and one rescue man; the two turret men and the second rescue man were actually in the back cab, separated by a sliding glass window. This was *my* truck and when I was assigned to be a driver on our shift, I always tried to get Unit #5.

All the crash trucks not only had water tanks, they also had a separate tank for firefighting suppression foam, technically known as Aqueous Film-Forming Foam (AFFF), but more commonly known as "light water." Mixed with water and air in the pump, it produced white foam that the trucks (both the turrets and the hand line) would use to spray on the fire.

We used to show just how powerful light water was by taking a small bucket, filling it half with water, and then pouring in some gasoline which floated on top of the water. We would then light the gasoline and pour about a tablespoon of the light water on top of the flames. In about two seconds, the light water would spread out over the top of the flames, depriving it of oxygen, and putting out the fire. That was *some* powerful stuff. The light water came in five-gallon blue plastic containers and each truck carried a couple of dozen of them in addition to what was carried in the light water tank.

At the time I was on Guam, all the crash trucks were painted standard Navy issue traffic signal yellow. Around that time the Navy was also testing other colors for emergency vehicles. While yellow was easily seen during the day and no color really stood out at night, the tricky time was dawn and dusk. They didn't change the truck colors when I was on Guam, but soon thereafter the Navy discovered that a fluorescent lime green color was the best color for fire trucks. According to the Navy, this was the best color to be seen throughout the day and the night.

The runways at NAS Agana Guam/Guam International Airport were about 12,000 feet long—that's more than two miles. As a comparison, the runways at LaGuardia Airport in New York are only 7,000 feet. There were five taxiways that crossed the parallel runways labeled A, B, C, D, and E. The alert spot was located about halfway down and between the runways. It was not on a taxiway since that is where the aircraft would roll, but it was located right next to one.

Sitting out on the runway in the alert spot, I got pretty good at identifying aircraft, both Navy jets and civilian airliners. I could even tell at night what type of jet was landing simply by the number and placement of the aircraft's landing lights. There was not much to do while out on the alert spot and we were not supposed to take anything out there, but most of us brought a book to read or a deck of cards which helped to pass the time.

I wrote a lot of my letters home while out on the alert spot, many of them at O-dark-thirty (between midnight and 0600). We all worked on our tans, too, especially during the noon to four shift. We would lay our asbestos coat out on the ground and lay down with our shirts off and our pants legs rolled up. All of us wore sunglasses.

During the day, if we were not out on the alert spot, we would either be cleaning the Crash Barn or in training. We had regularly scheduled courses for ABHs and our training petty officer was a cool lifer named Tom Cullen. He was a second class petty officer and I thought he did a good job training. In fact, I decided a few months into my tour on Guam that I would like to be a division training officer one day. It didn't happen on Guam, but I was assigned training officer duties while aboard Kitty Hawk when we were in the Bremerton shipyards.

Most of the guys in the Crash Barn smoked cigarettes and I'm sure a lot of the guys smoked marijuana. There were only a few of us in the division that didn't smoke either. Both my parents smoked cigarettes, but thank God I never picked up the habit though I did try one every now and then when I was growing up.

Did the guys ever smoke marijuana while on duty out on the alert spot? I'm sure they did, even on my truck, but they were very discrete about it. I probably knew more than I should have but when I got a whiff of a joint, I would say something out loud like "I better not catch any of you smoking on my watch." They would laugh and put out the joint. I'm sure someone in the control tower with powerful binoculars could see what they were doing out on the alert spot, too. That might have also served as a deterrent to smoking dope while out there.

I never reported anyone for smoking and my crew respected me for not smoking. No one ever really tried to get me to smoke which I very much appreciated. It was one of those things that I think my crew admired about me and respected my wishes. Either that or they figured they would have more to smoke since they did not have to pass the joint to Chet.

During our normal workday, we would schedule hot drills several times a month. At the end of the runways to the northeast up on a small hill, were parts of old jets, each part put into place to resemble a single jet. This is where we practiced fighting fires. Also up on the hill was an old tanker truck that held discarded contaminated aviation fuel. The training petty officer would spray a couple hundred gallons of gas all around the jet and carefully lit it. We practiced putting out the fires just like we did in A School. I really enjoyed donning the asbestos firefighting suit, walking through the fire, and knocking down the flames. It turned out those would be the only fires I would fight during my tour of duty on Guam. There were no plane crashes on my watch though there were plenty of emergencies.

After I had been in Crash and Rescue for about six months, I would periodically get assigned to man the Phone Office. It was on a rotation schedule and I would spend eight hours in the office at one time, then someone else would take over for eight hours, then another after that. It beat the hell out of spending two, four-hour shifts out on the alert spot.

All emergency calls came into the Phone Office from the ATC on what we called the Batphone, a dedicated phone line directly from the tower to the Crash Barn. If an aircraft reported an emergency, the tower would call the Crash Barn and give instructions about the emergency to the person on duty in the Phone Office. After that, the fun began.

The Phone Office Watch would press the Crash Barn emergency alarm which was a Klaxon alarm. There was a Klaxon alarm in every room, just in case we had a deaf sailor on duty. He would hit that three times, each alarm blast lasting a second with a second in between. Everyone would run to their trucks and suit up. Everyone kept their asbestos coats on the truck and their pants and boots would be beside the truck, ready to jump in, pull up, and buckle up. It was pretty exciting since most of the time we didn't know what was happening—was this an incoming emergency or did an aircraft actually crash? As the trucks headed out onto the taxiways, the Phone Office Watch would radio the information about the emergency to us.

The Klaxon alarm is an extremely loud buzzer that would almost knock your socks off. If you have not heard one before, you would definitely know it when it went off. If you've ever watched a submarine movie and heard the alarm when you heard the command, "Dive, dive," that's a Klaxon alarm. It would almost knock you out of your rack though I knew a couple of guys who slept through them once or twice.

Every so often, we would get checked out on a new Navy jet or a commercial airliner. Because we would be the ones fighting the aircraft fires and rescuing people, it was important that we understood the various types of aircraft that flew in and out of NAS Agana Guam. For example, most Navy jets have ejection seats. Those ejection seats are armed during flight and there are safety pins that the air crewmen put into place to keep the seat from ejecting while on the ground. When ready for takeoff, the air crewman pulled the safety pins and give them to the pilot for storage in the cockpit.

We needed to know where they were located in the cockpit and how to insert them into the ejection seat before attempting a rescue. Otherwise, and this had happened in the past, the rescue man might pull the pilot out of the cockpit and accidentally catch the ejection seat handle, activating the rocket-powered ejection seat, sending both the pilot and the rescue man flying. Not a good day for either man.

We had to be familiar with all the planes on the base, new as well as old. We had a couple of C-121 "Constellations" which were really old, four-engine, gasoline-powered propeller planes that flew with a crew of six. They were built by Lockheed and had two unique features: a triple tail and a clear observation dome on top of the aircraft for the navigator to look out at night to navigate using stars. The main mission of the "Connie" was to provide cargo loads during three wars: World War II, Korea, and Vietnam. It was also the presidential aircraft for Dwight D. Eisenhower. The only problems we had with the C-121s were either accidental fuel dumps, in which case we would be called to wash down the fuel spill, or if one of the engines had a problem and the pilot was landing with only three engines operating.

We got checked out on commercial airliners since we were also the firefighters for the international airport. Most airliners were from the Boeing class: 707s, 727s, and 747s. The 747s were the biggest and Japan Air Lines (JAL) had one of the largest 747s ever made. I think they told us that three hundred and fifty people could fly on one of those behemoths.

Most people do not think about it, but if one of these babies came creaming in, we would have one hell of a mess on our hands. You try not to think about it, but as a crash truck driver one of the things the instructors tell you is that there may be bodies all over the ground and you have to figure out how to maneuver around them to get to the fire without driving over them. A gruesome thought to say the least.

There were also several squadrons stationed at NAS Agana Guam. We had a squadron of P-3 "Orions" which are four-engine turboprop planes. Their main mission was to scout for enemy submarines. It flew low over the water and dropped electronic, submarine detection devices called sonobuoys in a straight line helping to locate enemy submarines. There were six of these patrol planes in the squadron.

We had a squadron of C-130 "Hercules" aircraft that were also four-engine turboprops. These were big honkin' cargo planes. You might be familiar with them today as Hurricane Hunters. I think we could have parked four of the crash trucks inside one. There were three C-130s on the base. We also had an A-3 "Skywarrior" squadron with three jets next to the Crash Barn. I would see these same A-3s again on Kitty Hawk during the WESTPAC cruise.

All aircraft emergencies were called into the Crash Barn directly from the control tower. Usually, there would be distress calls from an aircraft coming in to land or from one of the squadrons on the base. We would often get routine calls for accidental fuel dumping on the tarmac. In those cases, one of the trucks would head over to the aircraft, stay upwind in case a fire broke out, and use the turrets on the truck to spray out fresh water, washing down any spent fuel. In those days, we sprayed out enough water to disburse the fuel. Eventually, it would evaporate. I got one of those calls my first day on the job. I thought it was pretty cool—the other guys on the truck thought it was boring. But then, I was the FNG.

We did have a few close calls though. One dark and stormy night (no kidding, it was night and we were having one hell of a thunderstorm), we were called out around midnight because a China Airlines 707 commercial airliner was on approach and had one engine out. A Boeing 707 has four jet engines and on this one, three were working well. But for standard procedure, we were called out just in case.

It was raining so hard we couldn't make out the landing lights on the aircraft until it was almost over the end of the runway. At that point, its starboard landing gear was touching down on the grass just to the right of the runway. For most emergencies like this, we had a crash truck positioned on each of the five taxiways about a hundred feet away from the runway. That means that the plane's wing would be close to clipping the tops of our trucks. In an almost totally synchronized move, all the drivers put their trucks in reverse and hit the gas backing up another hundred feet or so. Fortunately, the plane landed without further incident, though we had a lot of runway lights busted out. It was a scary few moments, too, especially for the first couple of crash trucks since they were so close to the aircraft.

Another close call involved an HU-16 "Albatross," a Navy seaplane capable of landing in the water as well as land. The bottom of the plane is shaped like a boat hull and there are small pontoons hanging from each overhead wing. There were a couple of HU-16s assigned to NAS Agana Guam and they were used mostly for search and rescue missions. Like any other squadron, they trained at night as well as during the day.

One night I was watching TV in my barracks room when the phone outside in the hallway rang. I went out to answer it and about that time the barracks crash alarm went off. If there was an emergency such as an actual airplane crash or a pending crash, the Phone Office Watch would call all off-duty guys in to help out. That's what this was—a potential, pending disaster. We were told that an HU-16 was coming in without any landing gear. So we gathered up all the sober, off-duty crash crew we could find and took off running to the Crash Barn which was about a half a mile away.

When we got there, we were told the HU-16 was still flying around, burning fuel and trying everything they could to get the landing gear down and locked. After an hour, the control tower called and told us that the plane still could not lock its gear and we needed to foam the runway. Our tanker truck headed out and started spraying fire suppression foam on the runway, putting about a three inch deep layer of foam across the runway for about the first half mile of the runway. This was supposed to keep sparks from flying around when the plane landed on its belly, hopefully to keep it from catching fire.

We saw the plane flying around trying to burn down as much fuel as it could. For some reason it couldn't just dump fuel and we knew there were four- to five-foot seas, so it could not land in the water. Besides, it was night and there were no landing lights in the water. So we were expecting the worst and the pucker factor was pretty high for most of us.

On the plane's short final approach, everyone was alert and ready and I bet most were praying for a safe and uneventful landing. The plane landed very softly and thank God the gear did not collapse. When it came to a stop, all the crash trucks were rolling up to it. We had never seen a crew come out of a plane faster than those three guys did. I'm sure they were due for a skivvy check. The gear on the starboard side of the plane was bent in an obvious distorted manner. We found out later that one of the crew had braced a two-by-four piece of wood against the airplane bulkhead, shoring up the gear to help keep it straight as the pilot landed the plane. The pilot and crew were very thankful for us being there. They came around and shook everyone's hand. We all were really glad they landed safely.

On another occasion, we were out on the alert spot and I was the driver/operator. I had brought out a game of Monopoly. I figured it would help pass the time of day. There were four of us in one of the smaller MB-5 trucks, so we had a little extra room in the cab to lay out the board.

We were on the noon to four shift so there was plenty of daylight. The air traffic was slow and there was a P-3 Orion flying in the pattern practicing touch and gos. I noticed the first few times that the P-3 was landing a little harder than normal. Most people would not notice such trivial things, but when you're out there on the alert spot and all you have to do is watch airplanes take off and land, you get to know some of their idiosyncrasies.

I kept my eye on the P-3 all the while playing Monopoly. About the third go round, the P-3 landed really hard and I could tell it blew a tire—time for an emergency. However, the pilot did not know it and kept heading down the runway ready to take off again. I turned on the emergency lights and the siren and took off chasing the plane down the runway while my crew suited up. I radioed the emergency into the tower, but for some reason the radio was full of static and they could not understand a word I was saying. However, they did see us take off after the P-3 so they called the Crash Barn and all the trucks rolled.

They apparently radioed the P-3 pilot too, because the P-3 started to slow down toward the end of the runway which was a good thing since it wasn't the best condition to land a turboprop aircraft, or any other aircraft for that matter, with a flat tire.

The plane was in the middle of the runway and there was not enough room for me to drive the truck past the plane on the runway, so I skirted out onto the grassy field on the port side of the runway to catch up and get in front of the aircraft. When we finally got there, the pilot had come to a full stop and my rescue guy, Gary Cuzner, got out with a fire extinguisher which was the standard operating procedure for an emergency of this type.

Gary signaled the pilot to cut the engines, all the while the pilot did not have a clue what was going on. He was probably confused and pissed at the same time. But after cutting the engines, the co-pilot climbed out and looked around, saw the flat tire on the starboard side of the plane, told the pilot and came back out and thanked us for being so alert. No telling what would have happened had they gone around for another touch and go with a flat tire, but it wouldn't have been a good day. We did the right thing at the right time and I was proud of that and my crew.

7 NAS AGANA GUAM
Off Duty

I ventured into downtown Agana quite a few times during my first few months on Guam, mostly at night. There were quite a few bars and plenty of massage parlors. Yes, I'll be up front. I had a few massages during my stay on Guam. At that time the real massage was about twenty dollars for an hour. Anything more would depend upon the girl and the other service, but you could count on spending another ten to twenty dollars.

I turned nineteen years old in December 1973 after only a few weeks on Guam. I had frequented the bars on my off duty days, but this particular night was special. The guys took me to a new bar called Frenchy's where there was an all-girl Filipino band playing country music. I was in hog heaven. The place was hopping and my drink of the night was a sloe gin fizz. I had no idea what was in it other than gin, but it tasted good and I was feeling great as the night wore on. The band played Happy Birthday for me and the bar owner gave me a free drink. I think it was a little stronger than the others.

The guys talked me into getting onto the stage. Boy, were we all in for a treat. A couple of girls in the band put a long, blonde wig on my head. They also put a couple of water filled balloons attached with a string around my neck so they dangled in front of me and I put on a long sleeve, button-down shirt. The band started playing and I started dancing, a little wobbly, but I was having fun. I must have looked like an ass up there on stage with the balloons bouncing all around under the shirt (ala Mae West), but at the time I didn't care.

When we ventured into town, several of us would often travel together. Not for safety reasons, but mostly because we got along well and we were drinking buddies. Besides, not too many of the guys owned a car so it made sense to travel together.

41

Guam bars were no different than other bars located near military bases. Just like in the movies, you would be sitting at a table and one of the local ladies of the night would come over, sit on your lap, look you in the eyes and ask, "Is your father as handsome as you?" Most of the time, I would reply, "almost." "Buy me drinkee?" "No, sorry, I don't have any money." She would leave and a few minutes later you would hear a Champagne cork pop and the standard Navy issue response from everyone else was "Sucker!" Drinks in Guam were expensive. Beer was a dollar and mixed drinks were $1.50. A guy could go broke during one night of drinking.

Downtown Agana was about two miles from the main gate. Because public transportation was almost nonexistent on the island, we either hitched a ride or walked. A few of the guys had bought cars which were double and triple hand-me-downs, meaning when a sailor got transferred off the island, he would sell his car for a decent price to the next guy. We would usually all chip in for gas. I didn't have a car so I usually tried to bum a ride or hitch-hike into town.

One night about eight of us were headed out on the town and we crammed into a small Datsun (now known as Nissan) and it was like packing sardines. There were three of us in the front seat. One of the guys was lying across the laps of the four guys in the back. As we got closer to the guard gate, the driver stopped the car and told us that we would never get off the base like that—the guards would think it was too dangerous to travel like that.

The smallest guy got out of the car and the two biggest guys, me included, sat next to the doors on the passenger side. We picked up the small guy, cradling him outside the car and held him parallel. The driver started the car and we slowly approached the guard gate. The guards didn't notice anything (they were Marine Grunts), waved us through, and we headed towards town. About a hundred yards down the road, we stopped and let the little guy back in.

When I first got to Guam, I was probably out on the town almost every night when I was not on duty. I was nineteen years old, new to the bar scene, and wanted to explore what I could. Most of our bar outings were to downtown Agana Guam since that was the closest to the base.

About three weeks into my new duty station, I wrote one of those real serious letters home to my dad. I know I had disappointed him and my mom when I flunked out of FSU. At the time, it wasn't any big deal to me to flunk out of college, but the nagging feeling was that I let my parents down. It was hard to explain and even an eight page letter didn't do it justice, especially one mailed eight thousand miles away from home. But, I laid all my thoughts down on paper as to why I joined the Navy and what I hoped to do with my life. As I write this today, those words still ring true to my heart: "I want to make you and Mom proud of me." I guess most kids grow up and go through different phases in life and it is not until you leave home that you realize what a great home you really have.

I wrote a lot of letters home to my parents, my sister, and my girlfriends. I didn't have a girl in every port, but when I was at FSU, I had a lot of friends who were girls. I thought it was great to write because when you are in the military and you write to girls, they usually wrote back. There is something romantic about writing a serviceman or servicewoman even today though most people now use email.

I would get several letters a week and we would have mail call at the Crash Barn after muster. The letter writing from my girlfriends didn't last too long though. I guess they found other guys or other things more important than to write to a lonely serviceman. I didn't mind though since I got regular letters from my family. I tried to write home once or twice a week, too.

I also periodically got packages from my mom and my sister, Anne. Those were always a surprise and so welcomed. They usually contained some sort of baked goodie. My mom baked the world's best pound cake and my sister baked the world's best M&M chocolate chip cookies. I always shared with the guys in my section, as did they when they received goodies from home. I don't think my mom or my sister ever realized how much these packages meant to me—some good cooking from home, baked with so much love. Best of all, it only took a week to get a package from Florida to Guam, except during the Christmas season.

One day I got a package from my sister. I was in the Division Officer's office just shooting the bull with the section Crash Chief while I opened the package. It was a cracker and cheese type package; you know the kind of gift you buy at the mall right before Christmas when you either can't think of anything else to get your relatives or you forgot and needed something at the last minute?

Anne sent me this wonderful package and it even had a small sample bottle of wine in its own little box. I opened it up and was talking "big time" about the wine I had while on duty when I noticed a little something extra in the bottle. I knew immediately what it was, but I quickly closed the box up and told the chief I would put it away until after duty.

That little something extra was a marijuana joint. Talk about a surprise— and from my own sister, no less. I had certainly seen my share of joints on the base, even though I had never taken a drag or smoked one. I told her about it years later and while I did appreciate the gesture, I am so glad I didn't share this particular package from home. That was a close call, to say the least. I ended up giving the joint to another guy in our section since I knew he smoked.

43

I bought a guitar off one of the other crash crew members for $60. It was a 12-string Greco and had a decent sound. The biggest problem I had with it was that I played hard and always broke one of the strings. Instead of replacing the broken string every time, I just played it with eleven strings. I was a decent guitar player with a decent voice, but this guitar would travel with me all over the world in my Navy career. I would learn all kinds of new music and new pickin' styles. I would eventually earn my nickname "Chet Adkins."

There were several other guys in the division that also played guitar so we would often get together and jam, both on duty as well as off duty. I never took my guitar out on the alert spot though I was tempted several times. But I would get together with guys on the Starboard shift when they were on duty. We would jam a lot in the Crash Barn. Since the floors were vinyl tiles and the walls were concrete block, the sound was unusually good.

I also learned to sing better and felt more confident in my voice. Some of us sang, some of us played guitar, others played other instruments and while we never really formed a band, we found ourselves spending many hours jamming away. My favorites were the older country songs from greats like Hank Williams, Merle Haggard, and Patsy Cline. Some of the other guys liked the newer country artists which at the time were Johnny Rodriguez, Freddie Fender, and Lynn Anderson. Anyway you sliced it, we all had a good time jamming and singing together.

It took a few weeks, but my first venture into the water was nothing short of spectacular. Several of us went snorkeling off the beach and the water was so clear one could almost see forever. I saw something about a hundred feet away swaying back and forth with the tide. I swam closer and discovered it was a three-foot octopus. It took off as I got closer, but the fact that I saw it from so far away truly amazed me. The water was a lot clearer here than off the coast of Panama City Beach or the St. Marks River in Florida. It was only about four to five feet deep for a couple of hundred yards off shore, then it dropped off to about forty to fifty feet. We snorkeled around for an hour or so, diving down to see the coral reefs and fish. That was the most beautiful water I have ever dived.

One of the best services offered to military personnel on Guam was the USO. They catered to all military men and women and besides having a great recreational hall, they held monthly Boonie Stomps where they would take a bunch of us out on tours all over the island. I was able to explore places, beaches, and World War II battle sites that I would probably never go to on my own. It also provided a much needed relief away from the nightly bar scene.

I met several other guys and girls from the other Naval stations and Anderson Air Force Base on the boonie stomps. While I didn't make any long-lasting friends, there were several of us that were regulars and it was interesting to learn more about the other military branches. Some of my favorite boonie stomps included Cetti Falls, Inarahan Zoo, Gadao's Cave, Gun Beach, and Bali Hai Falls. I went on about a half dozen different boonie stomps during my stay on Guam.

Every few months the division would allow us to throw a section party. We would get as much food as we wanted at no cost from the mess hall. We usually chose one of the beaches (this *is* an island) that had grills and picnic tables. With about twenty-five to thirty guys in the section, we would load up one of the utility pickup trucks with chicken, hot dogs, and hamburgers, and then stop by the PX to pick up a dozen or so cases of beer, soda, and ice and head out to the picnic.

Sometimes we would cook a bunch of sliders (hamburgers and cheeseburgers) or tube steaks (hot dogs). A lot of us pitched in to do the cooking and we would play volleyball, football, softball, Frisbee, and of course we would swim. Come chow time, it was a mad dash to see who could load their plate up the fastest with the mostest. There was always so much food, we would never run out and often we would have seconds and thirds. We always had good times since we worked so close together and most of us drank at one time or another. "Work hard, play hard" was our motto.

I also made friends with several Seabees while on the base. "Seabees" is a nickname for Navy men assigned to the Construction Battalion, "CB." Remember the movie, *The Fighting Seabees*, starring John Wayne?

The Seabees were responsible for construction projects on the base. They typically worked during the day and as such, were also assigned other collateral duties on the base. The Seabees drove the base taxis (there were two on the base). If you wanted to go from the barracks to the Enlisted Men's Club, you had three choices if you didn't have your own wheels. You could call the base taxi which was driven by the Seabee on duty. You could walk, but since the Enlisted Men's Club was located across the base and you couldn't walk across the runways, it was about a three mile hike. Or, you could take your chances walking across the runway which was illegal though I did that a time or two during my stay on the island.

I got to know a couple of the Seabees fairly well. They were decent guys and since their barracks were located next to the WAVES' barracks, it helped having friends in good places. One of the Seabees had a love of country music almost as much as I. He played the harmonica, so one night I was riding in the taxi with my guitar and we started jamming—right there in the taxi. We both knew a lot of the same songs so we got along well.

There were plenty of nights when I didn't have anything else to do and I knew my Seabee buddy was on duty driving the base taxi so I would call him to pick me up and we drove around the base jamming. He played the harmonica while driving and I played the guitar and sang. We got to be pretty good and the passengers got entertained along the way. We even had a few of the Chief Petty Officers give us a tip.

The Enlisted Men's Club usually had a band on Friday and Saturday nights. They would rotate between rock, jazz, and country bands. I didn't care much for the rock or jazz bands but I very much enjoyed the country and western bands. My favorite was a four-man group called The Westerners. They were all Air Force pukes, but they were a tight band. I would often go to the club with some buddies just to drink and listen to The Westerners.

One of the songs they sang was an old Leroy van Dyke song, *The Auctioneer*. When I was a kid growing up, my dad had an eight-track tape player in his Oldsmobile '98 and he had a tape of Leroy van Dyke's Greatest Hits. I really liked it and as a kid in high school, I would often just ride around at night or on the weekends playing that tape, singing along. My favorite which I constantly sang along with, was *The Auctioneer*.

I had heard that The Westerners were going to be playing at a New Year's Eve party up at the enlisted men's club at Anderson AFB, so I made arrangements with a buddy who had a car to go to the AFB for the party. We were all having a good time as usual and on one set, The Westerners played and sang *The Auctioneer*. Since I was feeling pretty good and it was closing in on midnight, I asked them on their break if they would sing *The Auctioneer* again and let me sing with them. Sure enough when the next set started, they called me up on stage.

I sang *The Auctioneer* on stage and nailed it. This is one of those songs you sing the last chorus several times, each time faster than the previous. I outdid the drummer who couldn't keep up with me and I'm sure I had more to drink than he did. This was my first performance ever in front of a live audience and would certainly lead to more along the way both in my Naval career as well as when I got out.

One of the barracks on the base served as a recreation room, complete with a television, a pool table, a ping pong table, a soda vending machine, and a beer vending machine. During my time in the Navy, only "3-2" beer was allowed on base. Instead of the regular beer which contained five to six percent alcohol, 3-2 beer contained three-point-two percent alcohol. I guess the idea was that it would fill you up quicker than regular beer. And this was before the beer commercial, "Tastes great—Less filling."

It was common to try to empty the beer vending machine and one night three of us tried to do just that. The beer was only twenty-five cents a can and I figure I drank at least two dozen cans of Coors by myself before giving up. This is where I learned that you really don't buy beer, you merely rent it. Thank God we weren't called in that night for any crashes or emergencies.

My first Christmas on Guam was my first Christmas away from home. I called my mom and dad a few days before Christmas because it was reported that oversees phone lines might be tied up during the holidays and we should try before Christmas Day. Guam was nine hours behind, but a day ahead of Florida. They say "America's day begins in Guam" because Guam is on the other side of the International Date Line.

I had received a Christmas package from both my parents and my sister, each with some presents and baked goodies. If we were going to mail packages home, we needed to do so by the end of the first week in December. I bought some small gifts on the island, wrapped them and packaged them up to send them off. I think they got home in time for Christmas.

I also had two birthdays when I was stationed on Guam. I turned nineteen and got pretty soused, dancing on stage in a blonde wig. I marked my second birthday by writing a letter home telling my mom and dad, like they didn't know, that I was no longer a teenager. I celebrated at the Enlisted Men's Club with The Westerners.

Guam is located between Asia and the United States. Back during my time in Guam, it was also a major gateway for drugs headed from Southeast Asia to the U.S. or Mexico. I wasn't into drugs and never have been, but apparently there were some guys on the base who were, big time. We got constant inspections and almost every time some guy got busted, even some from our own division.

I had seen marijuana before and the Military Police (MP) gave us a lecture one time about hashish, holding up a brick about five inches by ten inches by a half-inch thick. I had never seen hashish before and didn't really know what it was, but some of the guys in the division were literally drooling. I think one of the guys at one time showed me a hit of LSD though it was so small and plain looking that I thought he was pulling my leg. No one ever tried to persuade me to do dope for which I am eternally thankful. I know at the time it was rampant and this may sound self-righteous, but I literally got high off of life. There was a lot more to life than drugs and I was living proof.

Despite my not doing drugs, every so often we would have a surprise inspection and everyone would be tested for drugs by supplying a urine sample. This was fondly known as piss test day; some of the lifers also called it Operation Goldenflow. There were several guys who tried to get others to pee in their cup, but the corpsman had their standard orders and watched every guy pee. God, what an awful job. These corpsmen were nicknamed "dick-smiths" or "meat gazers." If someone tested positive for drugs, they would get written up, confined to the base, and had to take a piss test every day for six straight weeks.

A couple of times the base commanding officer, or Old Man as we would call him behind his back, would venture over to the Crash Barn. He usually showed up at night after chow and would often sit around shooting the bull. I thought he was just being a nice guy, getting to know the guys in the division. I found out later that he was really trying to stir the pot looking for signs of drugs. I was so naive at times.

After a few months on Guam, several of the guys in our division received orders to immediately transfer to Diego Garcia, a small island in the Indian Ocean. By immediate, I mean they got their orders one day and shipped out the next day. Seems the Navy recently built a Naval Air Station there and needed some help setting up the Crash and Rescue Division. They would be TAD (Temporary Assignment of Duty) for sixty days.

My name was at the top of the list, but because I was taking flying lessons at the time, the Division Officer decided to send some other peon. At least that's what they told me. I wouldn't have minded going since it would have been a new adventure. But after these guys came back a couple of months later, I'm glad I didn't go. They said there wasn't anything to do there—only one Enlisted Men's Club, and that was on the base. I don't believe there were any women on the island either.

I was promoted to an E-3 (Airman) in March 1974. That meant instead of earning $363 a month I would be earning $377 a month. I had taken the exam while in Lakehurst at A School and this would be an automatic promotion. That also meant I could take the E-4 exam in a few months and possibly become a new Petty Officer in the United States Navy—the goal of every young recruit.

I took the Third Class Petty Officer exam in August 1974. I knew it would take a few months before I got the results back, but it seemed to drag on and on. Meanwhile, it was business as usual at the Crash Barn. When the results came back in November, I found out I passed and would become an ABH-3 on Sunday, November 16, 1974. My good buddies, Gary Borne and Glenn Law also passed. It was a big day for me. I went down to the PX and bought standard Navy issue ABH-3 patches for both my utilities and my whites, ready to sew on Saturday at midnight.

I was so happy that I had passed my exam and was now an official United States Navy Petty Officer. That meant a lot to me, not only because I was no longer a simple peon, but because I could let my folks know that I was promoted. I was still trying to prove to them that I wasn't a flunky.

I had heard all kinds of rumors about what some of the guys did when you got promoted and I even participated in a few of these traditions, but for some reason nobody bothered me that night. Maybe it was because I didn't get plastered or maybe it is because I had let them know I knew karate. We all celebrated like we always did when one of us got promoted—we went out drinking.

In 1973 and 1974, two major political events happened that caught my attention. Richard Nixon was impeached and resigned as President of the United States and Saudi Arabia declared an oil embargo on all countries that supported Israel. I wasn't that much into politics at the time and from what I had read, Nixon was a liar and a crook and deserved to be impeached. While he was the only president who was forced to resign, there are several others since that time that should have resigned, in my opinion. Nixon's resignation didn't affect those of us on Guam one iota.

However, the oil embargo in late 1973 did have an impact on us. Like in the U.S., there were days when 150 to 200 cars would be lined up for gas at the Post Exchange (PX) gas station. Gas prices were outrageous during this time: about fifty-nine cents per gallon, up from about forty-five cents, and gas was rationed to only four gallons per car.

I didn't have a car and it didn't affect me personally, but I do recall several of the guys sneaking gas out of the crash trucks. This was before they put locks on gas tanks and you could use a garden hose to siphon the gas out. Back home, we called these Florida Credit Cards. A couple of our guys got caught stealing gas and were busted down a rank. The Division Officer, Bos'n Joye, started gas watches which meant someone had to keep an eye on the crash trucks around the clock. Frankly, it was a royal pain in the ass.

While on Guam, I was introduced to a few new Navy traditions. There were the standard Navy issue traditions like personnel inspections, barracks inspections, locker inspections, and piss tests. Then, there were the non-standard Navy issue traditions which were more fun and practical. I'll elaborate on some of the more memorable ones. Actually, they were probably more like pranks than traditions, but since certain people were pinpointed at a certain milestone in their Navy career, I guess it could technically be called a tradition.

During my tour on Guam, several of my buddies got orders to transfer to another duty station. It was a tradition to "wet down" the short timer on his last day of duty. That meant a bunch of us would wrestle him down out in front of the Crash Barn and hose him down. Sometimes we would use a garden hose, but most of the time we tried to get him with one of the crash truck hoses. I found it quite funny since this would probably be the last time we saw these guys.

I was also introduced to the tradition of "lighting a fart." For many years this has been a tradition, not just in the Navy but in all branches of our fine military. It *is* an art, because not everyone can do it properly and those that can could probably make a decent living in a circus or at a busy intersection in downtown Manhattan, New Orleans, or Las Vegas. It was funny watching some of the guys try this; some were much better than others. I guess you have got to have the right mixture of gas and air and the lighter has to be at the right distance. I think it also depends on what you ate a few hours earlier—Navy beans are said to be the best gas producers.

It is a big thing when a sailor gets promoted to the next rank, especially when he was promoted to a petty officer. There is a third class petty officer (E-4), a second class petty officer (E-5), and a first class petty officer (E-6). We would always go out and party when one of the guys was promoted. As a matter of fact, we would always go out and party even if nobody got promoted. After all it is a Navy tradition to drink, plain and simple.

Sometimes the promotee would drink a little too much and make an ass out of himself. The drunker he got, the easier it was to handle him. By that I mean there were several times when a newly minted petty officer would wake up at the Crash Barn, butt naked, tied tightly to the telephone pole, and greased up from head to toe with standard Navy issue axle grease. That stuff is hard to get off and takes several weeks to get the stink out.

It was not unusual to see or hear about someone who was promoted in one of the squadrons to wake up, butt naked, tied to a chair, and dangling from a rope about twenty or thirty feet off the hangar deck. Sometimes, if they didn't wake up, they would get hosed down by their crews.

After several months on the island and living in the old open barracks, we were able to move into newly remodeled barracks that included rooms that would hold four guys. They weren't really that new, but a fresh coat of paint worked wonders. We even had wood paneling in our rooms and best of all, an air conditioner. There were four men to a room, each with their own locker. The rooms were about twenty-five feet by ten feet, plenty of room for the four racks (we had bunk beds), four lockers, a couch, and a couple of chairs. My roommates were Glenn Law, Bill Riggs, and Chris Nottingham. We got along fine and became good friends.

Back in the early 1950s, my mom was learning how to fly airplanes when she first met my dad. I don't know if he asked or if she decided on her own, but she quit flying soon thereafter. One of the guys in our division, Bruce Hallowell, was taking flying lessons on the base. There was a flying club with several airplanes and he was in the process of getting his pilot's license. I liked that so I inquired about flying lessons. Since we were on Port/Starboard duty sections, I had a whole day off every other day, so I certainly had the time to learn.

My first flying lesson was in early May 1974. I arrived early at the flying club, checked in, paid my money to start, and was so excited of what I was about to do. My first flight instructor was Larry Watkins, a civilian contractor for the Navy. The total cost for the first hour's flight instruction was $25: $16 for the plane rental and $9 for the instructor. After showing me how to pre-flight the plane, we taxied out to the runway and took off, Larry in the right hand copilot's seat and me in the left hand pilot's seat.

We were in a Cessna 150, a small two-seater airplane, about the size of a large can of tuna. The whole introductory flight only lasted an hour and Larry gave me a good overview, even letting me fly the airplane a few times. This is where I literally learned the term "white knuckles." I can't tell you how many times Larry told me to "Relax, the plane will fly itself." We landed and taxied back to the flying club.

Back then, you had to log ten hours of flying time with an instructor before you could do your first solo. During those first ten hours, there was a lot of flying to learn, including takeoffs and landings and stalls. I was getting pretty good but in a small airplane like the Cessna 150, the wind could easily push you around during takeoffs and landings.

My first solo was, to say the least, nerve wracking. There wasn't going to be anyone in the plane with me—that's why they call it a "solo." I stopped on the taxiway to let Larry out, closed his door and got clearance from the Tower to take off. "Just take off and land, Chet, that's all you have to do. You've done this dozens of times and this will be no different."

You know what? Larry was right. I was able to take off, circle the airport and come back in for a nice smooth landing. I was so proud of myself. I picked Larry up and we taxied back to the flying club. We celebrated in style with a couple of cold cokes.

There were several others at the flying club that day, all happy for me because they remembered their first solo and this was a reason to celebrate. Larry told me to turn around and close my eyes. I had no clue what was happening. He took hold of my T-shirt, cut out the back with a pair of scissors, laid it on the table, and wrote "First Solo, May 26, 1974, NAS Agana Guam." It was a tradition to cut one's shirttail off after their first solo. I still have it, too. It was a proud moment and I had only been flying for a little over three weeks.

Part of the requirement to get your pilot's license is to fly a cross-country flight. The problem in Guam is that there is no cross-country; it is only thirty-two miles by eight miles. And, at that time, you had to fly at least one, one hundred-mile segment. As I understand it, now you have to fly three, one-hundred mile segments for your cross country flight.

The only place to fly in a chain of islands is to fly to another island, so the cross-country flight for me would be to the island of Saipan and back, about a three-hour round trip. The first two cross-country flights were with an instructor, just to make sure you knew how to get there and back. All you have to do is fly over water on a straight compass heading, find the right island, do a touch and go landing, and come back. Flying over water requires you to carry a life raft in the plane and you also have to wear an inflatable life preserver on the trip.

My cross-country flight instructor was Mary Hoy, who I really liked. Her husband was an Air Force pilot who flew C-130s out of Anderson AFB and was also a Hurricane Hunter. In Guam, as in the western Pacific, hurricanes are called typhoons, but these guys preferred to be called Hurricane Hunters instead of Typhoon Hunters. It turns out that during one of her husband's flights as a Hurricane Hunter, they had to ditch in the storm; that's all they knew. The plane disappeared and they could not find any survivors or any sign of the wreckage, even though the search and rescue squad looked for a couple of weeks after the plane went down. This happened several months after I got my pilot's license.

From Guam, the first island you fly over is Rota. Next is Goat Island, then Tinian, and then Saipan; all are in the Marianas. Tinian, by the way, is the island where "Big Boy" was loaded onto Paul Tibbits' B-29 *Enola Gay*, the A-bomb that was dropped on Hiroshima, Japan. The flight to and from Saipan was great, over open water, and clear as could be. I only did a touch and go landing on Saipan but I would make that trip three more times.

In order to get your pilot's license you also had to attend ground school, learning all the aviation rules and regulations. Ground school lasts several weeks and covers a lot of ground, pun intended. The test is given every few months and I was bound and determined to pass. I wasn't going to flunk out of school again. The day of the test, I was ready, but for the first few minutes I pushed the test and the books away and closed my eyes. I was so worked up that I didn't want to jump in with both feet before I had a few quiet moments to myself.

I don't think I prayed. I wasn't that into God at the time. I think it was what is called meditation. I wasn't trying to remember what I had read and I wasn't trying to anticipate what types of questions might be on the test. It was slow breathing and focusing on something relaxing. I thought about Kingsley Lake and all the good times I had out there as a kid. After a few minutes, I started taking the test. I actually did quite well on the test, passing it the first time. I wrote home to my mom and dad and told them that it wasn't that hard.

Over the next few months I would continue my flight training, both solo and with an instructor. Most of the training dealt with the "what ifs" which means that the plane usually flies well all by itself, but "what if you lose power," or "what if you stall on a tight turn." I did a lot of touch and gos and practiced in cross winds.

I had started flying in May and I took my check ride October 21, 1974 with John Brandenburg, a retired Navy Captain. In fact, he used to be the Commanding Officer of NAS Agana, Guam. I passed the test with flying colors and was so happy. I was now a private pilot, "Airplane Single Engine Land," and I had a license to prove it. Wow, I was a scuba diver, I was a skydiver, I was a firefighter, and now I was a pilot—all by the time I was twenty years old.

After I got my pilot's license, I was allowed to take passengers. The Cessna 150 had only room for two people, the pilot and one passenger. But the Cessna 172 had room for a total of four. I took a couple of check flights with one of my favorite flight instructors, Mary Hoy, in the Cessna 172. I was then able to take up more people. It was great, flying some of my buddies around the island. They all enjoyed it and got lots of good pictures.

I also got checked out for night flying. That wasn't too tough and I only needed a few check rides with an instructor at night before I could fly solo or with passengers at night. Mary Hoy was also my night instructor. Flying at night is obviously a totally different environment.

First of all, if you don't have any of the island's night lights, like the downtown area, then there is no horizon. Trying to fly over the ocean at night would be close to impossible without relying on your instruments. The instructor takes you through a lot of that though, just in case you get turned around. It was something to look down at night at the downtown Agana area to see all the lights. It wasn't Las Vegas, but it was pretty.

I always thought a WAVE had something to do with the ocean, but WAVES are "Women Accepted for Volunteer Emergency Service," a term originating from WWII. At my time in the Navy, it simply meant a woman sailor. We had lots of WAVES on the base, but none in Crash.

I met a WAVE at the base swimming pool one day while off duty. We started talking and it turned out she played the guitar, too. Robin had a 12-string guitar like I did. Well, I could see this going somewhere. I didn't know any women on the base. We seemed to get along fine and she invited me to a party one night, so I went carrying my 12-string guitar with me.

It turns out the party was at a local downtown church and she was very much into Jesus. At that time, I would have labeled her a "Jesus-freak" since every time anyone mentioned Jesus, the entire group would scream out in chorus, "Hallelujah!" That was a big thing back in the seventies. Don't get me wrong, I love Jesus, but that was a little too much for me.

Having said that, I was inspired one night while attending a Christian celebration with Robin. I've always been a country music fan and Hank Williams was one of my favorites. He had written a song, *I Saw the Light* which is a really easy song to sing and during my solo, I added an extra verse that just came to me:

> *I just walked through that big wooden door*
> *I look up and said I want more.*
> *I look around at all my new found friends*
> *I pray to the Lord, I hope it never ends.*

I had been on Guam for almost a year before I got to know some WAVES. I actually was introduced to them through the Seabees since their barracks were right next to the WAVES barracks, lucky bastards! The old saying, "once you know one, you know them all," was almost true. I initially got to know one or two and since I played guitar and sang, that helped break the ice.

Many nights we would gather a group of five or six of us (Seabees and WAVES) in the stairwell at the barracks to jam, sing, drink, and generally have a good time. Why the stairwell? It was a legal meeting place because you couldn't go into the WAVES rooms and they couldn't go into yours (like *that* would stop us), but since the stairwells were bricks and ceramic tile, the sound was awesome for jamming.

Several of these WAVES were what we called "buns" or sexually active women. To be honest, Navy guys were called "hot dogs" or sexually active men. Get it—hot dogs and buns? Hey, I don't make this stuff up. Remember, this is the Navy and it *is* a second language. Besides, I had learned that G.U.A.M. really stood for "Give Up and Masturbate" so getting to know some attractive, sexually active women was *not* a bad thing.

I almost got married while on Guam. I met a girl; actually I met several WAVES in my last few months on the island. I dated a few and almost ended up marrying one. I'm certainly glad I didn't, but at the time, I was twenty years old and I thought I was madly in love. I would spend most of my off duty time with her in the barracks which by the way was not allowed, and we even spent a couple of weekends at the Guam Inn, the local, cheap, rat-infested hotel close to the base.

Looking back, I think I was enamored because I had been without a girlfriend for a long time and longed for female companionship. I was also very inexperienced, having only been with a few girls before meeting her and when we spent so much of our time together, I think the loneliness one feels doesn't really hit until you're no longer lonely.

Bonnie worked in the base dental clinic and while I didn't have dental problems, I tried to find excuses to go see her on my days off. Likewise, she knew the times she could come by the Crash Barn while I was on duty. While we couldn't fool around, it was kind of nice having her visit when I was working. I liked showing her off, so to speak, to the other guys. They knew we had the hots for each other and I think several of them were jealous.

I do remember the division training officer telling me that "No, you're not in love. You're letting your Johnson Bar get in the way. Besides, she's like a railroad track and gets laid all over the place." That one hurt and I ignored him and defended her. I really didn't know if she had been around the block and frankly I didn't care. I was at the tender age where love was blind and I ignored anyone else's thoughts on the subject.

When I left Guam, Bonnie rode with me up to Anderson AFB to see me off. We would see each other again since she would be transferred a few months after me to San Diego. It was a tearful parting, both for me and for Bonnie, but she was pretty devastated. I was the one leaving and happy and would be going home to my family. She was the one staying behind. I ended up giving her my silver dollar necklace, a token that I would see her again soon. I had been wearing that silver dollar since my grandfather gave it to me when I was twelve years old.

8 NAS AGANA GUAM
New Orders

The Navy is good about planning your every move and your next duty station. About six months before your scheduled departure date, someone starts to work with you on where you want to go for your next duty station. I personally think that is a crock since the Navy is going to send you wherever it wants you to go. But I guess in the long run, it is a morale booster since they do ask. The person in charge of this horse hockey is called a Detailer.

The Navy actually sent a detailer out to Guam to meet with a bunch of us and ask us where we wanted to go. I told him my choice would be either Key West or Italy. I lived in Florida so Key West was a no brainer and would be closer to home. I had heard that NAS Naples, Italy was a great duty station so that was an option. The detailer told us that since we were on the west coast already, we would probably be assigned to a ship on the west coast, most likely San Diego or San Francisco—so much for the dream sheet.

I was scheduled to leave Guam sometime in February 1975 and wasn't quite sure where I was headed. That would come later. I did think about extending my tour of duty on Guam for another nine months, but a couple of beers and a few more ass chewings from the senior petty officers helped me decide different.

Each of the Navy billets typically comes with a sea/land rotation schedule. For ABs, that rotation is 4/2. You spent four years on sea duty and two years on a land base. Funny thing, even though an overseas duty station like NAS Agana Guam was on land, it was considered sea duty. I would have to keep that in mind at re-enlistment time.

My orders finally came through on January 15, 1975. I had learned earlier that I would be assigned to the aircraft carrier USS Kitty Hawk, CV-63, stationed out of San Diego, California. I wasn't sure when I had to report to her, but I finally found out, "No later than 20 MAR 1975." That was plain and clear. I knew I would be leaving Guam sometime during February, but not sure when. The Navy always waits until the last minute or at least the last month before they lay the big date on you. But you are so ready to leave that it does not matter.

I also knew that several of my good buddies would also be transferred to Kitty Hawk. Glenn Law and I would leave Guam and head back to the states on the same flight. Gary Borne had already transferred to Kitty Hawk. James Young, who was with me at boot camp, A School, and Guam, would also be on Kitty Hawk.

As time gets closer to your departure date, you become what is known as a Short Timer. It definitely affects your attitude about things. Everyone gets the GAF (Give a Fuck) attitude, some worse than others. Some guys even make a short timer chain that hangs from the belt of a short timer for everyone to see and admire, with one link representing one day, (signifying too short to care) and usually starts with thirty links. The mantra then becomes, "thirty days and a wake-up," or whatever amount of time is left. I didn't make a short timer's chain, but towards the end, I certainly came on duty with the "twenty days and a wake up" attitude.

I was also on a roller coaster ride with emotions about leaving and what I would do during my leave time between duty stations. I probably drove my parents crazy. In one letter I wrote them I would be home for three weeks; another letter said I might have to transfer directly to Kitty Hawk without coming home; still another letter said I might stay a few days in California to visit some friends before I came home. I'm sure they were also on an emotional roller coaster ride. After all, their little baby boy had been gone for fifteen months and they certainly wanted to see him.

It didn't help that the Navy waited until the last minute to let *me* know when I would be leaving. But when they did, I had my orders to leave Guam on February 10, 1975 flying out of Anderson AFB. My orders would get me to Travis AFB in San Francisco and then to San Diego which the Navy paid for. What I needed to do was to get back to Gainesville, Florida to see my family. That would come out of my pocket.

Our freedom flight was a Northwest Orient 707. Glenn and I had made arrangements for his girlfriend and Bonnie to take us up to Anderson. After a tearful goodbye for both of us, we climbed on board and settled down for a long flight. It was about an eight hour trip back to Hawaii, a couple of hours layover, then onto a military aircraft to Travis AFB near San Francisco.

I had left Guam in my summer whites because Guam is a tropical island. We got to San Francisco in February—it wasn't tropical weather. In fact, it was hovering around freezing and my peacoat was stowed away in my seabag. To top that off, when we got to the San Francisco airport terminal about five in the morning, it was closed and didn't open until six. We had to stand outside waiting for about an hour before we got in. You can bet your sweet ass I dug in my seabag to get out my peacoat. It definitely made a difference.

I didn't hang around California. I booked the first flight home I could find. I called my mom and dad and I think we all shed a tear of joy that I was coming home. I flew into Jacksonville and my mom picked me up. I couldn't believe it had been fifteen months since I had seen her.

I drove home and we were talking about so many things I forgot the turnoff to Gainesville and ended up in Green Cove Springs without realizing where I was. It was funny since this would take us home through Penney Farms, the place I had gotten my speeding ticket right before I enlisted. I spent three glorious weeks at home on leave before heading out to my next adventure—USS Kitty Hawk.

So, what experiences did I walk away with from Guam? I can think of a dozen things, but the most prevalent was how much I appreciated my family and my home. This was by far the longest time I had ever been away from my parents and my sister—fifteen months, including two birthdays and two Christmases. Letters, packages, and the few phone calls I made were so important to me and I know they were to my family. I made some good friends, several of which I would be with together again on Kitty Hawk.

Fighting fires? Well, the only fires I fought were the hot drills. We had no real fires, no aircraft crashes, and no disasters on my watch. Was I disappointed? Hell no. Part of me wanted to know how I would react in such an emergency, but the other part of me said that I would have done fine since I had been through so much training in so many different situations.

I was a pretty confident kid at the ripe old age of twenty. Besides, my training would be tested several times a few months later aboard Kitty Hawk. When I got out of the Navy, I became a civilian firefighter with the City of Gainesville for a few years—a natural progression. I would be on duty for six months in Gainesville before I fought my first house fire.

One of the more important qualities I think I picked up was leadership. I was now a Third Class Petty Officer and I had men (hell, they were boys like me) that I was responsible for. Sure, we would play grab ass every now and then, but when it came down to duty and orders and all that other important Navy crap, I had to learn how to give orders and more importantly, how to handle some bent shitcan that was ignoring my orders. But it comes with the territory and I would have to learn how to deal with it one way or another. There would be more of these tests aboard Kitty Hawk.

#

After fifty years of service, NAS Agana Guam "Gateway to the Orient" was closed March 31, 1995 by decision of the BRAC (Base Realignment and Closure) '93 Commission. The land and buildings were eventually handed over to the government of Guam. The Guam International Airport was renamed the A.B. Won Pat International Airport and remains a major Pacific airline crossroad.

9 USS KITTY HAWK
I'm Too Early

After Glenn and I left Guam, I flew home to visit my mom, dad, and sister. I found time to visit some other friends, too, but most of the time I spent at home. It felt good, especially since I had never been gone from home for so long. Winter was winding down in Gainesville which meant the temperatures were getting back to the fifties and sixties and the flowers were starting to bloom.

One of the best things about the Navy, and I guess all military branches, is that you earn thirty days of leave (vacation) each year. Since I had to report to Kitty Hawk no later than March 20, 1975, I had about four weeks I could take.

It was great being home, but I also had the itch to get to my next duty station. Instead of taking a full month's leave, I decided I would only take three weeks and head out to San Diego and Kitty Hawk. I left the fifth of March and got to the Naval Station in San Diego. I was to report in to Kitty Hawk, but she was out on maneuvers in Hawaii and would not be back for a few weeks. Well, that sucked. I asked if they would fly me out, but for some reason they wouldn't and I had to stay at San Diego Naval Station in a temporary holding company until Kitty Hawk got back to port the end of March.

There were three of us in the holding company and we had the entire barracks to ourselves. That was fine, except that the three of us had to *clean* the entire barracks. We started duty at 0730 and after cleaning the barracks, we could do whatever we wanted until we had to muster again at 1245. After muster, we could take the rest of the day off. We didn't have to stay on base, so I took it upon myself to explore more of San Diego. I didn't have any friends in San Diego and the other two guys were hanging out with their girlfriends and didn't want extra company.

There were a few things to do on the base, but after a while swimming, bowling, and playing pool got boring. At the time, downtown San Diego was loaded with bars, massage parlors, and X-rated movie theaters. I think they've cleaned it up now, but there were a lot of temptations back in the mid-seventies.

On one of my outings just outside the base, I was waiting at a crosswalk for the traffic light to turn. There was a slight drizzle and I wasn't in any hurry to get anywhere. All of a sudden, a motorcyclist hit his front brakes a little too hard and I saw him fly over the handlebars and land in the middle of the intersection. I ran over to him like a lot of other people, but everyone was standing around doing nothing. I checked to see if he had any obvious broken bones—he had broken his ankle, but wasn't in too much pain.

One of the few A's I got while attending FSU was for First Aid; the other was for Scuba Diving. The guy was conscious and coherent. I talked to him for a little and tried to comfort him until an ambulance arrived. We did not have cell phones back then, but we did have 911 and you could place a free call at a phone booth for an emergency. It had been raining that day and he was lying down in the water, so I took off my jacket and placed it under his head which he greatly appreciated.

When the ambulance arrived, the paramedics jumped out and came over to examine him. One of them was a very attractive female with a large bust and let people know it, if you know what I mean. I looked at the guy on the ground and made some crude comment like, "You hit the jackpot. Look at the size of those jugs." He started cracking up and I could hear him laughing as they loaded him into the ambulance. He was going to be alright.

I think in my entire Navy career, short as it was, the time spent in San Diego in a temporary company was by far, bar none, the most boring. There were a few working parties which helped pass the time, but there was almost nothing to do and no one to do it with. I was getting anxious to get on board the ship, but I would have to wait three weeks until the end of March when Kitty Hawk returned from Hawaii. I didn't get into any trouble. I did, however, tour some of San Diego and went to the San Diego Zoo, Balboa Park, and SeaWorld. What else was a bored sailor supposed to do?

10 USS KITTY HAWK
Welcome Aboard

Finally, I got on board Kitty Hawk on March 30, 1975. I had enough of the boring barracks life in a temporary holding company, but I was mature enough to realize that's the way it was in the Navy, "Hurry up and wait! It's not just a job, it's an adventure!"

Kitty Hawk's home port was North Island Naval Station, just west of San Diego across the bay. When I first arrived on the pier, I was looking up at this magnificent aircraft carrier which was to be my home for the next two and a half years. I wouldn't say she was beautiful (that would come later), but I would say it felt right.

My good friend Glenn Law was already on board. He came in a couple of weeks before I did and was aboard when Kitty Hawk left for Hawaii. When I first arrived on board and checked in with the personnel department (commonly called processing), he came down to greet me and we shook hands like old friends. It was good to see him. He told me that Gary Borne was already on board and in the crash crew—they called it Crash and Salvage on the ship. That is probably where I would be going since I came from Crash and Rescue in NAS Agana Guam.

Glenn told me that Kitty Hawk had been on a RIMPAC (Rim of the Pacific) exercise off Hawaii and that was probably why they didn't fly me out. RIMPAC was a major ten-day exercise designed to test and evaluate nearly every facet of modern naval warfare and usually involved ships, planes, and men from other nations in the Pacific Rim. This exercise was done in preparation for an overseas deployment.

While I had already been in the Navy for a year and a half and I had learned some colorful language in boot camp and on Guam, I was about to learn more of this second language aboard Kitty Hawk. As many Navy traditions I experienced in Guam, there would be more aboard Kitty Hawk.

During my first week on board, Kitty Hawk sailed for a "Family Day Cruise" which was a one-day cruise allowing sailors' dependents on board for a day. Since this was my first time on the ship when at sea, I was told to stay off the flight deck and hob knob with everyone else. I could watch flight deck operations from Vulture's Row, an open air balcony on the ship's island overlooking the flight deck. I was OK with that, because I got to see for the first time flight deck operations: Navy jets being shot off the catapults and landing on the carrier. It was pretty exciting and I couldn't wait to get onto the flight deck.

The ABH rate has two types of jobs. One is the aircraft firefighting that I had done in Guam. The other is a combination of tasks that involve handling aircraft, hence the rate Aviation Boatswain's Mate *Handler*. These tasks include directing jets around the flight deck, driving aircraft tow tractors, and tying the aircraft down to the flight deck using chains. I would learn it all soon enough. My first assignment aboard Kitty Hawk *was* with Crash and Salvage and that was fine with me. There were fourteen guys in Crash. I would find out later just how short-handed we really were.

While we were in port at North Island, I took an opportunity to attend a presentation about the Navy's Explosive Ordnance Disposal (EOD) team. I met the initial qualifications ("Press hard, the third copy's yours") and from what I could tell, there were only about four hundred EOD members in the entire Navy. It wasn't as dangerous a job as a Navy SEAL, but it could be very exciting. EOD teams help to identify and disassemble explosive devices when called upon. The training at the time was about thirty-nine weeks and involved scuba diving for those bombs that may be underwater.

Besides a written qualification exam, I had to also take a physical qualification test which consisted of pushups, pull-ups, sit-ups, and running. I didn't have any problem with any of those, I was in great shape. In fact, I ran a mile and a half in under ten minutes—barefoot. I had never run that fast before.

A couple of days after the EOD qualifying exams, I thought about it some more, but after finding out that it would require another two-year commitment, I wasn't so sure anymore. I decided that I didn't need to spend any more time in the Navy than I had already committed.

I was in San Diego on board Kitty Hawk with some old friends and meeting new friends. Bonnie was still in Guam and I would not see her for several more months. I called her several times from a pay phone on the pier and it was expensive—thirteen dollars' worth of quarters for only three minutes. We talked and it seemed there was a lot of crying on her end; I wasn't quite sure why. But I still tried to call every week or so, just to stay in touch.

I had written my dad a long letter a couple of weeks after I arrived on the ship asking for his advice. "Dad, how did you know Mom was the right one for you?" I asked. I was beginning to question myself and while I know I loved Bonnie, I wasn't sure I loved her enough to marry her. How does one really know?

Bonnie wanted to get married right away. I wanted to wait a little while, get to know each other better, and find out if we were really meant for each other. It's hard to do that when you are six thousand miles apart and only get to talk a few minutes on the phone once a week. Email did not exist back then and letters usually took a week. Besides, Kitty Hawk was gearing up for a Pacific cruise and I would be gone for six months. I just didn't know. My dad wrote back a very serious and purposeful letter telling me that while I was growing up and maturing in the Navy, there was no reason to hurry these things. If it was meant to happen then it would. Give it some time. Dads have such great advice.

Over the next couple of months, Kitty Hawk would be getting ready for a forward deployment cruise called a WESTPAC (Western Pacific). It would be a six-month cruise and we were scheduled to deploy May 21. Before that, we would be at sea training for a week here and a week there and I would be learning what an AB does on board an aircraft carrier.

One of the things that pissed me off at the time was the drinking age in California. On Guam, the drinking age was eighteen. I was twenty years old now and had been drinking like a sailor for a couple of years. The drinking age in California was twenty-one so I didn't have any luck going out drinking with the guys and I even got kicked out of a bar or two. That meant that I would not be able to drink legally in California until Kitty Hawk returned from the WESTPAC cruise. That sucked!

A United States Ship (USS) typically has three birthdays: laying the keel, launching the ship, and the ever popular and public commissioning. USS Kitty Hawk was built by the New York Shipbuilding Corporation, Camden, New Jersey. Her keel was laid down December 27, 1956. She was launched May 21, 1960 and commissioned April 29, 1961 at Philadelphia Naval Shipyard. It was the second U.S. Navy ship named after the small North Carolina town near which Orville and Wilbur Wright flew the first manned aircraft on December 17, 1903. At the time when she was built, Kitty Hawk *was* the largest ship in the world.

Kitty Hawk would be the first of four carriers of the *Kitty Hawk* class of super carriers, all built in the 1960s: USS Kitty Hawk (CV-63; 1961-2009), USS Constellation (CV-64; 1961-2003), USS America (CV-66; 1965-1996), and the USS John F. Kennedy (CV-67; 1967-2007). Before her decommissioning in January 2009, she would be the oldest, longest-serving, active aircraft carrier in the Navy.

Her sister ship, USS Constellation (CV-64), was being built at the same time. Both ships were behind construction schedules though. On December 19, 1960, the "Connie" was heavily damaged by fire while under construction when a forklift moving through the hangar bay pierced a fuel tank. Fuel was spilled on welders below decks which ignited a fire, claiming fifty lives and injuring 323 shipyard workers.

There have always been rumors that the Connie was *supposed* to be the first carrier in this class and named USS Kitty Hawk (CV-63), but because of this fire and the subsequent delay, the other ship being built at the same time was re-designated USS Kitty Hawk, CV-63.

Kitty Hawk's first Commanding Officer was Captain William F. Bringle. Captain Bringle brought her out of the shipyards, conducted extensive sea trials for several months in the Atlantic, and then headed for her new home port in California.

On October 8, 1961, she rounded Cape Horn and officially became part of the Pacific Fleet. After stops in Brazil, Chile, and Peru, she arrived in San Diego on November 1, 1961 to a warm, home port welcome. As she entered the 42-foot deep channel in San Diego harbor, newly dredged to accommodate her, a swing band on board a nearby ship played its rendition of *California, Here I Come*. Her first extended deployment was underway September 13, 1962.

Kitty Hawk has enjoyed a rich history over her forty-eight years of dedicated service. Some were good; others, not so good. Beginning in late 1965, she made six combat WESTPAC deployments during the Vietnam conflict and performed with consistent distinction. In 1969, Kitty Hawk was awarded the Presidential Unit Citation by Lyndon B. Johnson in recognition of her performance during 1967-68. This was the first time the Presidential Unit Citation was awarded for service in Vietnam.

On the not so good side—on the evening of October 12, 1972 immediately following flight ops, a series of incidents broke out wherein a group of black sailors, armed with chains, wrenches, bars, broomsticks, and other dangerous items, went marauding through sections of the ship disobeying orders to cease, terrorizing the crew, and seeking out white personnel for senseless beating with fists and with weapons which resulted in extremely serious injury to three men and the medical treatment of many more, including some black sailors.

It was reported that the initial fisticuffs started in the mess hall. The Marine detachment was called in to help quell the situation. Both the ship's CO and XO tried to help calm the situation, but apparently the situation started to sour between the armed black sailors and the Marines. The XO was a black man and seemed to be able to communicate to the rioters helping to calm them down. The riot lasted for about six hours.

These events were investigated by a special subcommittee on disciplinary problems in the United States Navy. The subcommittee was unable to determine any precipitous cause for rampage aboard Kitty Hawk. Not only was there not one case wherein racial discrimination could be pinpointed, but "there was no evidence which indicated that the blacks who participated in that incident perceived racial discrimination, either in general or any specific, of such a nature as to justify belief that violent reaction was required."

However, it was obvious that the participants perceived that racial discrimination existed. The subcommittee's position was that the riot on Kitty Hawk consisted of unprovoked assaults by only a very few men, most of whom were, according to the published reports, "below-average mental capacity, most of whom had been aboard for less than one year, and all of whom were black." This group, as a whole, acted as thugs which raised doubt as to whether they should ever have been accepted into military service in the first place.

There were probably several reasons for the riot. First of all, Kitty Hawk was on an extended deployment—we were at war with Vietnam—and just when the crew thought they would be heading home to the United States, they learned they would return to the combat zone after a port-of-call in Subic Bay. There were a couple of small scuffles reported in port though there were *always* scuffles when in port. Second, this was the early seventies—the United States had been working to desegregate schools all over the country and even these schools experienced racial tensions.

In 1970 when I was in high school, the predominately white school and the predominately black school were desegregated and brought together in the white school and I remember it being a very tough time. We had more than a thousand kids graduate in my class in 1972. Lots of fights and gangs and beatings. Some even called them riots. But as I understand it, that was happening all over the country. Kitty Hawk was no different. There were racial tensions all over and unlike my high school, there wasn't anywhere anyone could go to get off the ship—it was at sea.

Fortunately during my tour aboard Kitty Hawk, 1975-1977, there were no major racial incidences. I think for the most part, the crew got along well. The black sailors did have a special handshake, called the Dap. It became very popular during the Vietnam War, but apparently had been traditional in many African communities for centuries. I saw some of our black shipmates spend hours trying different adaptations of the Dap, but it was something I never got into.

Kitty Hawk is 1,065 feet long from bow to stern (about as long as the 77-story Chrysler Building is tall), 282 feet wide at the flight deck level, and displaces more than 83,000 tons with a full load. She has a draft of 38 feet and is powered by eight steam boilers with four bronze screw propellers (each 21 feet in diameter and weighing about 30 tons), producing 280,000 horsepower, giving her a top speed of about 35 knots. She carries about 2,000,000 gallons of fuel. She also had onboard a desalination plant that turns salt water into fresh water making about 340,000 gallons a day.

When on deployment, she carried a compliment of more than 5,500 officers and enlisted men and more than 75 aircraft. Ship's company (those men who were permanently assigned duty aboard the ship) comprised about 3,000 officers and enlisted men. The rest of the 2,500 men were the air wing (those men who were permanently assigned duty to the various air squadrons, but *temporarily* assigned to the ship). In 1961, her cost was about $265,200,000. In comparison, today's aircraft carriers cost more than $4 billion. It took $9 million in ship support and another $22 million in airwing support *each year* to enable Kitty Hawk to perform her mission.

Carriers came into real service during World War II. The Japanese proved that—the attack on Pearl Harbor was carried out by aircraft launched from Japanese aircraft carriers. It took us a while to catch up, but there is a rich history of United States aircraft carriers over the years. Today's super carriers and their extended families, the air wing and the battle groups, are unmatchable anywhere in the world.

One of the biggest obstacles in today's neopolitics is how to get our country's air power to countries that need it. We can't fly and land our jets just anywhere. We need permission which often takes a lot of diplomacy and time, and the time this process takes could mean the difference between victory and defeat. We've heard about it on the news time and time again— a country refuses the United States permission to land jets in their country or even let our jets fly over their airspace. It is also estimated that eight-five percent of the world's population lives within one hundred miles of a coast.

So with an aircraft carrier, we can bypass that political and diplomatic bullshit. Like Dominos or your favorite Chinese restaurant, "we deliver." We may not be able to deliver in thirty minutes or less, but we can place our aircraft carriers pretty much anywhere in the world in a matter of days. Under the International Freedom of Navigation laws, aircraft carriers and other warships are recognized as sovereign territories in almost the entire ocean. As long as the carrier respects the territorial boundaries, we're home free. And the best part? With more than seventy-five aircraft aboard, fifty of which are strike fighters, the U.S. Navy has a more powerful air force on a single carrier than about seventy percent of the countries of the world.

So what does CV-63 stand for? The Navy has specific designations for its ships depending upon the ship's mission. The number is typically a sequential number for the major designation. For example, 63 meant Kitty Hawk was the 63rd aircraft carrier built for the U.S. Navy. The first letter in the designation is a general classification: "A" for auxiliaries, "B" for battleships, "C" for cruisers, "D" for destroyers, "L" for amphibious vessels, "M" for mine warfare vessels, "S" for submarines, "T" for Military Sealift Command, and "Y" for service and yard craft.

Despite common misconceptions, CV does *not* stand for Carrier Vessel. CV was derived from cruisers since carriers were originally seen as an extension of the cruiser mission: sea control and denial. The "V" stands for aviation *fixed wing* ("H" would be aviation *rotary wing* aircraft, or helicopter). If there was an "A" following the CV, it would designate "attack."

When Kitty Hawk was first commissioned, she was designated CVA-63 which meant she was designated as an attack carrier. In January 1973, Kitty Hawk was converted in the shipyards from an attack aircraft carrier to a multi-mission aircraft carrier and re-designated as CV-63. That meant she was also outfitted for anti-submarine warfare. If there is an "N" following the CV, it would designate the ship was "nuclear" which now accounts for all U.S. Navy aircraft carriers.

Over her forty-eight years, Kitty Hawk completed eighteen deployments in support of operations including Vietnam, the Iranian hostage crisis, Operation Restore Hope in Somalia, and air strikes against Iraq. She underwent three major overhauls in Bremerton, Washington Naval Shipyard in 1976, 1982, and 1998. But its most significant maintenance period was in the Philadelphia Naval Shipyard in 1987. Called a SLEP (Service Life Extension Program), the four-year overhaul added an estimated twenty years to the originally planned thirty-year life of the ship.

Since 1961, Kitty Hawk sailors have experienced liberty in many different countries during these deployments, most of them in the western Pacific including Japan, Hong Kong, Hawaii, Philippines, Kenya, Singapore, Bahrain, United Arab Emirates, Australia, Guam, and Thailand. She's also stopped in ports at Spain, Trinidad, Brazil, Chile, and Peru.

When I was active duty, 1973-1977, there were twenty-seven carriers in the U.S. Navy. When Kitty Hawk was decommissioned in January 2009, she was the last of the diesel-powered aircraft carriers. Now, there are only ten active aircraft carriers in service. The latest commissioned carrier is USS George H.W. Bush (CVN-77). All are nuclear powered.

11 USS KITTY HAWK
A Tour Of The Ship

To board a ship, you've got to somehow get from the pier to the ship. Unlike the Starship Enterprise, you can't just "Beam me up." An aircraft carrier is huge and on Kitty Hawk, two of the starboard flight deck elevators were lowered. A Brow is a long metal walkway extending from a platform with stairs on the pier to these elevators. The Forward Brow is reserved for officers and VIPs. The After Brow is for the rest of us riff-raff.

When a sailor boards a ship, she or he first faces the stern and salutes the flag, then turns to the officer on watch at the brow, shows his or her military ID card, salutes the officer on watch and asks, "Permission to come aboard, sir?" The salute is smartly returned with "Permission granted." When disembarking a ship, the reverse is true: the sailor shows his military ID, salutes the officer on watch and asks "Permission to go ashore, sir?" which is then returned with a salute and "Permission granted." The sailor then salutes the flag and walks off the brow. This tradition is followed by both officers and enlisted personnel. These are time honored Navy traditions and I've seen many sailors, drunk as a skunk, stagger aboard but still manage to salute the flag and the officer on watch.

One reason I am no longer in the Navy is because as a petty officer, one of my less than glorious duties was to stand watch at the After brow when the ship was docked at port. To make a long story longer, one night I had the dog watch: 0000 to 0400 (12:00 a.m. 'til 4:00 a.m.). As you might guess, sailors have a reputation for drinking and most bars around the port closed at 0200.

About three o'clock one morning while on watch, I spotted an obviously inebriated sailor walking up the After brow. He was swaying to and fro and as he got closer, I recognized him as a friend of mine. We had nicknamed him J.J. because when in port, he always seemed to have a bottle of Jack

Daniels in one pocket and a bottle of Jim Beam in the other. It is against Navy regulations to bring liquor on board and is punishable up to thirty days in the brig with nothing but bread and water.

J.J. was staggering up the After brow grinning from ear to ear with a bottle in each pocket. When he got to the ship, I stopped him and started my Navy lifer lecture. "Now J.J., you know bringing liquor on board is against regulations. I'm supposed to report you and have you thrown into the brig. But you and I have been through a lot together on the flight deck. So this is what I'm going to do: I'm going to turn around and I want to hear two splashes." I was going to give J.J. a break. After all, he was my buddy and a fellow flight deck director.

I turned my back and after waiting a few seconds, I heard a gentle "kerploosh, kerploosh." I turned around planning to give J.J. another lecture about bringing liquor on board. He was still there, swaying side to side, grinning ear to ear, and completely barefoot. J.J. had thrown his shoes overboard. He did what I asked, so I decided that since no one else was around, I had to let him pass. I have to admit that was really funny. It just goes to show you that what you want to hear, what you think you hear, and what you actually hear are not necessarily the same.

On most ships, the main deck is the uppermost deck that is continuous from the bow to the stern. The second, third, fourth decks and so on are continuous decks *below* the main deck and numbered in sequence from topside down. On Kitty Hawk, the main deck is the hangar deck. Any decks *above* the main deck are called the "0 (pronounced 'Oh') decks" and sometimes called the "O level." For example, one deck above the main deck is called the 01 deck or 01 level; the second deck above the main deck is called the 02 deck, and so forth. A carrier typically has about 18 total decks, eight above the flight deck and ten below.

Aircraft carriers are so big, it is easy to get lost your first time aboard. Today's aircraft carriers are comprised of more than 2,400 compartments, each compartment with its own number or address. Once you understand the system, it is easy to find your way around the ship.

Every space in a ship is assigned an identifying letter-number symbol which is marked on a label plate secured to the hatch (door) or bulkhead (wall) of the compartment. Each compartment number contains the following information: deck number, frame number, port or starboard relation to center-line of the ship, and the use of the compartment. This is similar to how different states identify people by their driver's license number—each part of the number has a specific meaning.

The *deck number* is the first part of the compartment number and obviously tells you what deck you are on. The *frame number* at the forward bulkhead of a compartment is its frame location number in relation to its location from the bow. The next number designates where the compartment is located from the center of the ship outwards. Compartments located on the centerline of the ship carry the number 0, those to the starboard side have odd numbers, and those to the port side have even numbers. The fourth and last part of the compartment number is the letter which identifies the *primary usage* of the compartment. "E" designates engineering spaces, "F" for fuel/oil stowage, "C" for ship and fire control operations, "L" for living spaces, and so forth.

For example, a compartment numbered 03-64-01-L S-5 means the compartment is located on the 03 deck (three decks above the hangar deck), 64 frames aft of the bow, 1 frame to the right of the centerline, and designated a living space. The S-5 means the Supply Division takes care of the space.

There are two parallel passageways on the 03 deck just below the flight deck, often called the Hall of Mirrors because they almost run the entire length of the ship, almost a quarter of a mile long—one on the port side and one on the starboard side. While there are plenty of knee-knockers along these passageways, not all knee-knockers have hatches. They are called "knee-knockers" because the bottom lip of the passageway is about shin height and every sailor who serves onboard a ship sooner or later hits that lower metal lip. I, as most other sailors, still bear several scars on my shins from hitting those knee knockers while running to my duty station during General Quarters.

To get from one deck to another, at least in the main passageways, there would typically be a steep ladder with an open hatch often called a "stairwell." As far as I know, there were no stairs on board Kitty Hawk, only ladders. The handrail on the ladder was usually made of chain though there were a few made of solid tubing—these were the ones you see in movies where the sailors would slide down on their elbows with their legs sticking out in front of them.

Each passageway consisted of a series of compartments, even though the main passageways were about the width of a regular hallway you would have in your house. Each compartment in the passageway had a hatch which was oval, about five feet tall and two feet wide. Most of these hatches were closed and dogged down during General Quarters.

You probably know that the bow is the front of the ship and the stern is the rear of the ship. When you are describing things in the front part, they are typically expressed as "fore" or forward; those in the rear of the ship are expressed as "aft." Thus, the landing area on the flight deck is aft.

On Kitty Hawk, as on most large Navy ships, there are two anchors on the bow—one on the port side and one on the starboard side of the ship. The anchor chain is threaded through portholes onto a large deck located under the flight deck called the forecastle (pronounced "folk sol"). Each

71

anchor weighs about thirty tons; each link in the anchor chain weighs 360 pounds. There is enough room for more than a thousand feet of anchor chain. The only time Kitty Hawk weighed anchor when I was aboard was when we stopped in Hong Kong.

Besides the flight deck and the hangar deck, the forecastle is the largest open space on the ship. Sunday Mass is celebrated on this deck. It is also one of the more prominent visitor's spaces for VIPs—everyone wants to see the forecastle. It is impressive to see these massive chains. Most Navy ships also display their awards, lineage, and honors in the forecastle.

Living quarters aboard a Navy ship are called berthing compartments. Each division has their own space and as you might expect, it is cramped living quarters though it is a luxurious Four Seasons hotel compared to the living quarters aboard a submarine. I didn't spend much time in any other division's berthing compartment, but let me briefly describe the V-1 Division berthing compartment.

First of all, we had a cleaning crew of V-1 Division peons that kept our space spotless. These guys were blue shirts and would rotate duty on and off the flight deck. Kitty Hawk's CO would often bring VIPs into our space when we were in port because it was one of the cleanest and neatest spaces on the ship. Even the pipes in our heads (bathrooms) would shine, it was so clean.

All berthing compartments were open, meaning there wasn't a lock on the hatch. Anyone at any time could walk right in; that is why we still had watches or patrols in the compartment all during the night. We had a rotating two-man team that would patrol the compartment at night in two-hour shifts to make sure no one was in our compartment that didn't belong there.

There were a couple of different ways to get to our compartment. The one most people came through was an almost direct walk from the forward hangar deck. We were on the 02 level forward towards the bow, located just under the flight deck. That also made it interesting, especially for those who worked the night shift and tried to sleep through the day during flight ops. You could definitely hear aircraft launching, but we were so tired, most of the time we were able to sleep right through it. The nice thing about having the compartment in the bow of the ship was that we were often rocked to sleep by the ship's movement through the ocean. Since Kitty Hawk is a huge ship, it easily sliced through the waves as compared to a tin can destroyer that bounced all over the place.

Coming into our compartment, the V-1 Division first class petty officers had their own little space to the starboard side of the compartment with four racks. The main compartment also had a small common space, about ten feet by twenty feet with enough room for a few chairs, a card table, and a television set. The rest of the compartment was filled with our racks and storage lockers. The deck was black vinyl tiles—you know, the eight inch square tiles you get from Lowe's or Home Depot and lay down yourself; or maybe *your* kitchen or bathroom doesn't have black vinyl tile.

You've seen bunk beds? Well, on the ship we had three racks, one above the other, each with a total rack space of about three feet wide, two feet high, and six and a half feet long. I'm six feet four inches tall, so it was a tight fit for me. The bottom rack was about three inches off the deck and was hinged on one side to allow the compartment cleaning crew to prop it up when swabbing the deck under the rack. To climb up to the top rack, you had to step on the side of the middle rack. My rack was the middle rack and there were many times when I was sleeping when the guy on the top rack woke me up when climbing into his.

There wasn't enough room to sit up in your rack though there was a small fluorescent light over your head. There was about three feet of horizontal space between stacks of racks. Not a lot of room, but then again, we didn't spend much time in our berthing compartment when at sea.

Most guys still had their boondockers issued from boot camp, but I wanted high tops so I bought a pair of lace up flight deck boots. I spent a lot of time polishing them, just like I did when in boot camp. It was relaxing and I could carry on a decent conversation with someone who was also polishing their boots.

Most ships have racks that you lift up to store your personal belongings in lockers located directly under your rack, commonly called a "coffin rack." However, on Kitty Hawk we had two lockers built into the side of the rack space so you would have to lean over your rack to get to your personal belongings. This is where I kept my folded working uniforms, toiletries, books, a small radio/tape player, and other personal items. Not much room, but that's why we learned how to fold and stack clothes in boot camp.

Everything was locked—you didn't trust anybody. With these two lockers, plus a six-inch wide by three-foot tall by two-foot deep vertical locker in the rear of our berthing compartment to hang our whites and dress blues, and a personal locker in the crash crew quarters on the flight deck, I had four different Master combination locks.

I had a small AM/FM radio cassette player that I kept in my locker. It was the same one I had bought earlier in Guam and I still listened to Lynn Anderson, George Jones, Olivia Newton-John, and Merle Haggard. CDs didn't exist back then, so tape cassettes were our source of music. If we listened to music, we were supposed to use headphones. Most of the guys did unless there was a small party or card game going on, then nobody really cared or complained. Usually the card game would get louder before the music bothered anyone.

While there wasn't a lot of room in our personal space, we did have heavy black plastic blackout curtains, giving us a little privacy and helping to block out any light. That really helped when we worked the night shift since we slept during the day. The mattress, or fart bag as some old salts called it, was about three inches thick and filled with down. It may not have looked that comfortable, but after working sixteen to eighteen hours on the flight deck, it was the most comfortable and most homey spot a guy could find. We had sheets and a blanket, but the temperature was usually very comfortable in the berthing compartment even during the cold winter season.

The head was located on the port side of the compartment and had four shower stalls, four sinks, and four toilets. The shower stalls had curtains and while the toilets had partitions between them, they didn't have doors or curtains. The thing I remember most about the head, other than a couple of knee-crawling, commode-hugging drunk nights, was that the berthing compartment crew also kept this place spotless and shiny.

The Navy issued everyone shower shoes which were really just flip flops, and some of the smart asses stenciled the left one "port" and the right one "starboard." That was pretty funny and when you think about it and it certainly helped on those mornings with a bad hangover. We were supposed to wear our shower shoes in the compartment and not go barefoot—something about dirt, grease, and grime we tracked in from the flight deck. Most guys abided by that rule. We also used towel wraps so no one walked around naked in the compartment. Mine was bright red.

I learned about Navy showers during my time in boot camp and while it was lax in Guam, you didn't have any choice on the ship. There were about eighty guys in the V-1 Division and after flight operations or first thing in the morning, there were a lot of guys who needed to use the head.

The Navy shower is a three-minute shower and is quite simple: Turn the water on and rinse down (1 minute), then turn the water off; lather up, including shampoo (1 minute); turn the water back on and rinse off all soap (1 minute); get out and let the next guy do it. It wasn't that bad or embarrassing now that I think about it. That's just the way it was. You learned quickly to be conscientious and respect your fellow shipmates. The Navy also helped with these showers—you couldn't turn them on and leave them on. The facets were the kind you had to hold on in order to keep the water flowing.

There were times on the cruise though, during water hours when there was no hot water available and we had to take cold water showers. That was the Navy's way of helping to conserve water. They figured that if there was only cold water available you wouldn't take a long shower. They were right.

When at sea, we were able to have our laundry done aboard ship. We had our names stenciled on everything we owned, at least what the Navy issued us, except for our standard Navy issue white socks. We even stenciled our skivvies. To get our laundry done, we would tie our socks onto the belt loops of our pants and then throw everything into a laundry bin. The berthing compartment crew would put them into cloth bags and haul them down to the ship's laundry.

A day later, it would be delivered back to the compartment. No, they weren't ironed and no, we didn't iron when we were out at sea; it just didn't make sense. We did have an iron and ironing board in the compartment, but we only used it when in port. The berthing compartment crew would sort the clean laundry and throw it onto our bunks. It was up to us to fold and stack our clothes. That is something I learned well while in boot camp.

Because we worked on the flight deck, we were allowed to wear Army fatigue pants. You know, those olive green (a.k.a. olive drab, or OD) pants. Back then, we didn't have camouflaged pants, so ODs were it. I had a few pair and they were very comfortable. Most of the time I wore skivvies, but there were a few times I didn't have any clean ones and I went skivvyless. Same with socks; there were times when I was sockless in my flight deck boots. I didn't do that too often, because if it rained or got wet, I knew I would be getting some blisters.

Most of the time, my standard Navy issue flight deck uniform consisted of a pair of white skivvies, a pair of white socks, a pair of army OD pants, a white t-shirt, a red crash and salvage crew shirt, a red life vest, a red cranial helmet, a pair of goggles, my flight deck boots, and a pair of gloves.

The first few times on the flight deck, I wore my blue utility pants that were issued to me in boot camp and I had also worn in Guam. Some of the guys told me that I should get some ODs, so I asked where. They told me there was a warehouse on the pier in San Diego close to the carrier and just go over to pick some up. The first day back in port, I headed over and found the warehouse. I asked the Quartermaster about them, he pointed me to a pallet full of ODs, both pants and shirts and I could take what I wanted.

I looked through them and found several pants that fit and headed back to the ship, thanking the Quartermaster on the way out. It took me a few days to realize that the pants I was wearing were once owned by a GI who had been killed in Vietnam. I obviously didn't know the guy, but it did hit me that when a GI was killed, they often shipped his military belongings back somewhere and they were divvied up. I think it bothered me at first, but after wearing them on the flight deck, I took more pride in knowing that.

The mess hall or galley was located on the second deck, two decks below the hangar deck. There were three galleys on Kitty Hawk. The main galley was located aft and served the main meals which typically included meat of some kind (in the Navy, all meat is called "Roast Beast" which is actually *any* meat served aboard the ship that even the cooks who prepared it don't know what it is), a starch (usually potatoes or rice), gravy, and a vegetable or two. Rolls were always available as well as soup and crackers.

Most of the time, chow was good. It was served buffet style, but unlike today's Navy chow lines, the cooks and stewards would serve you when you put your tray out. My favorite meal was roast beef, mashed potatoes, and gravy; we called it Kitty Hawk Steak. Like I said before, I never went hungry and always tried to eat everything on my tray. We had to bus our own trays so we just took them over to the scullery, dumped excess food into a shitcan, and gave our trays, glasses, and utensils to the dishwasher.

For drinks, we often had whole milk for the first few days at sea. After a few days, the galley would run out of fresh milk and started serving powdered milk. That tasted like crap so I learned to eat cereal only the first few days at sea. After that, breakfast consisted of anything other than cereal. I did try putting bug juice (Hawaiian Punch or Kool Aid) on my cereal once. That was pretty bad, but since I had made a bet with another Crash crewman, I didn't want to back down. But after that episode, I didn't try that again. In fact, bug juice is not really in my diet these days and that is probably because I had enough of it while on the ship. We also had iced tea, water, and the standard assortment of sodas.

Chow lines were often long, especially when at sea. It would not be unusual to wait in line for an hour to get chow, it was that slow. On Kitty Hawk, the galley needed to feed more than 5,500 men every meal. That's about 17,000 meals served a day, including more than nine hundred loaves of bread when the ship was underway. That's a lot of meals to cook and serve.

The lines would wrap around and through several different passageways. I learned early on to bring a book down to the chow line and I read a lot of books while waiting for chow. Since I worked on the flight deck, every now and then we would get a special chit to "go to the head of the line" so the chow line traffic cop (Master-at-Arms) would allow us to butt in. But, that didn't happen all the time.

We ate in shifts, so to speak. While flight ops were going on, we had to maintain a minimum crew of yellow shirts and crash crew on the flight deck so each unit would send five to six guys down at a time. Most of us would get our chow, eat like the dickens, and then head back up to relieve another crew man.

I also ate a lot of Saltines since they were readily available. I didn't know it at the time because I just liked Saltines, but for some reason, they helped settle my stomach so that I didn't get seasick. During my time on the ship, I never got seasick which is more than I can say for a lot of other guys, especially the FNGs. There were times when I would have a bag of buttered popcorn and see some new guy a little green and offer him a handful of greasy popcorn. He headed for the side of the ship, tossing his cookies. I know it wasn't a nice thing to do, but it was just one of those things I did to show off I was an experienced seaman.

A second galley called the Express Line was located forward also on the second deck. This was like a fast food drive-in, serving mostly hamburgers, hot dogs, French fries, spaghetti, and whatever else the cooks could scrape up quickly. I ate a lot of my meals there, not because I was a burger or dog freak, but because it was fast and with eighty guys in our division to feed and long times in the chow line, I needed to get something, choke it down, and get back on the flight deck to let another group of guys come down.

The officers had it made—they ate in wardrooms which had round tables, tablecloths, real dishes, and better yet, a wait staff. Most of the wardroom stewards were Filipino and served as both cooks and waiters. I never ate a meal in the wardroom.

Another thing that proves "Rank Has Its Privileges." Officers also had staterooms which had a lot more room and a lot more privacy than our berthing compartments. I peeked in one or two just to see how the other side lives and there seemed to be a lot more personal and storage space.

Most officer staterooms housed two men with bunk bed style racks. In other words, there were only two stacked as opposed to our three-stack racks. They also had larger lockers for their uniforms and personal belongings, a sink with running water, and a table with chairs. Some had rigged in their own television set and they had electrical outlets, something we didn't have in our racks. Their doors locked, too, so that no one could just rummage around when everyone else was on duty. Most of the time, staterooms did not have their own toilet; that was shared somewhere down the passageway. Officers did have their own heads identified with big red letters: OFFICERS HEAD. All in all, they had a good life, or at least a good a life as one can expect on a ship of 5,500 men. I wasn't complaining though, because I knew my place and I was fine with that.

Midnight rations (Midrats) were always available for those working late into the night. They were served from the forward galley from 2300 to 0100 (11:00 p.m. to 1:00 a.m.) and usually were pretty good. I ate there many times when I was assigned the night shift when at sea.

Also just forward of the main galley was the Gedunk shop. This small onboard store was like a small neighborhood convenience store and had an assortment of snacks and cigarettes. While I didn't smoke, some of my friends did and their standard line was "Where else can you buy a carton of cigarettes for ten bucks?"

There were times when the chow line was too long for me to wait so I would head to the Gedunk shop and pick up a bag of chips or crackers, some canned cheese, and a can or two of sardines. It wasn't that healthy, but it was something to eat. Unfortunately, while standard Navy issue meals came with the job, the Gedunk shop did not and this came out of our pockets.

Most people think of an aircraft carrier as a place to launch and land aircraft. That is true, but it takes a lot of men (and now women) to accomplish that mission. You've got 3,000 ship's company plus 2,500 air wing personnel. This is, in reality, a small city. You've got power and water plants, telephones and computers, cooks and dishwashers, stores, a post office, and gas stations. You've also got the executive branch, the legislative branch, and the judicial branch. It *is* a small city and you've got all the same types of problems that small cities have.

Having said that, an aircraft carrier requires an infrastructure similar to a small city. The duties of the Commanding Officer parallel those of a mayor. The CO is ultimately responsible and accountable for the welfare of the ship and her crew and establishes the guidelines under which the ship operates. Next comes the Executive Officer (XO) similar in many respects to a city manager. The XO ensures the CO's guidelines are implemented and the ship runs smoothly. There is also an Officer in charge of every department and every division within that department.

When I think about it, there were probably about three thousand sailors (including WAVES) stationed at NAS Agana Guam. We had barracks, a mess hall, medical and dental facilities, and recreational facilities. NAS Agana Guam sat on about 1,700 acres.

Take that same number of sailors, add 2,500 more for the air wing, and cram all those sailors and facilities into one giant floating city—*that* my friend is an aircraft carrier. A lot of people doing a lot of things in a lot of different places, all day long and all night long, in a small cramped space with nowhere else to go. It was truly amazing that it even worked at all, but that is what you do on a ship—you *make* it work.

12 USS KITTY HAWK
A Tour Of The Flight Deck

The first time I walked out onto the flight deck of Kitty Hawk, I was totally awestruck. It reminded me of the excitement I felt when I first walked through the stadium gate of the University of Florida football field—I was ten years old. It was huge and larger than any place I had ever seen. And in 1975, I was still a kid barely twenty years old, but this would be where I would spend most of my waking hours for the next two and a half years.

The flight deck of Kitty Hawk is a little more than a thousand feet long (more than three football fields) and about 250 feet at the widest part—a total of about four acres sitting about sixty feet above the water. To answer your next question: No, sailors in their right minds do not dive off the flight deck though there were rumors of this one kid who jumped while we were at sea.

The superstructure, called the island on an aircraft carrier, is located aft of amidships on the starboard side of the flight deck. On Kitty Hawk, the island rises about 150 feet above the flight deck, is 120 feet long, but only twenty feet wide at the base. By the way, 120 feet is the exact distance that the Wright brothers flew the first airplane in December 1903 at Kitty Hawk, North Carolina.

The island is but a mere footprint compared to the rest of the flight deck. Here you will find the command center for not only flight deck operations, but for the entire ship as well. The top of the island is much wider than the bottom, allowing for more personnel and more equipment. On top of the island, you'll find an array of radar and communications antennas which track surrounding ships and aircraft, intercept and jam enemy radar signals, target enemy aircraft and missiles, and pick up satellite TV and radio signals.

79

The Captain, or Commanding Officer, of the ship hangs out on the bridge which is located forward on the island. On an aircraft carrier, the captain is a Naval Flight Officer (a.k.a. Naval Aviator) with hundreds of hours experience flying aircraft, launching from a carrier as well as landing. He must be intimately familiar with all flight operations. As long as they are in command of a carrier, they are prohibited from climbing into the cockpit to fly a plane themselves. Just below the bridge is the Flag Bridge where you'll find the Admiral in charge of the entire carrier battle group.

Just above the bridge, aft on the port side of the island is Primary Flight Control, or PriFly, where you'll find the Air Boss and his assistant, the Mini Boss. No, I don't make this stuff up. Both are also experienced Naval aviators and are constantly facing outward to the port side watching all flight deck operations. PriFly controls all movement on the flight deck as well as a five-mile radius air space up to an altitude of about a mile above the ship.

At the flight deck level, you'll find the Handler. His compartment is on the forward side of the island and his main job is to track all aircraft on the flight deck and the hangar deck. He is Flight Deck Control. All flight deck directors, also known as yellow shirts, report directly to the Handler. He also has several assistants working with him to help track the 75+ aircraft assigned to the carrier.

The Handler's primary tracking tool is a two-level transparent plastic table with etched outlines of the flight deck and hangar deck on a scale of 1/16 inch to one foot. The board is about six feet long and two and a half feet wide; the flight deck is on the top and the hangar deck is on the bottom. Using scaled cutouts of all aircraft on the ship, including aircraft tail numbers, he spots (places) them in various locations on the flight and hangar decks where the real aircraft will be located. Different Handlers use different tools, but you'll find an assortment of colored nuts and bolts to represent various maintenance activities, such as repairs, ordnance loading/unloading, and fueling/defueling.

This "Ouija Board" provides at-a-glance where all aircraft will be during launch and recovery operations. Theoretically, anything that fits on the Ouija board in Flight Deck Control will fit on the flight deck or the hangar deck. When a real plane moves from one point to another, the Handler moves the aircraft cutout accordingly. When the plane is out of service because it needs repair work, the Handler turns it over.

Prior to launching aircraft, the Handler will spot where all aircraft will park and in what order they will be launched. Most aircraft are parked along the outer edge of the flight deck with their tails extended over the water in order to conserve deck space. One of his assistants then draws this layout on a sheet of paper, makes copies, and gives them to all flight deck directors.

This way, all the yellow shirts know where the aircraft will need to be moved. Every yellow shirt gets a copy of this spot sheet and carries it with him all over the flight deck. You'll even find some yellow shirts that direct airplanes with the spot sheet in one of their hands. This is done for each launch cycle *and* each recovery cycle during flight ops. During the time I was on Kitty Hawk, we didn't have copy machines (they hadn't been invented). Instead, we used mimeograph machines.

This low tech approach to aircraft flight deck control has seen relatively few changes since World War II. Most everything today aboard ships is computerized, but the main reason this remains low tech is simple: if the ship ever took any sort of battle damage, electronics are usually the first thing to go. With the Ouija Board as is, you won't lose a thing. It's cheap, it's reliable, and it's effective.

The LSO, or Landing Signal Officer, also known as Paddles, is stationed on what is called the LSO platform, an area on the port edge of the flight deck aft toward the stern. He himself is a pilot and each carrier-based squadron will typically assign two or three junior officer pilots to be LSOs as collateral duty, meaning they also fly jets during flight ops when they're not LSOing.

His job is to direct pilots in for a smooth landing with the plane's approach, visually gauge altitude and speed, and relay that to the pilot. He has to almost put himself in the cockpit and think like the landing pilot and get a feel for the landing. He is the only person allowed on the flight deck during flight ops who doesn't wear a cranial helmet though he does wear foam ear plugs. He must be able to hear as well as see how the aircraft is flying.

The LSO can give guidance over the radio to the approaching pilot, but won't unless necessary since radio traffic is kept to a minimum at all times. Typically, the LSO will only provide a few brief commands over the radio: "Power," which means the aircraft is settling below the guide slope, give it some throttle; "Right for line-up" which means the pilot needs to make a brief wing-dip to correct his line up; and finally, if the pilot has screwed it royally, he'll issue a "Wave Off!" command. The pilot can generally tell the severity of the deviation from the pitch of the LSO's voice.

Pilots learn to trust their LSO, because the LSO can usually detect whether the aircraft is going above or below the glide slope before the pilot can. He can tell by looking at the attitude of the plane whether it is fast or slow and he can spot every throttle movement made by looking at the smoke from the plane's exhaust.

Because the LSO is located so close to the landing area, there is a safety net all around him just in case he needs to jump out of the way in a hurry. During flight ops, there can be anywhere from a few to a dozen men and women on the LSO platform. There is also a windbreak on the forward side of the LSO platform to provide a little shelter from the thirty-plus knot winds that blow down the flight deck.

Before today's sophisticated electronic landing systems, the LSO would have in each hand a colored fabric-covered paddle similar in size to a Ping-Pong paddle—hence the nickname "Paddles." As the aircraft would come in for a landing on the flight deck, the LSO would hold the paddles out horizontally at arm's length and help guide the aircraft in by raising or lowering the paddles.

Today's landing systems are sophisticated electronics with lights that resemble a movie set from *Close Encounters of the Third Kind*. The most prominent visual landing aid is called the "Meatball." This collection of lights represents the aircraft's position in relation to the glide-slope.

The meatball is basically a Fresnel lens which is a light array, about six feet high and twenty feet wide, just to the left of the landing area on the flight deck and mounted on a gyroscopically stabilized platform. The lens is named after Augustin Fresnel, a French physicist who in 1822 invented a lens that resembled a huge glass beehive with a light at the center. This is the type of lens that has been used in lighthouses for years. It focuses the light into narrow beams that are directed into the sky at various angles.

The meatball has a horizontal row of green lights called "datum lights" and an amber light, or meatball, that rides up and down centered between the green lights to indicate the pilot's position relative to the optimum glide slope. The lowest cell on the display is red and used to indicate that the pilot is about to get into trouble. The LSO will issue the pilot a "Wave Off" if he is too low. He does this by triggering a button on a hand-grip, called the "Pickle," that he holds up high. This makes the meatball flash and is his signal for the pilot to add full throttle, abort the descent, climb back into the traffic pattern, and go around for another try.

Many of today's Navy aircraft are designed to land on a carrier hands off, meaning the on-board computers control the plane's descent and throttle all the way through the landing. They may be designed that way and test pilots may have proven that they work, but I've never met a Navy pilot who has performed a hands off landing. That just takes all the fun out of a carrier landing.

The Crash crew compartment was located aft on the starboard side of the island on the flight deck level. It wasn't that big of a space, but had room for a desk, a TV, a couple of cushioned benches, several storage lockers, and the most important thing—a 100-cup coffee maker. Access to the Crash compartment was through a single hatch on the starboard side of the island.

Also, on the starboard side of the island, there is about a twelve foot wide space between the island and the catwalk. This is a place where squadron ordnance crews stored bombs waiting to be loaded aboard aircraft. We called this area the Bomb Alley. It's called the Bomb Farm now. It took a little while to get used to walking out of the crash crew compartment and seeing dozens of 700-pound bombs and Sparrow and Tomahawk missiles just right outside.

The Sparrow missiles were about ten feet long and about six inches in diameter. The nose cone was made of some sort of ceramic material that could take the heat of friction during supersonic flight. They were also great for sharpening knives and since I always carried a four-inch Buck folding knife with me, I would stop every now and then and sharpen my knife on the missile nose cone. Of course, no one was around to tell me not to.

Before I got to Kitty Hawk, one of the crash crew decided he wanted a personal knife sharpener. The rumor was that he walked outside the crash compartment one night and wacked the nose cone of a Sparrow missile with a ball-peen hammer, cracking it into several large pieces. He never got caught for it, but when he left, he forgot to take his souvenir with him. I got his locker when I first checked into Crash, so I was the proud owner of a piece of a Sparrow missile. I still use it as a knife sharpener, too. The curvature of the piece of cone fits right on my thigh—perfect for sharpening knives.

Kitty Hawk had an angled flight deck, meaning that you could launch aircraft off the bow catapults while simultaneously landing aircraft on the angle. Since the early 1950s it has been common to direct the landing recovery area off to the port side at a twelve- to fourteen-degree angle to the centerline of the ship. The primary function of the angled deck landing area is to allow aircraft that missed the arresting gear wires, referred to as a "bolter," to become airborne again without the risk of hitting aircraft parked on the forward parts of the deck. This also meant that aircraft would not be landing directly into the wind. They would be landing at a slight angle which would be very difficult since the landing area would be in a constant, angled, slightly forward, and sliding motion.

The angled deck was not initially developed by the United States. It was developed by the British in the early 1950s by Capt. D.R.F. Campbell, Royal Navy in conjunction with Lewis Boddington. The first American aircraft carrier with an angled deck was the USS Antietam (CVA-36) which was retrofitted in the shipyards in 1953.

There are two major missions on the flight deck: launch aircraft and recover those aircraft. It is that simple. But, like anything else in life that is simple, it is all that other stuff in between that makes it complex.

Kitty Hawk had four launch catapults. From a bird's eye view starting at the bow, the launch catapults are numbered one through four, starting with the catapult on the starboard bow. The bow catapults are #1 and #2. There are also two more catapults on the angle, #3 and #4, commonly called the "waist cats." The four catapults are capable of launching more than sixty aircraft in less than twenty minutes.

Behind each catapult is a Jet Blast Deflector or JBD. The JBD is a hinged trap door built into the deck and is raised at an angle of about seventy degrees when an aircraft is on the catapult ready for launch. It is about twelve feet high and twenty feet wide.

The reason for the JBDs is simple: when aircraft are ready for launch, the jet blast, whether the jet is in afterburner or not, is enough to blow men and equipment overboard. That would be a bad day. Though I was blown down several times while working on the flight deck, I never went overboard and I never saw anyone else get blown over the side.

The catapults are steam powered using fresh water compressed into super-heated steam to help launch the aircraft into the air. Before the advent of the steam driven catapult, aircraft carriers used a cable-driven system with pulleys and a hydro-pneumatic rotary drive mechanism—something like the proverbial hamster cage as compared to today's more powerful steam-driven catapults.

The concept is quite simple. Each catapult consists of two pistons that sit inside two parallel cylinders positioned just under the flight deck. These cylinders are eighteen inches in diameter and about the length of a football field. The pistons each have a metal lug on their tip which protrudes through a narrow gap along the top of each cylinder. The two lugs extend through synthetic rubber flanges which seal the cylinders, and through a gap in the flight deck where they attach to a small shuttle.

The shuttle is about three feet long, about four inches wide, and about four inches tall. It has a grooved, horizontal slot in the front where the aircraft's tow-bar fits for the launch. Super-heated pressurized steam from the carrier's boilers builds up behind the pistons to the tune of about six hundred psi.

When released by the launch button, the steam pressure pushes the pistons forward, literally throwing the aircraft off the carrier. At the end of the catapult is a water brake, designed to stop the piston and therefore stop the shuttle while the plane keeps flying. It is as simple as that.

Normally, land-based military jets require about a mile of runway to take off. However, on an aircraft carrier, these catapult launch systems are capable of taking a 60,000 pound aircraft from zero to more than a hundred and fifty miles an hour in about two seconds and launch them in about three hundred feet. They repeat this incredible feat every thirty to forty-five seconds during flight ops. When we were on water hours which typically occurred after being at sea for more than a couple of weeks, we would say "There goes another two hundred showers" each time a jet was launched because the catapults used fresh water to create the steam.

Each aircraft has two components that connect it to the flight deck for launch. The "tow-bar" is attached to the aircraft's nose gear strut which is lowered into place by the pilot. This tow-bar is placed in a grooved slot in the front of the shuttle. The "holdback" is just to the rear of the nose gear. Its purpose is to prevent the aircraft from moving forward until the launch button is pressed.

A small disposable fastener called a "breakaway link" is connected between the aircraft holdback and a three-foot bar that is anchored to the flight deck. The breakaway link looks like a mini dumbbell, aptly called a "dog bone," and is designed to break at a specific tension when the catapult fires to allow the shuttle to push the aircraft down the flight deck to launch speed. These breakaway links are color-coded by type of aircraft to prevent them from being used mistakenly on the wrong plane. Each breakaway link and each steam pressure setting must coincide with the aircraft's type and weight to ensure a successful launch.

The landing area is aft and is angled about twelve- to fourteen-degrees (depending upon the particular carrier) to the port of the ship's centerline. It is not a long runway. In fact, there is only about five hundred feet of total landing area from the stern to the angle. Four arresting gear wires are stretched across the landing area, #1 the most aft, #4 the most forward, spaced about forty feet apart. Each braided wire cable is one and three-quarters inches in diameter and is raised about four inches above the flight deck by springs that closely resemble an upside down car leaf spring. This helps the landing aircraft's tail hook catch the wire. Landing on an aircraft carrier is called a "trap."

Both ends of the arresting wires are channeled down below decks in a mass of hydraulics and gears that are designed to help bring the landing aircraft to a stop within a few hundred feet. The hydraulic pressure for the arresting gear wires is set to stop each aircraft at the same place on the deck, regardless of size or weight. An A-3 "Whale" which weighs about 80,000 pounds must have a different setting than an A-4 "Skyhawk" which weighs about 35,000 pounds. If you leave the A-3 setting on for an A-4 that is landing, the A-4 will probably rip out the tail hook. Likewise, if you leave the A-4 setting for an A-3 that is landing, it would probably pull out enough cable to drop off the angle into the water. Not a good day for either.

When a plane traps, a total of about eight hundred feet of arresting gear cable is pulled out. Keep in mind landing speeds are between 120 to 150 mph and aircraft stop on a dime, so to speak. The goal of most pilots is to catch wire #3. Wire #1 is not a good choice because it is too close to the stern. If the pilot comes in too low, he could easily crash into the stern of the ship—not a good day. Wire #4 is also not a good choice because it is too close to the end of the angle and the pilot may not have enough power to take off in the event he misses a cable.

When the aircraft's tail hook snags an arresting wire, it pulls the wire out and the arresting gear engines and hydraulic systems below decks absorb the energy and bring the plane to a stop in less than three hundred feet. The arresting gear requires constant maintenance and the V-2 Division takes care of both the arresting gear and the catapults. It is a dirty, greasy job, but somebody's gotta do it.

One of the worst things that can happen on the flight deck is for the arresting wire to snap when an aircraft traps. Though this never happened during my time on Kitty Hawk, we saw several training videos showing what happened—all of them were not pretty. First, the plane keeps going toward the angle like normal but because it has been somewhat significantly slowed by the arresting gear cable and even though the pilot has applied full power, the aircraft doesn't have enough speed to take off. The plane heads to the water and hopefully the pilot recognizes this is a problem, punches out, and ejects safely.

You think a rubber band stings when you stretch it and it snaps? Picture a high tensioned two-inch steel braided cable snapping in two. Two pieces of the cable are flying over the flight deck at ankle or knee height, still connected to the arresting gear engines below decks. If the cable snapped in the middle, there would be two, three hundred to four hundred feet of death flying a few inches across the flight deck at high speed. It is a bad day for anyone on the flight deck to get their legs taken out by this cable. If they're not severed on the flight deck which is the usual case, chances are the ship's surgeon will be performing an amputation before the day is over to remove what's left of the leg.

If you are aware and see the cable snap, God's on your side but all you can do is jump up and raise your knees as high as you can. I've known yellow shirts that have witnessed this and lived to still talk about it. In fact, one of our instructors in A School told us a story of a night recovery when the arresting gear snapped. He saw out of the corner of his eye something sparking along the flight deck and instinctively jumped up high. He said the cable took off the heels of his flight deck boots. He had a guardian angel watching over him that night.

Also on the flight deck, there is what is called the aircraft barricade. This gigantic barricade which resembles a twenty-five foot tall tennis court net, would be raised in the event a pilot could not get his aircraft tail hook down or there was some other problem with his landing gear. The barricade has expandable nylon webbing with two arresting gear size cables, one on the top and one on the bottom, and is stored on the starboard side in a compartment located just underneath the flight deck. If needed, the barricade would be pulled and stretched across the deck using a tow tractor and connected to two stanchions hinged to the flight deck and then raised. All flight deck personnel take part in raising the barricade and the requirement is to "rig the barricade" within five minutes. Thank God we never had an incident of a jet taking a barricade.

So why doesn't an aircraft in trouble just fly to another airport with a longer runway? When you are in the middle of the ocean, you *are* the airport. It is called "blue water flying" when there is no Bingo spot (i.e., an alternative airport) to land. We trained constantly on various emergency situations and rigging the barricade was one of those. We would drill for that at least once every time we were underway.

A two-inch wide, alternating red and white painted line lies along the starboard side of the landing area from the stern to the end of the angled deck. This is called the Foul Line and during recovery operations, no one is allowed to cross over it unless there is an emergency. The reason is that if one stays on the starboard side of the line (i.e., the safe area), then there is less chance of injury should a mishap occur.

There is also a foul line on the port side, but the only people allowed on the port side of the flight deck during flight ops are the LSO and his assistants. The only persons allowed inside the foul line area during recover ops are the Hook Runner from the V-2 division and the Gear Puller, a yellow shirt from the V-1 Division that directs the pilot out of the landing area after he has taken a wire and landed safely.

There are four aircraft elevators on the flight deck. These are about thirty feet by thirty feet and can carry two aircraft and tow tractors between the flight deck and the hangar deck. Three elevators are located on the starboard side, two forward and one aft of the island, and one elevator on the port side, aft. When the elevators are in operation, an Elevator Operator (also from V-1 Division) first raises a safety guy wire which is about two feet high and supported by stanchions every eight feet that rise out of the deck. A yellow shirt is directing the entire operation.

The elevator operator sounds an elevator alarm, then raises or lowers the elevator. The hangar deck is about thirty feet below the flight deck and the elevators are actually over open water, so it is quite a sight to see these elevators quickly drop with two aircraft on them while the carrier is steaming along. You hope the engineering guys did their job of lubing the gears, working the hydraulics, and whatever else it is they do in order to maintain the elevators in prime operating condition. It would be a shame to drop a couple of fifty million dollar aircraft and crew into the ocean.

For those who work on the flight deck, it is divided into three areas: Fly 1 is the bow area, Fly 2 is amidships, and Fly 3 is aft. Fly 1 and Fly 2 yellow shirts are responsible for moving and directing aircraft onto the bow and angle catapults. Fly 3 yellow shirts are responsible for moving and directing aircraft on the aft part of the flight deck and out of the landing area after a trap.

The flight deck itself is painted with a non-skid coating of dark gray paint. It is a mixture of abrasive grit and synthetic rubber applied in a ripple-like pattern. Because aircraft on the flight deck use aircraft fuel and hydraulic oil, the flight deck would sometimes get slick, but the non-skid coating helped keep slipping and sliding to a minimum. Every six feet in every direction is a pad eye which are deck fittings about the size of cereal bowls and are embedded into the plating of the flight deck with a welded five-star bracket on top. This is where you would attach the chain to tie the aircraft down to the flight deck. It is also the first thing you would grab should you get blown down by a jet blast.

Aircraft are typically parked in designated areas all over the flight deck. During launches, aircraft are parked aft on the flight deck, both amidships next to the island and on the stern also called the "fantail." After launching from the bow and waist catapults, aircraft that were not launched are moved forward and parked on the bow in order to make room for recovery operations. Most of the time, they are towed by MD-3 tractors, small three-foot high, rectangular tow tractors, similar to the ones you see at major commercial airports, only smaller. Tractor drivers are also part of the V-1 Division.

You have probably seen pictures of aircraft parked nice and neatly on the bow of the flight deck along the starboard side of the ship, as well as on the stern. Aircraft are parked tighter than compact Smart Cars at a mall during Christmas shopping season. Because of the limited space and close proximity on the flight deck, Navy aircraft have wings that fold so they can be parked even closer. In fact, these multi-million dollar aircraft are literally parked with only a few inches between them. It was very tricky and required experienced yellow shirts to move them without bumping into each other.

When an aircraft bumps into another aircraft or scrapes one during a move, it is called a crunch. The yellow shirt that was directing it was put on report and taken off the flight deck to be re-evaluated. It may not be a long time, but it is a devastating blow to that yellow shirt, even if it wasn't his fault. But he was responsible for moving that aircraft safely. It doesn't happen often, but when a crunch occurs, those in charge want to make sure it doesn't happen again. As they say in the Navy, "One 'oh shit' flushes about twenty 'attaboys'." During my short time as a flight deck director, I was fortunate not to have any crunches, but several of my friends did during the WESTPAC cruise.

There are also other nicknames for specific areas on the flight deck. The "Street" is in the Fly 1 area between catapults #1 and #2. The "Crotch" is the area where the angled deck ends and meets with the port bow. The "Junkyard" is located aft of the island on the starboard side where the crash crew parks the crash truck and tractors, the aircraft crane ("Tilly"), forklifts, and tractors. The "Corral" is located between elevators #1 and #2 forward of the island and where the E-2C "Hawkeyes" and C-2 "Greyhounds" are parked. The "Patio" is located aft of elevator #3 on the starboard side.

Safety nets and catwalks are all around the perimeter of the flight deck. A safety net is just that: a wire mesh net that extends horizontally out from the deck about four feet. If you wanted to jump overboard, you would have to first step out onto the net, then jump, or you would have to take a running leap to get beyond the net. These were located on the bow (as well as the angle) and the stern of the ship. The rest of the flight deck is surrounded by catwalks which are open walkways with an outside bulkhead height of about four feet and enough room for two men to pass without bumping into each other. From the catwalk, there would be stairs that led up to the flight deck as well as down to another hatch to get inside the ship.

One last comment. When FNGs come aboard who will be a part of the flight deck crew, they first spend a little time watching flight deck operations from what is called "Vulture's Row," an open air balcony located on the 08 level port side aft of the island overlooking the flight deck. You can't see much on the bow catapults, but you've got great views of the waist cats and the recovery area. This gives the new sailor a chance to see how everything works on the flight deck including the sights and sounds and smells that he will come to know intimately.

13 USS KITTY HAWK
Flight Deck Operations

They say working on the flight deck of an aircraft carrier is one of the most dangerous jobs in the world and one of the most unforgiving places to work—there is little to no margin for error. It's loud, it's busy, it's smelly, and you have to keep your head on a swivel, constantly aware of what is going on around you. In one careless second, a fighter jet engine could suck somebody in or blow somebody overboard.

Being behind a jet exhaust is no fun, either. It stinks and sometimes it is so hot it can burn your nose hairs when you breathe in. There are usually between 175 and 200 personnel on the flight deck at any one time during flight ops. The average age of airmen on the flight deck is between nineteen and twenty years old. That is a lot of responsibility to throw at these youngsters, but most of them are one dedicated bunch.

Having worked on the flight deck, I can certainly attest to how dangerous an environment it is. But in the same sense, flight deck operations can be one of the most challenging, rewarding, and orchestrated performances you will ever witness. It takes teamwork from a group of men (and now women) who do not know each other, but they know and respect the important roles each must play during this command performance.

Flight deck operations involve many different people with many different jobs. The Navy figured out a long time ago that different colored jerseys with stenciled IDs would help to identify who does what on the flight deck. Because of these different colored jerseys, flight deck personnel are now sometimes referred to as "Skittles." Skittles is the name of a candy with many different colors; they hadn't been invented when I was in the Navy. Here's a quick rundown on the colors and who does what on the flight deck.

The V-1 Division is part of the Air Department and is responsible for moving aircraft on the flight deck and "spotting" catapults. They are also responsible for making sure the flight deck is free of foreign object debris (FOD). Aircraft directors wear yellow shirts and direct aircraft from one location to another. The number on their jersey designates what Fly the director works in though he is not limited to working in that one Fly. During flight ops on a flight deck re-spot, between twelve and fifteen yellow shirts are typically on the flight deck at one time. After our stint in the shipyards, I moved from Crash to being a yellow shirt. I was Flight Deck Director #36 and I was assigned to Fly 3.

Blue shirt aircraft handlers secure aircraft to the flight deck with special tie-down chains and chock the tires under direction of the yellow shirts. They also drive the tow tractors to move aircraft around the flight deck. There are a dozen or so tractors on the flight deck and a smaller number on the hangar deck. One designated yellow shirt is in charge of the tractors and is affectionately called the Tractor King.

Red shirts are the Crash and Salvage crew. Most yellow shirts start out as blue shirts and work their way up the proverbial food chain. There were about eighty guys in the V-1 Division when I was aboard Kitty Hawk. Now there are about 160 men and women in the V-1 Division on today's aircraft carriers.

The V-2 Division is also part of the Air Department. They maintain and operate the launch catapults and arresting gear. There were more than two hundred men in the V-2 Division and it was the largest division on the ship. V-2 Division personnel wear green jerseys. The Catapult Launch Officer, or Shooter, is part of V-2 and wears a yellow shirt with a green helmet. His yellow shirt and float coat are stenciled with "Shooter." Arresting Gear Officers also wear a yellow shirt with a green helmet. Their yellow shirt and float coats are stenciled with "Arresting Gear Officer."

You'll find the V-3 Division on the hangar deck, also part of the Air Department. There are about eighty people in the V-3 Division and they are responsible for moving aircraft around the hangar bay. They also wear yellow and blue shirts, similar to the V-1 Division.

The V-4 Division has about fifty to sixty people who work on the flight deck and hangar deck fueling aircraft, defueling aircraft, and repairing fuel stations. They are also part of the Air Department and wear purple jerseys. For obvious reasons, they are known as "Grapes."

The V-5 Division consists of approximately fifteen personnel who work in Primary Flight Control. This division works directly with the Air Boss and keeps track of all of the aircraft in the air wing assigned to the carrier. They wear a white jersey. When VIPs land or take off from the carrier, V-5 personnel are the ones who escort them to and from the aircraft. They also retrieve and deliver mail to and from the COD, or Carrier On-board Delivery aircraft.

All officers on the flight deck, no matter what division they work in, wear three, 1-inch vertical strips of red reflective tape on their cranial helmets. This is to help easily identify them on the deck as officers. If you are a WWII history buff, Army officers similarly wore a single, white vertical stripe on the back of their helmet.

Five people control operations on the flight deck: The Air Boss directs all aspects of flight deck operations from Primary Flight Control including the launch, recovery, and shipboard handling of the aircraft. The Mini Boss is the Air Boss' assistant and sits next to the Air Boss in PriFly. The Handler directs the movement and placement of aircraft on the flight deck and in the hangar bay. The Air Bos'n supervises the crash crew and fire parties in handling aircraft emergencies during flight ops and General Quarters. The LSO monitors and directs the final approach and landing of every fixed wing aircraft.

Aircraft are always in constant movement on the flight deck. Every plane in every squadron has an assigned Plane Captain who is an experienced airman in charge of that particular aircraft. Either the pilot or the plane captain is in the cockpit whenever the aircraft is moved. Pilots are at the controls when the aircraft is taxiing under its own power; plane captains are in the cockpit when the aircraft is towed.

Yellow shirts have the ultimate responsibility for all aircraft movement on the flight deck. They choreograph the "dance of danger," much like Tchaikovsky's Nutcracker Suite, by using distinct hand signals. They help direct aircraft from the hangar deck onto the flight deck, for fueling and maintenance operations, lining up on the catapult for a launch, and directing aircraft out of the recovery area after a trap. Anytime an aircraft is moved, there is a yellow shirt making it happen. While he is directing the aircraft, he is also trying to watch out for other flight deck personnel around and behind the aircraft. One short blast from the jet's exhaust could blow somebody down, or worse, overboard.

All yellow shirts and officers that work on the flight deck use two-way radio headsets built into their cranial helmets to communicate with each other, the Handler, and the Air Boss, but they don't communicate with the pilots. They are all on the same frequency and radio chatter is kept to a minimum. The microphone is built into a swivel arm, much the same as you see used by today's rock stars.

There are also other personnel that work with the air wing that wear different colored jerseys and helmets. Here is a quick summary of all the colored jerseys and helmets of flight deck personnel and their associated tasks:

Jersey	Helmet	Tasks
Blue	Blue	Aircraft Handlers; Tractor Drivers
Blue	White	Aircraft Elevator Operators; Messengers and Phone Talkers
Yellow	Yellow	Plane Directors; Aircraft Handling Officers
Yellow	Green with three red stripes	Catapult and Arresting Gear Officers
Green	Green	Catapult and Arresting Gear Crews; Air Wing Maintenance Personnel; Photographer's Mates
Green	White	Cargo Handling Personnel; Helicopter Landing Signal Enlisted Personnel
Green	Brown	Air Wing Quality Control Personnel
White	None	Landing Signal Officers
White	White	Air Transfer Officers; Medical Personnel; Visitors / VIPs
White	Green	Squadron Plane Inspectors; Liquid Oxygen Crews
Brown	Brown	Air Wing Plane Captains; Air Wing Line Leading Petty Officers
Brown	Red	Air Wing Helicopter Captains
Purple	Purple	Aviation Fuels
Red	Red	Ordnance men; Crash and Salvage Crew; Explosive Ordnance Disposal

During flight ops, it was almost impossible to hear anyone talking to you, especially with a nearby A-6 Intruder in full power, but you would cup your hand in front of the mike while simultaneously keying the microphone. It took a little while to get used to it, but there were several times I heard, "Chet, drop down!" That usually meant that I was about to get blown down by a jet's exhaust, so I would drop down to the flight deck and roll one way or the other, grabbing onto a pad eye. Like I said, we all tried to watch out for each other while working on the flight deck.

You can go through hours and hours of training and watch videos of horrendous crashes, fires, and other unpleasantries, but until you work on the flight deck of an aircraft carrier, you can't really get the feel for all the action. Flight operations hours vary depending upon the circumstances, the required pilot training qualifications, and the carrier's mission. Most of the time while I was aboard, flight ops started at ten in the morning and continued until midnight. We typically worked sixteen to eighteen hours a day on the flight deck since V-1 Division personnel needed to be on deck an hour or so before flight operations began and an hour or so after they ended and were on deck the entire time. There were times during the WESTPAC cruise though, when we flew around-the-clock for several days in a row.

Most civilians who tour aircraft carrier museums, such as the USS Midway (CV-41) in San Diego, the USS Yorktown (CV-10) in Charleston, South Carolina, or the USS Intrepid (CV-11) in Manhattan, walk out onto the flight deck and see a wide expanse with only a few planes on the deck. I have had the pleasure of walking out onto the flight deck of Kitty Hawk and seeing fifty plus planes parked all over the bow, the stern, and on both sides of the deck. You have to constantly remain alert and keep your head on a pivot. Otherwise you can easily find yourself in trouble.

An aircraft carrier, such as Kitty Hawk, carries a complement of different types of aircraft. These aircraft squadrons make up what is called the air wing. Typically, you will find a couple of fighter jet squadrons, a squadron of EA-6B "Prowlers" whose main mission is to jam the enemy's electronics systems, a squadron of E-2C "Hawkeyes" whose main mission is surveillance, a squadron of S-3 "Vikings" whose mission is anti-submarine warfare, and a squadron of helicopters which are used for anti-submarine warfare, search and rescue, plane guard, and cargo. Together, these various squadrons make up the air wing or strike force of the carrier battle group. The person in charge of the air wing is called "CAG" or Commander Air Group.

When I was aboard Kitty Hawk, 1975-1977, we also had a reconnaissance squadron of A-3 "Whales," a bomber squadron of A-6 "Intruders," two attack squadrons of A-7 "Corsairs," and an RA-5 reconnaissance aircraft. Our two fighter jet squadrons on Kitty Hawk were F-4 "Phantoms" during the WESTPAC cruise and later after the shipyards, the F-14 "Tomcats." The F-14 was the jet that Tom Cruise "flew" in the movie *Top Gun*.

When an aircraft lands on the flight deck, it is called a "trap." All fixed-wing aircraft that land on carriers have a tail hook—this is what separates Naval aircraft from other military aircraft. Depending on the type of aircraft, the tail hook is anywhere from three feet to eight feet in length but always hangs lower than the landing gear for obvious reasons. The pilot has control of the tail hook and lowers it for landing and raises it after he has trapped the arresting wire and landed safely.

The tail hook is held down with about nine hundred pounds of pneumatic pressure so that when it hits the deck, it stays down and shouldn't bounce around, allowing the hook to engage the arresting gear cable. Navy aircraft that are designed to operate from carriers have to withstand the shock of arriving on-deck at flying speeds and then capturing a cable with its tail hook and coming to a very quick stop within a couple of hundred feet. If an aircraft cannot land on board the carrier and there is no land nearby, the options are well, very undesirable.

If an aircraft misses the arresting wires, it is called a "bolter." Pilots are trained when landing on carriers to apply full power as they touch down, just in case they don't catch a wire. That way, they keep flying off the angled flight deck, climb back up to the traffic pattern, and try landing again. Besides the gut feel that he caught a wire, it is also up to a yellow shirt standing at the crotch of the flight deck to help the pilot know he is safely on board by using hand signals—the yellow shirt does not have radio contact with the pilot.

The first thing done before commencing flight ops is what is known as a FOD walk down. FOD can be anything from a small bolt or wing nut to a drunken sailor. Jets have large intakes and will suck in anything and anybody near them, so it is important to make sure there is nothing on the flight deck that is lose or not fastened down. You would be surprised as to the damage a small wing nut can do to a multi-million dollar jet engine.

This is the job of the V-1 Division, but usually every able-bodied person on the flight deck takes part in the FOD walk down. Everyone knows the importance of this exercise. A line of men extending from port to starboard across the flight deck walk the length of the ship, starting from the bow of the flight deck and working down toward the stern. FOD walk downs are usually done two or three times a day between flight ops cycles—usually just before the first cycle and again at dusk before night flight ops begin.

The job of Crash and Salvage is simple: sit around waiting for a crash and when it does, try to put the fire out and rescue the pilot and crew. Our motto was, and continues to be, "You light 'em. We fight 'em."

Crash was expected to be on the flight deck twenty-four hours a day while at sea. Throughout the night after flight ops, squadron maintenance crews were always working on aircraft, getting them ready for the next day's activities. We had to be on deck and available and because of that, we always had a night shift crew.

While everyone else went off duty and down below decks to the berthing compartment, the night crew would stay on the flight deck usually hanging out in the crash crew compartment. We did not have to sit in the crash truck all night long. We would get a radio call if we needed to man a fire truck or needed to be on deck for any reason. Many nights there was nothing going on and we would end up playing cards or reading all night long. I wrote a lot of letters home to my mom and dad during the night shift.

During my time on Kitty Hawk, Crash had one fire truck on the flight deck, an Oshkosh MB-5, the type which I had driven in Guam. So it was natural that I would be driving this baby. The biggest difference between driving a crash truck on the Naval Air Station in Guam and on the flight deck was, well, tight spaces. NAS Guam had hundreds of acres of paved runways and taxiways and side roads; the Kitty Hawk flight deck had a little more than four acres and lots of tighter spots. The truck was the same, but the driving conditions were *slightly* more complicated.

We still had a four-man crew in the truck: the driver/crew chief, the turret man, the lead rescue man, and the backup rescue man. Everyone had to wear asbestos hot suits during flight ops, the same kind we wore in Guam. The only exception was the driver who didn't have to wear the proximity suit pants, but he did have to wear the coat. While we didn't have to wear them on the Alert Spot in Guam, we had to wear them on the flight deck. The hood would be beside us, ready to put on quickly if needed. We had to wear our cranial helmets at all times on the flight deck during flight ops. The suits got quite hot at times, too, so we always tried to drink a lot of water. We also rotated our guys so the same rescue man wouldn't be in a hot suit more than a couple of hours at a time.

The crash truck parked in different places around the flight deck depending upon the flight ops cycle. During launches, we would park the truck on the point, a spot just forward of elevator #1 on the starboard side. That way we could watch both the bow and waist cats and be ready to roll in an instant should we be needed. During recovery, we would move the truck to different areas depending upon whether we were launching and recovering simultaneously or if we were only recovering aircraft. The yellow shirts were always giving us grief between launch and recovery cycles because no matter where we parked the truck, it seemed we were always in the way and had to constantly move from one spot to another.

In addition to the crash truck, we also had two MD-3 tow tractors that had been converted into special fire-fighting crash tractors. Instead of the usual traffic yellow paint job, these were painted white with black stripes. The rear of the tractor had been converted to include a basket to hold a tank of the PKP firefighting agent, often called "Purple Powder" because it was dyed purple, about fifty feet of hose, and a seat for the hose/rescue man to sit. The crash tractor driver wore only the coat, but the rescue man was fully suited up in the proximity suit. The crash tractors were also placed on the bow and waist during launches and moved accordingly during recovery. They were a lot easier to maneuver than the MB-5, but also always seemed to be in the way.

We had to know the emergency rescue procedures for every type of aircraft that landed on the flight deck. Everyone had to be familiar with everyone else's crash job, because during an emergency, anything could happen.

Most of the time during recovery, one of the crash tractors was parked alongside the foul line adjacent to the recovery area. In the event a landing aircraft couldn't raise its tail hook, the yellow shirt would signal the pilot to hold the plane and then signal the crash crew members, along with the V-2 Division Hook Runner, to run out to the plane and try to manually raise the hook a few inches off the deck to clear the arresting gear cable.

It was not uncommon for me to lie flat on my back under this jet right underneath the exhaust and use my feet to push the tail hook up enough for the hook runner to move the cable. This happened a lot with the A-6 Intruders. The A-7 Corsairs had a similar problem, but you couldn't crawl underneath it—there was only about a foot between the bottom of the plane and the deck. However, the A-7 had an override button in the starboard wheel well which you could press that bypassed the hydraulics; this usually raised the hook.

Once the tail hook was cleared, we would haul ass to get out of the way so the yellow shirt could quickly direct the plane out of the recovery area in order to allow the next plane to land. Sometimes the tail hook was stubborn and we couldn't get it up enough to clear the cable, so the LSO would have to wave-off the next incoming plane. Eventually, with several of us on the ground pushing up with our feet, we could raise it. Everyone in Crash knew these tricks.

During our time at sea, especially on cold nights, a bunch of us would huddle around the crash tractor and lean over it. The engine was always idling and it provided a source of warmth to us when we leaned over it. Between the warmth and the gentle vibration of the idling engine, it was pretty relaxing. There were a few times late at night during flight ops that I drifted off to sleep leaning over the tractor. I wasn't the only one, either.

In addition to manning the crash trucks and the crash tractors, Crash and Salvage was also responsible for moving aircraft that were damaged during a crash. We had a couple of forklifts and a huge NS-50 aircraft crane we affectionately called "Tilly." This huge crane stood about fifteen feet high at the driver's cab and the crane rose about twenty five feet. I really liked driving Tilly; something about driving a big crane and lifting big heavy rigs, but I guess that's a guy thing. We also had an assortment of aircraft cables and slings that were stored in the crash barn shed; one or two for every type of aircraft on board.

On the starboard side of the ship just aft of the island, there is a boat and aircraft crane, or B&A crane. It is attached to the ship and swings around toward the starboard side over the water. Its main purpose is to raise or lower either aircraft or boats from the ship to the pier or the water. I had the opportunity to lower the Admiral's boat into rough waters during our stop in Hong Kong; it got a little dinged.

I was in Crash before and during our WESTPAC cruise. Most of the time, I drove the crash truck. I enjoyed that too, especially since I didn't have to suit up. When I was a teenager, I wasn't that careful of a driver. I had four accidents and three speeding tickets before graduating from high school. Of course, none of them were *my* fault.

But something about driving a fire truck helped me grow up and become a much more careful driver. I tell people that I used to drive fire trucks ... on the flight deck of an aircraft carrier—that gets their attention.

We had good crews in Crash too, even though there was always some friction between some of the guys. I don't think I was ever racially prejudiced, but I'm sure being from the South it may have come across that way sometimes. At the tender age of twenty, I was still naive about many things. We had whites, blacks, and Chicanos in the crash crew. While I had been around black guys growing up and worked closely with several in Guam, including my good friend Glenn Law, this was the first time I had been around Chicanos—they could speak another language which I envied.

I think we got along well, but like I said, there were some times that I may have come across prejudiced. I don't know, maybe it was my ego. As a petty officer, sometimes you need to get guys to do things they don't want to do, but you've got to find a way. At twenty years old, there really wasn't a Human Resources School of Management in the Navy. You learned on the job in the School of Hard Knocks.

Usually I tried to ask nicely, but sometimes there were guys who still didn't want to get off their lazy ass to do some work. In those cases, you resort to the best threat a petty officer has, "Off your ass and on your feet, sailor; otherwise, I'll write you up!" That worked most of the time, especially if you had another petty officer with you as a witness.

So what do you do when you have an actual crash? The answer of course, depends upon the type of crash, what type and how many aircraft are involved, if there is any fire, and if you have injuries. We constantly watched training videos from actual crashes and fires and we constantly trained for all types of situations. We could not practice hot drills on the carrier, but we had plenty of pretend fires to drill.

While the emphasis in this book is on the V-1 Division and Crash and Salvage, there were always other personnel who also trained for flight deck fires alongside us. Kitty Hawk had dozens of firefighting stations located all around the flight deck in the catwalks, some with AFFF capabilities, and others with straight salt water. But during our deployment, we trained several times a week on all different kinds of emergencies.

Crash had all sorts of tools and equipment available. The first goal was to put out as much of the fire as you could in order to get in and rescue personnel. That was usually handled by the MB-5 crash truck and the two crash tractors. After the personnel rescue, the second goal was to put out the rest of the fire. Next, you needed to clear the debris if the fire was in the recovery area because there may be other aircraft circling overhead waiting to land. I've seen training films of crash crewmen using the crash forklift to push a wrecked plane overboard because it either couldn't be salvaged or the deck needed to be cleared in a hurry. There is not much time before the next plane lands.

There were times when we would train on an aircraft that just trapped. This would be the last one in the flight cycle so there were not any more planes waiting to land, but we would pretend that the aircraft crashed, there was a fire, and we had to put it out and rescue the crew. The flight deck personnel would man four fire hoses from the catwalks, the crash truck and crash tractors would be on the forward side of the plane all pretending to be fighting the fire.

On one particular training exercise, I was the hot suit rescue man, so it was up to me to rescue the pilot and co-pilot from the A-6 Intruder that just "crashed." I climbed up the plane's ladder, unstrapped the pilot, and inserted the ejection seat safety pins. Then I pulled him out and threw him over my shoulder. He was nervous and asked if I was sure I could carry him. I did and climbed down to the flight deck, then with the help of a couple of other crash crew, carried him over close to the island and gently laid him down on the flight deck. Not bad for a day's work.

We learned several things on that particular exercise. Not everyone was as big or as strong as I was and when we were debriefing the exercise, somebody asked why not rig a rescue basket on the forklift and use it to help get the crew out and onto the ground. That way, it would reduce the risk of dropping the pilot on his head when getting him out of the cockpit. That made sense to me, so Crash rigged up a basket and we used that for rescue training the rest of the cruise.

Probably, *the* most horrific flight deck fire in US Naval history occurred on the USS Forrestal (CV-59) on July 29, 1967. It was captured on one of the flight deck cameras and to this day, flight deck crews watch what started the fire and how it was fought. You can't evacuate the ship and call the fire department when you have a fire, you ARE the fire department.

The fire on the USS Forrestal started just before 1100. The second launch of the day was being readied when a five-inch Zuni rocket, for unknown reasons, shot across the aft end of the flight deck from an F-4B Phantom, starboard to port, rupturing the four hundred gallon fuel tank on an A-4 Skyhawk jet parked on the port side. The fuel ignited instantly and with the help of cross-deck winds, the fire spread causing adjacent fuel tanks and ordnance to rupture on other parked jets. Flight deck crews, ordnance men, and firefighters all struggled to clear away bombs and ammunition, even throwing ordnance over the side of the ship.

From there it escalated as more fuel tanks ruptured, more fuel dumped onto the flight deck, and more ordnance cooked off. The pilot of the plane that was first struck by the Zuni missile was Lieutenant Commander Fred White—he didn't survive. One of the other A-4 pilots, who was in the cockpit at the time, was John S. McCain, who is a United States Senator who ran for President in 2008. McCain jumped from his cockpit and out over the plane's refueling probe, dropped to the deck and escaped the fire.

Seven bombs detonated on the flight deck during this horrific disaster. The flight deck fire was under control within an hour, but below decks fires burned for more than twelve hours. A total of 134 men were killed, 300 injured, and fifteen were either blown off, fell, or jumped overboard. Of those killed, 50 were in their racks on the 03 level, just below the flight deck. A total of 21 aircraft were destroyed and another forty-one damaged.

Kitty Hawk also suffered several fires during her time in service. In December 1967, a serious fire broke out in a compartment on the 02 level which was utilized for tire storage, spreading smoke and heat throughout the 02 and 03 levels while Kitty Hawk lay moored at Subic Bay in the Philippines. According to published reports, "Medical facilities were taxed to the utmost during the first six hours." The crew bravely fought the blaze for nine hours, securing it the next afternoon. Some 125 sailors sustained injuries due to smoke inhalation though none seriously. All returned to duty.

On December 11, 1973, a fire erupted in #1 Main Machinery Room at approximately 1800. Five of the twenty sailors on duty in that space died. An additional thirty-four sailors were treated for smoke inhalation, several also receiving minor injuries. A fuel leak spraying into the machinery space from a strainer in the fuel line between the storage tanks and fuel tanks caused the blaze. My friend Jack Kuiphoff was on that WESTPAC cruise.

On March 31, 1987, a fire occurred in an oil pipe on the starboard side sponson in the hanger bay while the ship was getting steam up for standing out from her anchorage off Masirah, Oman. Prompt firefighting action by the crew contained the flames, preventing a major disaster without casualties.

On July 11, 1994, while approaching a severely pitching flight deck, an F-14A Tomcat from the VF-51 squadron struck the ramp, breaking in two and exploding into a fireball. Part of the Tomcat slid off the port side. Both men ejected and were rescued. However, the pilot landed in the inferno, suffering severe burns. The mishap occurred in the vicinity of Japan.

14 USS KITTY HAWK
Launch And Recovery Operations

When an aircraft carrier is ready to begin flight operations, the Captain turns the ship into the wind and increases speed—aircraft always take off and land into the wind. Because the launch area is such a short distance, the aircraft needs as much help as possible. Turning into the wind provides additional airflow over the flight deck and this air moving over the wings lowers the plane's minimum takeoff speed. But aircraft are not the only things affected by the ship's increased speed and wind—everyone on the flight deck also feels it. These are not hurricane force winds by any means, but there were many times on the flight deck where you would see personnel walking at an angle because the wind coming across the deck was so strong.

Meanwhile down below decks, the pilots are in the squadron ready rooms getting briefed on the day's missions. The CO, the CAG, and the Strike Operations Officer (SOO) create a daily air plan or flight schedule, usually twenty-four hours in advance and provides this to all squadrons. During wartime activities and training when there is more than one aircraft carrier in the theater of operation, flight ops for one carrier may be from noon to midnight while flight ops for the other carrier would be from midnight to noon. That way, there would be planes in the air twenty-four hours a day.

Flight ops are broken up into different events, or cycles, usually dependent upon the fuel capacity of the plane that uses the most fuel in the shortest amount of time. During our WESTPAC cruise, that was the F-4 Phantom which could stay in the air without refueling anywhere from thirty minutes to one and a half hours, depending upon the flight conditions and the mission (full afterburners versus cruise speed). Using this as a guide, flight operations would allow for eight to ten cycles per day in a twelve-hour flight ops day, each cycle lasting anywhere from forty-five minutes to an hour and a half.

Events are typically made up of about fifteen to twenty aircraft and are sequentially numbered throughout the day. Prior to flight ops, the aircraft on the flight deck are arranged, or spotted, so that Event #1 aircraft can easily be taxied to the catapults once they have been inspected and started.

Once the Event #1 aircraft are launched which generally takes about fifteen to twenty minutes, Event #2 aircraft are readied for launch about an hour later. The launching of these aircraft makes room on the flight deck to recover the aircraft launched earlier during Event #1. These aircraft from Event #1 are re-fueled, re-armed, re-spotted, and readied for Event #3. This sequence of launching and recovering aircraft is continued throughout the day.

Briefing in the squadron ready rooms usually starts about two hours before the actual launch. Briefings would be held on closed circuit TV in all the ready rooms, so everyone would hear the overall plan, the weather report, and any other special information that needed to be passed along by the CO, CAG, and the SOO. After the TV briefing, individual squadrons may have additional information to pass along by the squadron commander or senior flight leader.

After the briefing, the pilot heads to the back of the room to suit up or grab a quick snack. He then reviews the maintenance log of the particular aircraft he will be flying. If there are no concerns, the pilot signs off indicating he has accepted the aircraft for flight. Then the senior maintenance CPO or PO releases the aircraft to the pilot.

The pilot then heads up to the flight deck about forty-five minutes prior to launch. He conducts the pre-flight, verifies the ordnance load and fuel load, and coordinates with the plane captain. Once in the cockpit, the pilot continues his pre-flight check, including checking his instruments and radios. It is fairly common, especially in older aircraft, that one or two things aren't working one hundred percent. The pilot is the final decision maker, asking himself two basic questions: "is this aircraft safe to fly?" and "can I accomplish my mission?" If the answer is no to either of these questions, then the pilot will most likely not fly on that particular cycle.

On Kitty Hawk, the first aircraft launched and the last aircraft recovered were the SH-3 helicopters; they served as the "plane guard." They are launched a few minutes before other aircraft in case there is a problem with launching an aircraft and the plane's crew end up in the water. When I was on board Kitty Hawk, we usually had two rescue helos in the air at all times during flight ops.

The next aircraft to launch was the E-2C Hawkeye. This aircraft has the eyes of the air wing and is the airborne early warning command and control aircraft that keeps the big picture for the entire carrier battle group. The E-2C has sophisticated electronics and sensors to provide early warning, threat analysis, and control of counteraction against both air and surface targets. This Airborne Tactical Data System (ATDS) is linked to the ship's Naval Tactical Data System (NTDS) to extend the fleet radar out hundreds of miles. The E-2C Hawkeye is a twin-engine, turbo-prop plane. Its distinguishing feature is a large rotating "frisbee" on top of the aircraft.

Besides the above aircraft, the order of the launch sequence is determined by the Handler. While squadron leaders would like to think they are in charge, there is no particular rhyme or reason as to who gets launched first within the squadron. It is usually dependent upon where the plane is located on the flight deck. The Handler overrides all launch sequence decisions.

Launch operations are basically the same for all fixed wing aircraft. After the plane captain turns the plane over to the yellow shirt, the blue shirts are directed to remove the tie-down chains and wheel chocks. The pilot's eyes are then glued on the yellow shirt's signals. Yellow shirts use basic hand signals ("come ahead," "turn left," "turn right," "stop") to direct the aircraft. If, for example, an aircraft is initially parked on the fantail of the flight deck and is supposed to be launched off the waist catapult, a Fly 3 yellow shirt starts directing the aircraft out of its tight parking space. There may only be a few inches between parked aircraft and it takes precise small movements to keep the aircraft from bumping into another aircraft in those tight spaces. The pilot and the yellow shirt learn to trust each other during these difficult maneuvers.

The yellow shirt is not supposed to walk backwards while directing planes because he might trip over something, but we all did it. When we got the plane out of its parking spot, we would look over our shoulder to see if another yellow shirt was ready to take over then we would hand off the plane to a Fly 2 yellow shirt that would then use hand signals to direct the pilot forward. When the plane got closer to the waist catapult, another Fly 2 yellow shirt would take over, and slowly guide the plane onto the catapult.

Once the aircraft passes the JBD, a V-2 green shirt crewman raises the JBD to protect other aircraft and flight deck personnel from the jet blast. Most of the time, especially after several days of flight ops, the movement is smooth from one point to another with rarely any stops once the aircraft starts to taxi.

At this point, the yellow shirt at the catapult is about ten to fifteen feet directly in front of the plane, straddling the catapult so he and the pilot can see eye to eye. If he is standing directly on the catapult track, he will probably get knocked on his ass by the returning catapult shuttle—it only takes one time to learn that lesson, not because it hurts, but because of the humiliation that follows. He directs the pilot to unfold the aircraft's wings. The ordnance crews check the bombs and missiles, including shaking them back and forth to make sure they don't fall off. They also arm the ordnance by removing safety pins at this time. The squadron's maintenance checkers are looking the aircraft over again to make sure there are no leaks and that all aircraft surfaces and controls are working.

As the aircraft taxis slowly toward the catapult, a green shirt from V-2 holds up a black box sign with easy to read large numbers indicating the total weight of the aircraft and shows it to the pilot and to the Shooter. They both need to agree on the number, because that is the weight that the Catapult officer will dial in for the amount of steam to be used for the launch.

When the plane is almost to the catapult shuttle, the yellow shirt directs the pilot to drop the aircraft's front tow-bar and guides the plane ever so slowly until the tow-bar drops into the slot on the shuttle. At that time, the yellow shirt directs the pilot to stop and a V-2 catapult crew member then checks the tow-bar placement in the shuttle. This same V-2 crewman inserts the dog bone into the holdback bar. The shuttle is eased forward by the V-2 launch crewman to take up the slack and put tension on the holdback bar. At this point, there are about eight to ten various crewmen around the plane constantly checking to make sure everything looks OK.

Every now and then, either the yellow shirt doesn't issue the stop hand signal in time or the pilot misses it, but the aircraft may go a few feet beyond the shuttle. There is no reverse gear, so the yellow shirt directs the pilot to holds the aircraft in place, informs the pilot to reduce power, and gets as many people around the plane as possible so that they can help to push the plane back a few feet. It doesn't happen that often, but when you are in the middle of launching aircraft, you only have a few moments to push the plane back into the proper position.

In the catwalk, a V-2 launch crewman mans the actual launch control console. Meanwhile, another catapult launch officer has to dial in the correct steam pressure for this particular aircraft and deck condition which includes the aircraft's total weight. If the pressure is too low, the plane will not have enough speed by the time it reaches the end of the flight deck and will probably end up in Davy Jones' locker. If the pressure is too high, the sudden jerk may tear off the nose gear. Either way, it's a bad day. When everything is dialed in properly, the launch crewman holds both hands up, indicating to the Shooter he is ready to push the launch button when directed to do so.

The yellow shirt moves to the inboard side of the aircraft, still in control of the plane. When everything appears to be alright, indicated by all crewmen around the aircraft holding a thumbs up, he directs the pilot with hand signals to go to full power, one arm straight up, the other pointing directly toward the bow, then hands him over to the Shooter, who takes control over the launch.

The Shooter is holding up his hand, waving two fingers back and forth (like a "big whoop-tee-do" motion). The breakaway link is strong enough to hold the plane at a standstill, even at full afterburner; it is the release of the steam into the catapult that causes enough force to break the breakaway link.

At this point, the Shooter is checking everything and everybody. He wants to make sure before launching this multi-million dollar aircraft that the launch deck is clear, all maintenance personnel (checkers), all ordnance men, and the yellow shirt are signaling a thumbs up, and the pilot is ready, in full throttle or afterburner. The pilot checks all his instruments and move (wipes out) all the aircraft control surfaces so the checkers on the flight deck can see everything is working properly.

When the pilot is ready, he salutes the Shooter indicating everything from his viewpoint is ready. The pilot has the throttle at full power and is grabbing a bracket on the firewall with his fingers so the throttle isn't pulled back accidentally. Hopefully, he's also taken his feet off the brakes. At night instead of a salute no one will see, the pilot signals by turning on the aircraft's exterior lights. The Shooter smartly returns the salute. The pilot sits back in his seat, putting his head back against the headrest because of the anticipated sudden onslaught of g-forces.

The Shooter makes one more look-see making sure the ship's bow is either steady on the horizon or it is coming up. He doesn't want to launch when the bow is coming down—aircraft fly very well, but don't ski worth a damn. When everything is clear, he issues the launch signal which basically means he squats down and leans sideways toward the bow and touches his twirling fingers to the deck, then points to the bow. At this point, the V-2 launch crewman presses the launch button and as the old saying goes, "away we go."

The pilot experiences an instantaneous exertion of forces and the plane is slung off the deck like a giant slingshot. By the time the plane travels three hundred feet to the end of the catapult, it has reached take-off speed which can vary depending upon the aircraft, but upwards of 150 mph. Most aircraft pilots never get to experience this feeling, but Navy pilots have this edge; it is an adrenaline rush you won't experience anywhere else.

The aircraft accelerates so fast down the deck, the blood in the forward part of the pilot's eyes rushes to the rear and the pilot may experience slight tunnel vision. By the time the plane reaches the end of the catapult, he can barely see, but he knows it is a good cat shot. As soon as the plane breaks free of the deck, his vision quickly returns to normal. Pilots say if you don't experience this tunnel vision, you might think about ejecting because there is only a split second from the end of the catapult to the water.

All the way down the deck, it is nothing but noise and vibration every foot of the way, but as soon as the plane is in the air, it becomes silent. Some pilots compare it to snow skiing—the difference between skiing on ice (noise and vibration) versus skiing in powder (quiet and smooth).

As soon as the pilot breaks the deck of the carrier, he banks to the left if shot off the port cat, or to the right if shot off the starboard cat. He raises his landing gear and accelerates until he reaches climbing speed. The first thing to do is to get into a climbing turn—he's only sixty feet off the water.

In the older days of hydraulic catapults, pilots described this as an instantaneous shot, meaning there was no cushion effect in the acceleration. Everything happened at once; you were at launch velocity as soon as the launch button was pushed. Lots of pilots reported this was very uncomfortable. But with the newer steam catapults, the launch is not an instant acceleration, but more of a gradual acceleration even until the shuttle hits the end of the catapult.

Pilots are the most uncomfortable on the catapult because they have no control over the situation until they are airborne—they are at the mercy of the catapult until launch. Pilots describe catapult launches in different ways and the main difference is between getting shot off a catapult on a bright, clear day versus launching during a dark and stormy night. Even with hundreds or thousands of hours of flight time, it is still a scary thing to get shot off at night with no visible horizon. You have to trust your instruments and pilots learn this in all kinds of combat situations. But no matter who you talk with, getting shot off a catapult is a walk in the park compared to landing on the carrier.

Once the plane is off the deck, the V-2 launch crew member pushes another button on his console to retract the catapult shuttle, the JBD is lowered, and the yellow shirt directs the next aircraft onto the catapult. From the time the plane initially reaches the catapult for launch until the plane is launched, the whole process only takes about twenty to thirty seconds.

So why are there so many people involved in the launch? It is not that obvious, but during flight operations, there are so many things going on simultaneously, everyone has a specific job to do. If any one of us working the launch spots anything wrong, we immediately stand up, cross our wrists in front at head level which signals either the yellow shirt or the Shooter that there is a problem and we need to abort the launch. This happens more times than you would think, even when the aircraft is in full afterburner. Needless to say, it is a dangerous situation to abort a launch like this, but everyone trains constantly on these situations and in all my times on the flight deck, while there were plenty of aborted launches, we never had a deck crash or injury on a catapult as a result.

There was one time, however, during the WESTPAC cruise when we were in the Sea of Japan, flying twenty-four hours around the clock non-stop for six days straight. Toward the end of this crazy schedule on the fifth or sixth day, there was an F-4 Phantom lining up on catapult #3. It was during the day and there were no problems that anyone *noticed*. I know everyone was tired, even though we were working shifts. The yellow shirt directed the plane onto the catapult, the ordnance guys were checking the bombs and missiles, the maintenance guys were checking the plane over, and the yellow shirt handed the plane off to the Shooter.

The Shooter had the plane in full afterburner, ready for launch, when all of a sudden the Air-Boss comes over the 5MC (the flight deck PA system) and on everyone's radios and screams, "Abort launch, Cat 3! Abort launch, Cat 3!" The yellow shirt had forgotten to instruct the F-4 pilot to unfold his wings and nobody caught it except the Air Boss. That would have been a bad day.

The F-4 in this case was fine. The Shooter aborted the launch, signaled the pilot to reduce power, the breakaway link was removed and the tow-bar was raised. The yellow shirt directed the pilot off the catapult and into a safe area in Fly 2 so the maintenance crew could check the plane over again. While the plane didn't launch that cycle, it did on the next. That was a close one! Several people, including the yellow shirt and the Shooter received a good ass chewing.

Kitty Hawk had four catapults, two on the bow and two at the waist. Most of the time, launches would take place at either the two bow cats or the two waist catapults. Every now and then, we would launch aircraft using all four catapults. During these times, there was a lot of moving aircraft around the flight deck and during the launches, they were lined up one after another like dominos. There would be two Shooters, one to handle cats #1 and #2 on the bow and the other to handle cats #3 and #4 on the waist. The process would be that we would launch bow cat #1 first, then waist cat #3, then bow #2, then waist #4—each launch about ten to fifteen seconds apart. That gave us time to move planes onto the catapults, go through the launch steps, and then bring up the next one. I've witnessed Kitty Hawk launch forty aircraft in less than fifteen minutes—and with no foul ups.

After the last aircraft is launched and airborne on a particular flight cycle, the flight deck crew begins the re-spot for the next scheduled launch cycle which is about thirty minutes to an hour away. After the second scheduled launch is complete, the arresting gear crew readies the deck for the returning planes from the previous flight. The magic words from the Air Boss are "Standby to recover aircraft." One by one the planes are trapped. When the last plane is trapped, the flight operations cycle repeats again and again until late into the night.

Can you launch and recover aircraft at the same time? Absolutely—we did many times. Most of the time during these simultaneous launch/recover cycles, we would only launch cat #2, the port side bow cat. We couldn't launch off the waist cats, because that's also the recovery area. We needed a place to park recovering aircraft, so once they trapped, we directed them to park along the starboard side of the bow in Fly 1. It was tricky but exciting at the same time. There was this one time during the WESTPAC cruise, however, when I was caught between a rock and a hard place during a simultaneous launch/recovery cycle.

There weren't a lot of "old" guys in our division, but our LCPO (Leading Chief Petty Officer) Senior Chief Kenneth Breig, had been in the Navy for about thirty years. He and I didn't see eye-to-eye, if you know what I mean, but I tried to respect him—at least as much as a twenty-year old smart ass kid could at that age. But he had been around a while and he once told us, "Back when I was a young whippersnapper, before jets and before fast prop-driven planes, the flight deck didn't have arresting gear wires. Instead, landing aircraft would be 'caught' by a team of deck-hands who would run out and grab a part of the aircraft to slow it down after it touched down." Of course with heavier and faster jets, that would be impossible, but it was still funny to visualize.

The recovery process starts when the various returning aircraft "stack up" at assigned altitudes in an oval flying pattern near the carrier. The Carrier Air Traffic Control Center below deck decides the landing order based on the aircrafts' various fuel levels. Logically, an aircraft that is about to run out of fuel comes down before one that can keep flying for a while. Most of the time, there was also an aircraft tanker flying nearby, just in case that needle was a little too close to the empty mark, in which case the aircraft low on fuel would take on more fuel to make a carrier landing. During our WESTPAC cruise, a couple of the A-6 Intruders served as in-air refuelers. Their designation was KA-6, where the "K" represented a tanker.

The Arresting Gear Officer, called Hook, would ensure that the proper weight was set in the arresting gear engines for each aircraft. Each had a special maximum trap weight and they were designed and set to stop aircraft about the same distance in the recovery area, no matter what type of aircraft or weight. Hook stood on the starboard side of the flight deck directly across from the LSO.

I have heard pilots compare landing an aircraft on a flight deck to sex: "It's like having sex during a car crash. It feels wonderful, it's violent, and when it's over, it's over pretty quick." I've also heard it referred to as "the best sex you'll have with your clothes on." This was a common theme with the pilots that landed on an aircraft carrier.

The traffic pattern for landing on an aircraft carrier is like an oval race track, with the downwind leg at six hundred feet above the water, 180 degrees opposite to the Base Recover Course on which the ship is steaming. The traffic pattern varies, but is usually about a mile wide and about four miles long around the port side of the carrier. Civilian aircraft practice a box-shaped traffic pattern, with crosswind, downwind, base, and final approach legs. Because timing, spacing, and interval are more easily controlled with a race-track pattern, the Navy had adopted this more efficient method of recovery.

The landing aircraft enter the traffic pattern by flying at an altitude of eight hundred feet right up to the wake of the ship, passing close to the starboard side. If flying in formation, there will usually only be four aircraft in the formation at one time. The planes are flying at about 250 to 300 knots and unless the plane is set for a touch and go landing, the tail hook will be down. The pilots are talking to the Air Boss at this time and must spot any other traffic in the pattern and extend upwind to allow a proper time interval. Typically, they allow any plane ahead of them thirty to forty-five seconds to give them time to taxi clear of the landing area and reset the arresting gear.

Next comes the break turn which is a seventy to ninety degree bank, putting the aircraft into a three- to four-G tight turn. From the flight deck, this is such a cool maneuver; I can only imagine what it was like for the pilot. If the plane is in formation, the next pilot executes a similar break at a predetermined time, usually six to eight seconds after the first pilot. The first plane swiftly decelerates in order to extend the landing gear and flaps. As the pilot slows down and approaches the proper heading for the downwind leg, he descends to about six hundred feet. The pilot constantly trims the aircraft for the landing configuration. Once established on the downwind leg, he only has a few seconds to complete his landing checklist.

On the downwind leg, called "the 180," he passes down the port side about a mile out from the ship. He then begins his turn to final approach when abeam the LSO platform. The "90" as it is called, is ninety degrees of turn off the downwind heading. At this point, the pilot should be passing through four hundred and fifty feet altitude and is about a mile away. Here is where the LSO gives him the instruction, "Call the ball," meaning the pilot is now working off the meatball. There is very little radio exchange between the LSO and the pilot at this time and this radio silence is often called "zip lip." The only reason the LSO might talk on the radio is if the pilot is not properly correcting his flying attitude on the way down.

At the "45" (45 degrees from the ship), the pilot starts to pick up the meatball and is about three hundred and fifty feet above the water. The landing aircraft continues to turn and descend, lining up with the meatball for the trap. At this point he has reached his final approach heading and should roll out of his bank. He should be established on the extended center line that runs down the landing area on the flight deck.

Keep in mind the landing area is not aligned with the course the ship is steaming. The landing area on angled decks is canted twelve- to fourteen-degrees to port of the ship's centerline. This means that as the pilot approaches the final leg, he will cross the ship's wake at a shallow angle and continue his turn for another twelve degrees to align with the landing area. It also means that as he comes down on the final approach, the ship is slightly moving forward from left to right.

Once on final approach, also known as "in the groove," the pilot is about eighteen to twenty seconds out from the landing. He will hopefully see a centered meatball with no deviations. But to maintain this flight altitude, he'll have to make constant and tiny corrections. He does not look at the landing area which is called "spotting the deck." The plane that landed ahead of him will either taxi clear of the landing area in time or not. If it doesn't, the LSO will give the landing pilot a wave-off and he'll go around for another try. The LSO is constantly watching the approaching plane. If the deck becomes fouled for any reason and the LSO doesn't see it, then the Air Boss can also call a wave-off. The pilot's attention constantly bounces from the meatball to his line-up to his angle-of-attack gauge and his air speed indicator.

The pilot hits the deck with a solid thump, commonly referred to as a controlled crash. And since he is watching the meatball and not the deck, the exact moment of every landing is always a surprise. Hopefully, he has stowed away any FOD in the cockpit such as his knee pad, navigational charts, or cameras. Otherwise, it would go flying and possibly either hit the pilot or worse, hit something important on the aircraft's control panel.

This is one of the main differences between Navy landings and Air Force landings. Navy landings are a controlled crash whereas Air Force pilots land like a butterfly floating in with sore feet. This is also how you can tell if your commercial airline pilot is ex-Navy or ex-Air Force. The Air Force pilot brings the airliner in nice and easy. The Navy pilot brings it down quick and hard—"we're here!"

The ship has four arresting gear wires stretched across the deck in the recovery area and if he does it right, the pilot will put his tail hook down in the middle between wires #2 and #3. The ideal landing is a 3-wire. From the flight deck, most of these landings seemed so smooth, but I always saw the pilot straining forward against his seat straps because of the sudden deceleration. The aircraft traps about 150 knots and rolls out in less than three hundred feet in under three seconds. Do the math—it's about four Gs. Only when he is sure he is aboard does he pull the throttle back to idle and looks for the yellow shirt for taxi directions out of the recovery area and to his parking spot.

At the moment of touchdown, the pilot jams full throttle, sometimes called going "Balls to the Wall." This is because the tail hook can miss the arresting wires. Even if he makes a perfect approach, his hook could bounce over the wires. This is called a bolter and it is no big deal provided the pilot can accelerate and climb away as he rolls off the end of the landing area. The arresting wires will stop the plane even at full throttle.

The yellow shirt Gear Puller who is positioned at the Crotch runs up close to the plane and gives the pilot the power back signal. The pilot reduces power and takes his feet off the brakes. The arresting gear wire is pulled back a few feet by the V-2 Deck Edge Operator, pulling the plane with it, in order to give the cable some slack. The yellow shirt gives the pilot the "hook up" signal. The pilot raises the hook with his eyes still glued to the yellow shirt. The yellow shirt gives him the "come ahead" taxi signal moving the aircraft forward then gives him the "fold the wings" signal, turns him starboard, and passes him off to another yellow shirt in Fly 2 to get the aircraft out of the landing area and gets ready for the next trap. The Hook Runner signals the Deck Edge Operator to retract the arresting gear cable ready for the next trap. During the day, we tried to trap aircraft about every thirty to forty seconds so you can imagine that everything needed to run smoothly during recovery.

Meanwhile, two additional V-2 Division Hook Runners positioned on the starboard side of the foul line help ensure the arresting gear cable remains in the landing area during its retraction by using a five-foot steel bar to push and guide it as it is being retracted. They also make sure the wires are taut and resting above the springs ready for the next trap.

Parking the aircraft can also be dangerous, but the pilot follows the yellow shirt's instructions. After recovery, the pilot is usually directed to park the aircraft on the bow of the flight deck, along both the port and starboard edges of the deck, and facing diagonally toward the center and aft, so that the flight deck tow tractors can hook them up and move them to the stern of the flight deck for the next launch.

The Fly 1 yellow shirt aims the plane toward the forward starboard edge of the deck and signals "come ahead." The nose gear of some aircraft are ten feet behind the cockpit which puts the cockpit over the water and the pilot hopes the yellow shirt will turn the jet soon since it is about sixty feet down to the water. He instructs the pilot to come ahead slowly and then finally gives the turn signal. I have to admit there were a few times when I probably kept the pilot over the water a little too long, but I wasn't the only one. It took a lot of expertise to direct these aircraft in tight spaces.

The aircraft finally stops in its parking spot. The pilot goes through a pre-shutdown routine. The plane captain chocks the wheels and installs wing-fold and strut locks and the blue shirts secure the plane with tie-down chains. If there is still ordnance on board, the squadron ordnance men de-arm the bombs and missiles by reinserting the safety pins. On the plane captain's signal, the pilot shuts down the engine and climbs out of the aircraft making his way across the flight deck and down to the squadron ready room for a debrief.

The flight deck is dangerous and it is noisy. No one is allowed on the flight deck during flight ops without a float coat, a cranial impact helmet, a whistle, goggles, and ear protection. The float coat is an inflatable life vest with an attached strobe light and a sea dye marker, just in case you get blown off the deck into the ocean. The whistle is used to attract attention, such as some FNG that is about to get blown down because he has his head up his ass and is not watching what is going on around the flight deck. The sound of a whistle can also be heard much better on the water than someone's screams for help.

The cranial helmet is for protection against flying objects, such as other airmen who get blown around by the jet exhaust. Each helmet also had a six inch square piece of reflective tape on the back as well as a three-inch by six-inch piece on the front shell of the helmet that helps flight deck personnel to be seen at night. Officers have three, one-inch vertical strips of reflective tape on the back of their cranial helmets. The ear protection, or Mickey Mouse ears, are thickly padded and are there to help protect from hearing loss. Most of us also used foam ear protectors in addition to the standard ear protection. I came into the Navy with the ability to hear a rabbit fart at a hundred paces— I intended to leave with the same hearing capability.

We also wore safety goggles on the flight deck during flight ops. Everyone also wore steel-toed shoes, just in case an aircraft ran over your foot. We actually had a blue shirt who for some reason did not want to work on the flight deck. Nobody wanted to work around him either, because they were afraid he would have his head up his ass one day and someone would get hurt. One day, he decided he had had enough of the flight deck and stuck his foot under the wheel of an A-6 Intruder being towed. The steel toe was crushed down and severed his foot at the toe line. He got his wish—he didn't have to work on the flight deck anymore. What an ass! He had a bad day.

For those of us who worked on the flight deck, the Navy considered this hazardous duty and hence, we received an extra $110 flight deck duty pay per month in addition to our normal pay when at sea. That was good money back then. Flight deck hazardous duty pay is now $150 a month.

Just because the sun goes down doesn't mean we stop flying. No sir, we would fly in any condition, day or night, clear or stormy. As you can imagine, flight ops at night are much more dangerous. But in a way, they were also more beautiful. Watching an F-14 Tomcat in full afterburner on the catapult right before launch is a beautiful sight.

There were no floodlights shining on the flight deck during the night flight ops. We used flashlights with an eight inch yellow cone attached to it, called a wand, to direct aircraft at night. The hand signals with wands would still be the same, but we would need to be a little more careful and precise when directing aircraft. We also couldn't see the pilot's eyes like we could during the day, so we had to trust that he was watching us.

Instead of landing aircraft every twenty seconds or so, aircraft were recovered about every sixty seconds at night. It was even a longer gap during heavy thunderstorms and rough seas. Like I said, pilots needed to train in all kinds of weather and we would be right there training with them.

When the deck was foul that usually meant that a plane or a person was in the recovery area and the LSO would issue the pilot a wave-off. Most wave-offs happened at night. LSOs use the term "boarding rate." During the day, you would normally experience a 98% boarding rate, meaning only two percent of the aircraft recoveries were either bolters or wave-offs. The boarding rate dropped to 89% to 90% at night.

They say on a good day, you can see about seven miles to the horizon at sea level. From the flight deck of an aircraft carrier sixty feet above the water, it is about twelve miles. However, at night, we use red lights in the compartments that opened to the outside of the ship, including those in the island, because they put out the lowest amount of ambient light. That means all compartments that face the outside, including the compartments in the island, must be illuminated with a red light, not a standard incandescent light bulb or fluorescent lights. That made for some interesting times, especially when you were playing poker and using colored chips—it was hard to tell the red chips from the blue chips.

They also say you can spot a lit cigarette at two miles, so there is no smoking outside at night. Smoking is never allowed on the flight deck anyway, but a lot of guys would cop a quick smoke in the catwalks. At night that was considered an offense and if caught, you could get reported.

The deck does have lights built in and shine straight up, so that pilots can find the recovery area, but for the rest of us—tough shit. You have to really be careful at night when walking around, especially around aircraft. When you first come out onto the flight deck from a lighted compartment, even with red lights, it takes several minutes for your eyes to adjust to the night. Some guys can see better at night than others and fortunately I was one of them, but I still had my share of problems.

One of the most dangerous things at night, other than walking off the edge of the flight deck, is an aircraft tie-down chain. They are usually in high tension, holding down an aircraft. When it comes to your shin or the chain, your shin is the one that gives way. I can't tell you how many times I have tripped over tie-down chains at night and I've got the scars on both shins to prove it. But you pick yourself up after a quick tongue lashing of the chain (like it really does any good) and keep on going.

While night launches were spectacular, recoveries were a completely different story. Besides barely seeing anything at night, we still had to position the crash tractor alongside the foul line and that was my usual spot. If the night was clear, we could see the navigation lights on the landing jets—they never used landing lights at sea. But if it was stormy and raining, it was next to impossible to spot them, you could only hear them. There were several times that I've hauled ass out of the way of a recovering aircraft because I wasn't sure if he would make it down safely or not.

The scariest aircraft to recover at night was the E-2C Hawkeye, because it had a wingspan of about eighty feet and the landing area is only about 120 feet wide. There were a couple of times when it was raining so hard you couldn't see the plane until it was just about over the fantail. It looked like it was headed straight for us, so we hauled ass away from the foul line toward the starboard side, but the plane always managed to turn at the last second and trap. I guess I had watched too many training videos.

I cannot imagine what a pilot feels when landing on a carrier in those conditions. They learn to trust their instruments. But if the CO has done his job, he's found the biggest thunderstorm in the area with high seas to pitch the deck just to make things interesting. In those horrid conditions, I bet there are pilots who hit the deck hard and probably had to check their skivvies when they got below decks.

15 USS KITTY HAWK
On Board Routines

Now that I've given you a tour of the ship and the flight deck and you have a good idea of what goes on during flight ops, let me fill you in on the boring stuff—what we do at sea when not at flight ops. There were about 80 of us in the V-1 Division; six sections with 12-15 sailors in each section. Section leaders were usually 3rd Class Petty Officers, so I was a section leader during most of my time aboard Kitty Hawk.

First of all, we would muster for quarters on the flight deck every day at a prescribed time, usually 0730. The main reason is that we needed to find out if anyone was missing. In boot camp, I had the privilege of "losing" a recruit one time and paid a price for not knowing where he was. It does not happen often, but people do go missing for one reason or another even when the ship is at sea. They could be on another duty assignment or they could be in Sickbay. Most likely if they *really* were missing, it is because they either fell overboard or someone threw them over. That never happened during my tour of duty on Kitty Hawk, but I had heard stories of sailors not being found—*ever*.

We would constantly drill, not only on the flight deck, but also the entire ship. We would go to General Quarters several times while at sea, "General Quarters, General Quarters. All hands man your battle stations!" It was important to know where we were supposed to be and what we were supposed to do when we got there. For most in the V-1 Division, my battle station during General Quarters was on the flight deck. When a carrier goes into General Quarters, 5,500 guys hoof it to get to their GQ battle station as fast as they can. The traffic rules are simple: if you are going forward or up, you stay on the starboard side of the ship; if you are going aft or down, you stay on the port side. You would cross over from one side to another in any of the many passageways.

We would run mock torpedo drills which were announced over the 5MC (flight deck PA system). The Air Boss would state, "Brace yourselves. Torpedo impact starboard side in fifteen seconds," at which time we were to find something to hang on to, squat down, and brace ourselves. Most of us sat down on the flight deck and grabbed a pad eye. Thank God we never had anything real like that happen though there was one time during the WESTPAC cruise when the CO came over the 1MC (ship's PA system) asking, "Anyone with scuba diving equipment report to engine room #1, *with* your equipment."

Prior to the WESTPAC cruise, we would head out to sea for anywhere from a few days to a couple of weeks. This would be a continuous training exercise for the entire ship including the air wing. Most of the time flight ops would last from ten in the morning until midnight. Sometimes we would fly continuously twenty-four hours around the clock for several days in a row. That was always a challenge, especially since we did not have enough guys in Crash to cover two full, twelve-hour shifts.

The flight deck would get slippery after a few days because of jet exhaust, jet fuel, and hydraulic oils. The day before we pulled into port, most of the aircraft were flown off the carrier back to their squadron home bases. Those that could not fly would be stored on the hangar deck until we got back to port. Prior to coming into port, we had to scrub the flight deck—this was the job of the V-1 Division.

Back in my day, since things are different now, we would take a couple of the MD-3 tow tractors, tie a rope to it and rig it with a metal pallet that had several rows of large wooden scrub brushes attached underneath, similar to push brooms. A couple of two and a half-inch fire hoses were strung out by four to five man crews and the flight deck was first wet down with salt water. Another MD-3 tractor would lead the way with one guy driving and two guys on the back throwing out yellow-orange colored powder soap called ZEP that came in fifty gallon drums.

Following the guys throwing out the ZEP would be two tow tractors with the pallet scrub brushes. There were two guys sitting on the pallet in order to weigh it down. Everything was great until one of the tractor drivers got a heavy foot, then the other would speed up, and soon it was a race around the flight deck. Even though there were no planes onboard, when these tractors sped and turned a corner, the guys on the pallet would fly around on the pallet hanging on for dear life.

There were so many times the Air Boss or the Flight Deck LPO (Leading Petty Officer) would chew us out for such shenanigans, but it was worth it. Nobody ever got hurt, at least not during our tour. Once the flight deck was scrubbed, the guys with the hoses would start to wash down the soap which took a while since there was a lot of soap on the flight deck. During the summer when we were coming back into the Philippines port, it was hot as hell and the hose teams sort of slipped with the hose, starting a water fight. I think the CO and the rest of the crew on the bridge thought it was funny, because they did not put a stop to it. But, that's how we cleaned and scrubbed the flight deck. Today, they use manual stick brooms to scrub the flight deck.

Another thing I loved doing was what we called bow flying. I've tried to explain to my family and friends about the sensation of being on the bow of the flight deck, stretching out your arms, leaning forward over the safety nets so you are looking straight down at the water, and letting the wind coming over the bow keep you steady while you're leaning at a forty-five degree angle. It works better when you can stretch out your foul weather jacket like a flying squirrel since it picks up more air. The wind in your face and the water below you makes you feel like you are really flying. When the movie *Titanic* came out, Leonardo DiCaprio and Kate Winslet were up front on the bow of the Titanic—you know the scene. It was almost like that, except we didn't have anybody on board that looked like Kate Winslet; or Leonardo DiCaprio, for that matter.

I did not get sick very often, but when I got a stomach ache or a head cold, I would head down to Sickbay. Here you would wait in line, not quite as long as the chow line, but sometimes it would take a while before you could see a hospital corpsman. Once you did, the corpsman would ask a few questions, take your temperature, and usually give you a prescription right then and there.

Every now and then when the line was especially long, a corpsman would come out and walk the line, taking care of those of us who were not really that sick, but only needed something quick. Sort of like a fast food drive-in—"place your order please." I was fairly impressed with the Sickbay and the corpsmen onboard Kitty Hawk.

A lot of guys played cards and sometimes there were all-night poker games. I couldn't do that, not only because of the lack of sleep, but because I was not a very good poker player. I would rather play Hearts or Spades. It passed the time as well and you could walk away after a game or two. I also read a lot of books while on the ship. While there was a library onboard in the Chaplain's office, we usually passed books around the division. One of the more intriguing books I read while on Kitty Hawk was a new best-seller, *Helter Skelter*, by Vincent Bugliosi, the prosecutor for the Charles Manson case in Los Angeles. That one gave me the willies.

Mail call on ship was pretty much every day when close to a port like San Diego, Hawaii, or the Philippines. The Navy would fly a COD plane out to us which on Kitty Hawk was a C-1 gasoline-powered, twin engine, propeller plane. It took a couple of hours for the mail to be sorted and one of the most wonderful things to hear on the ship was, "Mail Call! Mail Call!" At that point, our division Yeoman would head down to the ship's post office, pick up the bag of mail for all guys in the division, and pass it out to us.

My mom would write a letter almost every week, usually anywhere from five to ten pages on a yellow legal pad. She would start writing on a Sunday and finish up the next Friday and get it into the mail. She would tell me about everything happening in Gainesville, talk about my dad (he was a lawyer), my sister, and my friends. Every now and then my dad would add a paragraph or two which made it that much more special.

I wish I had been able to keep those letters, especially now. But I did not have room in my locker to keep too many letters, so after a while I would have to toss them to make room for a new batch. These days, most ships have email capabilities—that did not exist when I was in the Navy. Letter writing has definitely taken a back seat in correspondence these days and I guess I can't complain. After all, hearing that you are a new dad a few minutes after a baby's birth with attached photos or even a video is probably better than waiting two weeks to get a letter and photos.

One of the pranks we would play on the new guys was to send them around to visit various air department divisions for different things. For example, we would tell an FNG to go to V-2 Division to get a left-handed screwdriver or a metric crescent wrench. They would head off and the guy in the V-2 Division would know what was going on and tell him, "We don't have one in the tool box right now, but I'm pretty sure V-3 does. You might want to head over there." It took two or three different trips before the new guy figured out we were pulling his leg.

Aircraft carriers are generally accompanied by a number of other ships, helping to provide protection for the relatively unwieldy carrier, to carry supplies and replenish the carrier, and to provide additional offensive capabilities. This is known as the "carrier battle group."

Carrier battle groups (CVBGs) vary depending upon the particular mission (e.g., we're gonna kick some ass versus carrier training qualifications) and available resources (how many planes can we put in the air at one time and how many sailors does it take to do that). CVBGs usually include a combination of the following types of ships: an aircraft carrier; two guided missile cruisers; one guided missile destroyer; one destroyer for anti-submarine warfare; one frigate also for anti-submarine warfare; two attack submarines; and one supply ship to keep the entire group supplied with fuel, ordnance, non-skid, and other essentials.

Today's nuclear-powered aircraft carriers can stay at sea for more than twenty years without replenishing fuel. They do, however, need to replenish supplies. After all, about 17,000 meals are made every day—that is a lot of food. Kitty Hawk was not nuclear powered and also needed to be refueled every week or so. All of the planes in the air wing also take a lot of fuel. It was quite a sight to watch an ocean escort ship come alongside about a hundred feet off the starboard side, cruising with us about fifteen to twenty knots.

The alongside connected replenishment, also known as CONREP, is a standard method of transferring fuel, ammunition, and bulk goods. The supplying ship holds a steady course and speed, generally between twelve and sixteen knots. The carrier then comes alongside the supplier at a distance of approximately thirty yards. A shot line is fired from the supplier to the carrier which is used to pull across a messenger line. This line is used to pull across other equipment such as a distance line, phone line, and the transfer rig lines. As the command ship of the replenishment operation, the supply ship provides all lines and equipment needed for the transfer. Additionally, all commands are directed from the supply ship.

Because of the relative position of the ships, it is possible for some ships to set up multiple transfer rigs, allowing for faster transfer or the transfer of multiple types of stores. We would often have two or three rigs at one time on the carrier. Besides fuel, we would take on ordnance, food, and other much needed supplies like non-skid (toilet paper). We did not have a neighborhood Super Wal-Mart, but this did the trick. Additionally, many escorts are set up to service two ships at one time with one being replenished on each side. I saw this several times during our WESTPAC cruise: Kitty Hawk on one side and a destroyer on the other side.

Aircraft carriers are always replenished from the starboard side of the carrier which would be the port side of the supply ship. The overhanging angled flight deck does not permit replenishment from the carrier's port side. The rigs and supplies would come onboard Kitty Hawk's hangar deck through two of the elevators on the starboard side of the ship that had been lowered.

Alongside CONREP is a risky operation, as two or three ships running side-by-side at speed must hold to precisely the same course and speed for a long period of time, sometimes several hours. A slight steering error on the part of one of the ships could cause a collision. For this reason, experienced and qualified helmsmen are required during the replenishment, and the crew on the bridge must give their undivided attention to the ship's course and speed. The risk is increased when a replenishment ship is servicing two ships at once.

Just before I got to Kitty Hawk when she was on the RIMPAC exercise in Hawaii, there was a collision on the starboard side between Kitty Hawk and the ammunition ship USS KISKA (AE-35). Not bad, but enough of a bump to damage a good part of the catwalk, and this was right outside the crash crew quarters. Fortunately, there were no personnel casualties.

In case of emergency during a CONREP, crews practice emergency breakaway procedures where the ships will separate in less than optimal situations. Although the ships will be saved from collision, it is possible to lose stores, as the ships may not be able to finish the current transfer. We practiced these emergency breakaway procedures almost every time after completing the replenishment.

Coming into port was always a special tradition, especially the first time back to San Diego after the six-month WESTPAC cruise. When we were out for a week or so before the cruise and then came back into Naval Station North Island, we would have assigned duty sections. Besides cleaning our spaces and compartments, the section on duty would have to prepare their duty stations. We had six sections so we had to stand duty every six days when in port. That meant everyone else was able to disembark and go home if they lived off the ship.

After a few weeks aboard Kitty Hawk, I usually took somebody's duty when we came into port, especially if they were married. I would charge ten dollars for taking their duty that night which was the going rate at the time. All I really did was sit around the compartment. Every now and then I would have to stand a watch on the After brow, but that was not any big deal. I also had to periodically take Shore Patrol (SP) duty, meaning we had to walk in pairs in our summer whites on the pier and the nearby baseball field to make sure nobody got into trouble or mugged. There were a couple of muggings, but never on my watch. The biggest problem I had on Shore Patrol was when the ball field sprinklers went off in the middle of the night with no warning. I got wet several different times.

A couple of weeks before we left for WESTPAC, I had the opportunity to witness one the Navy's oldest traditions: a burial at sea. It was a very solemn and momentous occasion. On April 24, 1975, the late Lieutenant J. J. King was committed to the sea from Kitty Hawk. It is quite a tradition. Those attending the ceremony wore their dress whites, initially standing at attention, then at parade rest. A burial service typically includes a few prayers, a reading of scripture, the committal, the benediction, then three volleys fired by the Marine guard, then a lone bugler playing Taps. I did not participate, but I was able to watch the ceremony from Vulture's Row.

When we came into port and the tugboats pushed us up next to the pier, the Boatswain's Mates secured the ship with mooring lines and they installed the rat guards which were funnel-shaped metal devices that fit around the mooring lines to help keep rats from climbing aboard. Then the shipyard workers would put the Forward brow and the After brow into place. Some of the signalmen on board had taught their wives or girlfriends (or both) how to signal, so it was funny watching them on the flight deck communicate with the women on the pier. We didn't have cell phones back then.

When in port, at least in San Diego, there would always be a Roach Coach on the pier during meal times. This was basically a large van, or canteen, with food and drinks. I cannot tell you how many times I headed down to the roach coach for a bean burrito and a soda. We called it the roach coach for a reason, but back then at my age, those were things you really did not worry about. I do remember though, that they had crispy, warm bean burritos. Plenty of ammunition in case one wanted to try his hand at lighting a fart, too.

Most of my time on Kitty Hawk was spent on the flight deck, either in Crash and Salvage or as a yellow shirt director. We had about eighty guys in our division and about five hundred in the Air Department. There were about 5,500 men aboard Kitty Hawk when at sea. It took a lot of men doing a lot of things to make everything work the way it was supposed to. That does not mean everything was perfect, but it means that there are a lot of men who did their job and did it well, and that made the ship operate.

We had cooks, now called culinary specialists, who made 17,000 meals a day and probably worked longer hours than we did. There were "snipes" or Machinists Mates who kept the engines and boilers running smoothly. We called them snipes because they worked below decks and rarely got up to see the light of day. We had Boatswain's Mates, the oldest rate in the Navy, that kept the decks running smoothly and knew how to tie some of the coolest knots. We had our own dental staff and our own medical staff that not only took care of us on Kitty Hawk, but also served the entire carrier battle group. If someone needed a doctor, these guys would often make house calls on the other ships.

There were so many people I never had the privilege to meet, but I know we worked on the same ship at the same time. When my daughter was in high school, I had given her my standard Navy issue jacket, complete with my patches of Guam and the Kitty Hawk WESTPAC cruise. She often wore it to school and one day she told me that one of her good friends asked her about Kitty Hawk. It turns out her dad was also on Kitty Hawk at the same time as I was. He married one of my high school classmates and we both lived in Gainesville only a few miles apart and both our daughters went to the same high school. Small world.

Figure 1 – Boot Camp. Seaman Recruit Andy Adkins in "Summer Whites."

Figure 2 – NAS Agana, Guam. John Melcher in crash truck on the Alert Spot.

Figure 3 - NAS Agana, Guam. Glenn Law and Gary Borne in crash truck on Alert Spot.

Figure 4 - NAS Agana, Guam. John O'Mara and Gary Cuzner on Oshkosh MB-1 crash truck; turrets in action.

Figure 5 - NAS Agana, Guam. ABH1 Gary Morey, ABHAN Eric Campbell, ABHAA Gary Borne, ABHAA Andy Adkins, ABHAN Bruce Hallowell. Taken after a "Whites" inspection.

Figure 6 - NAS Agana, Guam. Piss test day - Starboard Section (not happy).

Figure 7 - NAS Agana, Guam. Hot drills; note the two crash crew in the middle of the fire after a path had been laid down by the turret man.

Figure 8 - NAS Agana, Guam. Hot drills; Andy Adkins as driver/crew chief.

Figure 9 - NAS Agana, Guam. Andy Adkins with Unit #5 on the Alert Spot. This was my favorite truck to drive.

Figure 10 - NAS Agana, Guam. Traditional hose down of Marty Bley's last day on Guam.

Figure 11 - Author, Andy "Chet" Adkins. The photographer wanted to display this photo in his studio. Our boot camp class, Company 163, was the first to graduate with the new style Navy uniform.

Figure 12 - USS Kitty Hawk, CV-63 (Photo courtesy of U.S. Navy)

Figure 13 - USS Kitty Hawk. A-7 Corsair on Cat #1 ready for launch. Yellow shirt is directing the pilot to go to full afterburner before handing off to the Shooter. Also notice the crash tractor in the background, centered between Cats #1 and #2.

Figure 14 - USS Kitty Hawk. F-4 Phantom takes an arresting wire. The V-2 Division Hook Runner is seen next to the aircraft, signaling the V-1 Division Gear Puller (not seen) to direct the pilot to raise the tail hook.

Figure 15 - USS Kitty Hawk. Flight deck. Note the tractor on the left side with mail bags just delivered by the COD (to the left of the crash truck).

Figure 16 - USS Kitty Hawk. Underway replenishment. The black hoses are fuel lines. The escort replenishment ship is about 30 yards off the starboard side.

Figure 17 - USS Kitty Hawk. Hong Kong tour of Aberdeen with my friend, Steve Cummings.

Figure 18 - USS Kitty Hawk. Tokyo trip with Gary Borne, Tom Watson, Jim King, Bud Laney, Gary DeSaunier. None of us spoke Japanese.

Figure 19 - Bermerton Shipyards. USS Kitty Hawk bow on blocks in dry dock.

Figure 20 - Bremerton Shipyards. USS Kitty Hawk resting on blocks in dry dock.

16 WESTPAC '75

Kitty Hawk got underway on Wednesday, May 21, 1975 about 1430 (2:30 p.m.) on a WESTPAC cruise. This would be Kitty Hawk's tenth consecutive WESTPAC and it was my first and only. We were supposed to leave at 1000, but there was a problem with one of the ship's boilers, so we had a slight delay. Boy it felt good heading out to sea again, past the other ships docked in the bay, past Point Loma and the Old Point Loma lighthouse, and out into the deep blue. *The wind in our faces, the salt in the air, and the glory of another fine day in the Navy.*

During my first few months aboard Kitty Hawk, I made several good friends in the V-1 Division. My good friend Glenn Law was a yellow shirt. Gary Borne and I were both in Crash. The three of us had been in Guam together. It was nice to have some old friends to help break me in to my new duty station and show me around. Duty aboard an aircraft carrier was a lot different than duty on Guam.

The head of Crash and Salvage was Chief Warrant Officer CWO-2 Tyrone Robuck who was a proud Cajun from Louisiana. He was the Air Bos'n and was a little short guy, but previously had been a Marine and had fought in Vietnam. He had a lot of medals and we used to joke that he walked with a port list since he had so many medals above his left breast pocket weighing him down. He was a good guy though, knew his shit, and kept us working as a team. He also had a great sense of humor. Sometimes when I made a comment to him, he would look me straight in the eye and say, "Adkins, when I want your opinion, I'll give it to you!"

Lieutenant Commander Robert Leone was the V-1 Division Officer and also carried the title "Flight Deck Officer." He had flown A-4 Skyhawks prior to this command. He was alright too, very disciplined and didn't take shit off of anybody, but he would also to go bat for you when needed.

Senior Chief Kenneth Breig was the senior enlisted man in our division and therefore our LCPO. It was rumored that when he went home on leave, he would line his kids up for haircut inspection. He and I didn't get along all that well, so I tried to avoid him as much as possible. The biggest problem was that I got caught between him and Bos'n Robuck too many times.

"Adkins, what the hell are you doing?" Senior Chief Breig would ask. "I'm working on this truck like Bos'n Robuck asked me to," I replied. "Well, I've got something else for you to do," he would tell me. Then I would get chewed out by Bos'n Robuck because I didn't finish what he asked me to do. Petty bullshit things like that could get to you, but I quickly learned how to live with it. When my time in the Navy was about up, Chief Breig asked me if I wanted to re-enlist. I asked him how much of a bonus would the Navy pay me to reenlist? He told me that I could get a $1,200 bonus to re-up for six years. The Nukes were getting $20,000 to reenlist for *four* years. That was an easy no for me.

We had some good first and second class petty officers, too. PO Jeff Atteberry was the only first class in Crash and therefore designated the Crash LPO. He was a soft-spoken guy and easy to get along with, but he also knew his stuff. After his tour on Kitty Hawk, he was assigned to be a recruiter and he was not happy with that. Atteberry would more than prove his worth a few months into the cruise.

PO Mike Alford was the Fly 2 LPO. He had a unique talent of being able to spit out baseball and music trivia. Not a day would go by that he wouldn't ask, "Chet, who pitched three no-hitters in 1966?" Like I gave a shit. While I did play little league baseball when I was a kid and at one time had a hell of a baseball card collection, I didn't know half of what he asked. Besides, Al could be blowing smoke up your ass and you would never know it. I liked Al though; he was a good guy and an outstanding yellow shirt on the flight deck. Even though he was only a second class petty officer, he looked after and took care of his guys in Fly 2.

John Mayberry was a first class petty officer and the Fly 1 LPO. I've watched him direct an F-4 back into a tight spot between two other F-4s with three inches on each side of the plane's folded wings. He would climb up to the cockpit of the plane and tell the plane captain that he was going to back him in slowly, then for the plane captain to hit the left brake hard when he told him to; the plane would slide in just right. He was a marvel to watch directing airplanes.

PO Frank Bethune was the senior first class petty officer in the division and therefore the Flight Deck LPO. He was a cool guy, too. He was one of the biggest and tallest black guys I had ever met. Rumor was that he had been a former heavyweight boxing champion, so he wasn't one to mess with. I used to call him BUD for "Big, Ugly, and Dumb," but after a couple of "Yeah, that's funny Adkins," he got tired of it and let me know ... personally.

Dennis Mahon was a third class petty officer like me. He was the Tractor King. He was a short guy but had a big heart. I don't know how he did it, but he was able to keep the blue shirt tractor drivers in line. Dennis and I would often take duty for other guys so they could go home or go partying, charging ten dollars for the night. It was not a lot of money, but it certainly helped out.

Buddy Laney was also a third class petty officer assigned to Crash. Buddy was from Atlanta and always had a smile and good things to say about anybody and everybody. I don't think I ever saw Buddy pissed off or in a bad mood—he kinda helped the rest of us along on those not-so-good-days. He often hung around the foul line at the crash tractor with us. He was a fast runner too. When an aircraft was on its last few feet of recovery, if it looked like it was drifting toward the island, Buddy was right there with us, heading toward to Starboard side usually beating us out of the danger zone.

Jimmy Smith was also a third class petty officer assigned to Fly 3. Smitty was from Texarkana and had married his high school sweetheart, Connie. They both became good friends of mine during our year-long stay in Bremerton. Smitty was one of the few married guys I know who didn't screw around on the cruise. Whenever he went out the gate, which was rare, he stayed straight and faithful—I really admired that.

Another of my good friends was PO MacKay. He was also a first class petty officer and the Fly 3 LPO. Everybody called him Mac. He was a short and stocky red-headed guy with a goatee. Mac was from Colorado and had a bitchin' four-wheel drive Dodge RAM truck, complete with huge tires. He loved off-road driving. He was also one of the guys who didn't screw around in port when overseas. In fact, he and Smitty hung out a lot together since they could help each other from giving into temptations. One of the things about Mac—he had a pair of lips tattooed on his ass. Funniest thing you ever saw. Read: "Kiss my ass!"

Ed Boes, another third class petty officer, was also a good friend and a yellow shirt. He was a tall, skinny guy and had one hell of a handlebar mustache. Ed lost some stupid bet one time and for losing, he shaved his handlebar mustache off on the flight deck during one morning muster in front of the whole division. He, Gary Borne, and I would share an apartment when we got to the shipyards in Bremerton.

Charlie Brown was a second class petty officer in Fly 2. He was a good director, but drank a lot. A couple of times while in port, he stumbled back onto the ship, climbed into his middle rack, then promptly puked on the floor. He would then order a blue shirt to clean it up. I would be with Charlie when he headed into Hong Kong to get a tattoo of the Philippine flag with his girlfriend's name. Charlie was a married man too, at least until his wife saw the tattoo.

Tony Davis was also a third class petty officer in Fly 1. He was from Maryland and had a unique style of directing using hand signals just like everyone else, but he had his own style that I would call "loud and proud!" I saw Tony tackle a new Blue shirt on the flight deck one day—the blue shirt wandered a little too close to an A-7 Corsair and was just about to get sucked into the intake. Tony saw it coming and tackled the guy. That would've been a bad day.

One of the funniest guys I met was in the V-3 Division—Peter Head. He didn't have a middle name, either. He was built like a linebacker. His unique feature was that he had one eye that would look you straight in the eye and the other eye would float around. I guess they call this a lazy eye. You wouldn't call him Pete or anything other than Peter Head. When an FNG came into his division, he would introduce himself, "My name is Second Class Petty Officer Peter Head and I'm a prick!" We joked behind his back that his parents either didn't like him or wanted him to grow up mean. Either way, he was one of the straightest guys I met, but he also had that air about him that you did not make fun of him or his name. Otherwise he would beat the living shit out of you.

We were headed first to Hawaii, a trip that would take about six days. When the carrier first leaves port, there are no aircraft onboard. The air wing maintenance personnel are aboard, but the planes and the pilots fly out and land on the carrier. It makes sense when you think about it because trying to load and tow seventy plus aircraft on board off the pier would be a big pain in the ass. First you would have to get them to the pier to be loaded. It's not like the Navy would parade seventy aircraft down the interstate. So, they get to fly aboard.

As you head out to sea, there are all kinds of things that need to get done. We had maintenance on the crash equipment. We had training, drills, and other various activities to keep us busy. But I was always able to find a little time to walk around the flight deck and gaze out. The ocean seemed to get bluer and bluer the farther we went out.

There were many times during the cruise when we would see a school of dolphins swimming and jumping alongside the ship and with the water so blue and clear, it was a magnificent sight. A couple of times I saw whales off the starboard side, not right next to the ship, but a hundred or so yards out.

Many times I would be on the flight deck at sunset and sunrise and many of them were absolutely spectacular. For some reason, and I'm sure there is a scientific explanation for it, the skies are deep blue and deep orange at that time of the day especially over the water. There is an old sailor saying, "Red sky at night, sailors delight; red sky at morning, sailors take warning." I don't know how true that is, but both dawn and dusk were usually spectacular.

A few days into the cruise it finally dawned on me—while *I* work for the Navy, the *Navy* works for me. Where else could I work and get an all-expense paid trip to Guam, Hawaii, the Philippines, Hong Kong, and a bunch of other great places? And the best thing? I got paid for it. Sure I had to put up with a lot of crap, but I had learned how to circumvent most of it. My dad was giving me a lot of advice as to how he dealt with this type of military bullshit when he was in the Army during World War II. But he was an officer and I was an enlisted man and I learned early on that Shit Rolls Down Hill. This is a lesson that I would take and run with, not only in my brief Navy career, but also throughout my life. You can sit back and take it or you take it and run with it.

There are two kinds of shipmates in the Navy: those who want to do their jobs, and those who don't give a shit and skate as much as they can. I was the former and most of the guys I worked with had a good attitude though we did have a few that slacked off every now and then. In a world of constant danger on the flight deck, you cannot allow guys with GAF (Give a Fuck) attitudes to work on the flight deck. We had a way of dealing with it—blanket parties.

The blue shirts usually would take care of such things since most of the dickwads in our division were FNGs with an attitude and were in the blue shirt crew. When one of these guys copped an attitude, several of the older, more experienced blue shirts would find him alone, throw a blanket over him, and punch him all over his body. I'm not talking about wussy, girlie punches, either. I'm talking about black and blue punches from several different guys, but never to the head, only to the body. That way, no bruises showed. It rarely took more than one blanket party to straighten his sorry ass out. It may not have been legal, but it was very effective and usually only required one party. The next day, that guy learned to carry his own weight.

Sometimes we just wanted to have fun with a new recruit, especially if he thought he was better than the rest of us. One of the more painless methods of humiliation was the balloon shaving cream trick. There would be several of us that would gather around the recruit's rack in our berthing compartment. He would have his privacy curtains pulled down. We would fill up a balloon with shaving cream, blow it up a little, then while guys held the curtains down, one of us would open the corner flap and let the balloon loose in his rack. Once the balloon finished its duty, we would all split and run like hell—he didn't know what hit him. I have to admit, that was one of the funnier things we did on the ship.

Each Fly had its own compartment alongside the flight deck. Fly 1 would be toward the starboard bow off the catwalk, Fly 2 in the island on the starboard side, and Fly 3 aft toward the starboard stern off the catwalk. Crash was in the aft part of the island on the starboard side. There were anywhere from twelve to fifteen guys in each unit. The space wasn't big, about twenty feet wide (port to starboard) and about twelve feet long (fore to aft).

There wasn't enough space for everyone in the unit to be in the compartment at one time, but that would be a rare occasion. There were padded benches, a table or two, a TV to watch launches and recoveries, and the most important thing: a 100-cup coffee maker. We didn't have computers, DVD, or CDs back then, nor did we have VHS tapes, but we made do. There were also a few lockers, but not enough for everyone, so they were shared by two or more guys. The more senior guys in the unit had their own.

During the cruise, Bonnie and I exchanged a few letters. We had mutually decided that we weren't going to get married and we both agreed that while our time on Guam was special, things had changed since we had been apart. I was going on a cruise for six months and she was still in Guam—we both realized there would be temptations. I think she had found someone else which was good though she never said so. I did get a letter from her telling me that she would be transferred to the dental facility at the Naval Station in San Diego. I told her that I would like to see her when the ship got back at the end of the year. She agreed.

17 WESTPAC '75
Kitty Hawk Air Wing, CVW-11

There were about 5,500 officers and enlisted men on Kitty Hawk. About 2,500 of them belonged to the air wing. Every time a carrier goes out, it is accompanied by a group of Naval air squadrons which make up the air wing. Face it—an aircraft carrier would be pretty lame if it didn't have aircraft.

Kitty Hawk had twelve squadrons of aircraft onboard during the WESTPAC '75 cruise. Fighters, attack planes, early warning, electronic jammers, anti-submarine warfare planes, reconnaissance aircraft, and helos—all of them made up the Carrier Air Wing, CVW-11.

CVW-11 dates back to 1942 and has a rich history in Naval aviation. Among other accomplishments, it was the first Navy air group to down a Russian MiG jet fighter during the Korean conflict. It was also the first air wing to receive the Presidential Unit Citation for performance in Vietnam.

We had two squadrons of F-4J Phantoms: VF-114 "Aardvarks" and VF-213 "Black Lions." Where they come up with these squadron nicknames beats the hell out of me, but apparently there is rich history and the pilots and crew are extremely proud of their legacy. I loved the F-4 Phantoms—they just looked like they could really kick some ass. These fighter jets carried two crewmen: one pilot in the front and one RIO (Radar Intercept Officer) in the back. When these bad boys launched at night, the glow of the afterburners was awesome.

We had two squadrons of A-7E Corsairs: VA-192 "Golden Dragons" (actually, they called themselves the "World Famous Golden Dragons") and VA-195 "Dambusters." These were one-seaters. These were my favorite aircraft during the cruise. I thought if one guy could go out all on his own and kick some ass, well, there's got to be some gutsy guys in that outfit. Besides, when they landed on the flight deck and couldn't raise their tail hook, we would run over and press a "magic" button in the starboard wheel well which was actually just a hydraulic override, to raise his tail hook.

In my opinion, the loudest jets on the flight deck were the A-6 "Intruders," all-weather attack planes that carried two crewmembers side-by-side, a pilot and a copilot. We had one squadron of these, the VA-52 "Knight Riders" who were the most decorated squadron in the history of the A-6 Intruder. Besides carrying bombs, a couple of the Intruders were also configured to serve as in-flight refuelers for the other aircraft. These guys were loud and even with ear protectors and foam ear inserts, they would really make your ears hurt if you were anywhere near them when at full power.

I liked these two-seaters too, because when they couldn't raise their tail hook after a trap, we would run out and lie flat on our back on the deck under the plane and push the hook up with our feet. We would do this just to get the tail hook clear of the arresting wire, then the yellow shirt would direct him out of the recovery area with the tail hook still dragging on the deck. The squadron maintenance guys would be able to get the hook up later.

A close cousin of the A-6 Intruder was the EA-6B "Prowler." These four-seaters belonged to the VAQ-136 "Gauntlets." They're basically the same plane as the A-6 Intruder, but with an extended cockpit for four crew members instead of two and it was fixed up with all kinds of electronic gizmos to do bad things to the enemy's radar and communications.

We had two squadrons of anti-submarine warfare planes, both of which were gasoline powered, twin engine, propeller-driven S-2 "Stoofs," originally developed in the mid-1950s. They carried a load of sonobuoys which were electronic devices that were dropped into the ocean to help track enemy submarines. VS-37 "Hacker Trackers" and VS-38 "Claw Clan" joined us for the cruise. One of the outstanding features of this plane was the long antenna that was extended about twenty feet out the rear of the fuselage when searching for enemy submarines.

Our forward looking eyes were the E-2C "Hawkeyes." They were also nicknamed "Hummers" because they had a distinct loud hum when in full power. We had two of them onboard from the VAW-114 "Hawgs" squadron. They were usually the second plane to launch during flight ops after the plane guard helos because their early warning capabilities extended the battle group's radar out about three hundred miles. If any enemy aircraft were near us, these guys had a direct electronic communications link to the ship's CIC (Command Information Center) using the ATDS (Airborne Tactical Data System) and would let us know pronto if any danger was near. The Hawkeye carried a crew of five who would fly around all day. These planes scared me when they landed, mainly because their wing span was about eighty feet and if they were off so much a hair from the centerline of recovery, it looked like they were coming straight at us.

We also had a couple of RA-5C "Vigilantes" from the RVAH-6 squadron. These were all-weather, multi-sensor, tactical reconnaissance planes and when they landed and taxied out of the recovery area, one of the first crewmen to greet them was the squadron's photographer's mate—they had to pull the top-secret film out for analysis. I liked these guys, too. They were long and slinky, kind of like a dragster. They would usually launch off Cat #4 which the pilots hated. The nose wheel is about five feet in back of the cockpit, so when the yellow shirt taxied them onto Cat #4, the cockpit would be directly over the ocean for several seconds before the yellow shirt would turn him onto the catapult. It was a tight turn, but most yellow shirts knew what they were doing.

Our HS-8 "Sea King" helicopters served several roles, one of which was the plane guard. They would be the first to launch during flight ops, just in case someone had a bad day and went into the drink. This squadron's nickname was "Eight Ballers." They also were anti-submarine and often worked with the S-2s during anti-submarine warfare exercises. They could carry a load of sonobuoys, too. Two of these aircraft crashed during the WESTPAC cruise, one in the drink and one on the flight deck.

Last, but not least, were my old friends from Guam. The VQ-1 "Bats" flew the EA-3B "Skywarriors." We picked them up as TAD (Temporary Assigned Duty) on our way from Hawaii to the Philippines. These planes carried a crew of three and were huge—the biggest plane on the ship. It was so big, its other nickname was the "Whale." The A-3 didn't have ejection seats, mainly to save weight and because the A-3 usually flew at very high altitude and the old timers often joked about it calling the A-3D, "All Three Dead." How the crew could get out even at high altitude still puzzles me. The A-3s on Kitty Hawk during our deployment were outfitted for electronic warfare support.

Kitty Hawk had closed circuit television with three channels. We didn't have satellite TV back then. The first channel was the ship's local TV broadcast channel and would usually be used for the CO or the XO to make a speech though that didn't happen too often. We had a regularly scheduled newscast where the Public Affairs Office would report what was happening on the ship as well as the rest of the world. When that wasn't on, the department would show movies, usually only during the night and when we were not in flight ops. Contrary to popular belief, they didn't show stag flicks on board. Usually the movies were old movies or "B" movies and they would usually show the same movie several times a week.

During flight ops, there were also two other channels available. One was a live feed from one of two cameras located on the island that showed the planes being launched in real-time. It switched between the bow cats and the waist cats, depending what aircraft was launching and when. There was also another camera built into the flight deck in the recovery area, centerline of the angle between wires #3 and #4, called the Plat camera. You could see planes coming in for a landing and actually watch them trap.

There were also times during night Blue Water flight ops (i.e., when there was no other air base for the aircraft to land) when a plane just couldn't seem to trap for one reason or another. He would approach and either bolter or get a wave-off from the LSO. There would be a KA-6 Intruder tanker flying around and you know the pilot had visited him a time or two. Everybody that could would be watching the plane approach, hoping he would catch a wire and land safely. Sometimes, there would be more bolters and wave-offs than there would be traps—that was not a good day.

We spent a lot of time watching these two channels, mainly because there wasn't anything else on. But it also had a relaxing effect almost like watching waves crashing on the beach or watching a camp fire. Most of the training videos we watched of carrier crashes and fires came from these types of cameras.

18 WESTPAC '75
Hawaii, One Word: Beautiful!

We were in and out of Hawaii twice on the way out to the Philippines on the WESTPAC '75 cruise. The first time in, we had two days of liberty. My first stop was Waikiki Beach. I wanted to learn how to surf, so several of us headed that way. The water was so warm and clear, it was absolutely beautiful. I thought Guam was gorgeous, but this was much better. One of the big differences between Guam and Hawaii was there were so many women here. Every one of them was a 10! The bikinis, if that is what you would call them, were like shoestrings.

I was out in the water with a surfboard, not having a clue as to what to do, but I was enjoying the water and the scenery. I got up on my surfboard after a couple of tries, but was not able to hang ten very well. My buddy and I were scouting out the chicks and he pointed to one very nice looking girl who was surfing pretty well. He told me he had talked with her a little earlier and she seemed really nice. "Her name is Karen," he said.

So I swam over to her with my confident and cocky attitude and said something like, "Hi. Your name's Karen, isn't it?" She said, "Nope, it's Jennifer." Damn, I fell for that old sailor trick again. I apologized and then left with my tail tucked between my legs, or whatever it is when you're on a surfboard.

A few minutes later, I spotted another nice looking chick and started talking with her. I told her I wanted to learn how to surf but was not quite sure how. I was a water skier and had never been on a surfboard in my life. I asked her how much she charged and she replied that she charged a drink an hour. Well, I could tell this might go somewhere. She agreed to teach me and we spent the next hour or so together. I was starting to get the hang of it, too. It was hot and the sun was beating down on my back. I had not put any sun screen on, but I didn't care. I would pay for that one later.

After this young lady and I surfed for a while, we went up to the beach bar and I bought us both a drink. I was becoming more interested and she was becoming more interesting. We got into a deep conversation about something totally unimportant and then she told me she had to leave soon to go to the doctor. She looked great and I told her so and asked what was wrong. She told me that she had V.D. Goodbye, that's all she wrote. I guess I was naive, because I believed her.

After a glorious day of sun and fun at Waikiki, several of us went bar hopping. I can't remember the name of the bar we stopped in. The only thing I remember is that I was drinking something blue and there was a girl dancing on our table. I do remember that the drink prices were sky high—$3.50 for a cocktail. Back in Gainesville the same drink would have only been $1.50. After that, the night got kind of blurry.

We stopped by another bar, the Red Door Lounge. They had a country band playing so this was more like it (not that I didn't like women dancing on my table, mind you). Several of the guys egged me on to sing with the band, so what the hell, I did. The band welcomed an addition—another drunk sailor. I got through *The Auctioneer* easily, then the lead guitar player handed me his guitar and I stumbled through *Wildwood Flower*. I tried to sing *Rednecks, White Socks, and Blue Ribbon Beer* as a tribute to my fellow shipmates, but I was pretty shit-faced, so I quit in the middle of that one. Everybody in the bar was laughing, probably because I was making a fool out of myself. It was not the first time. We certainly did have a good time on the town though.

The next day, several of us went to the USS Arizona Memorial. We had to take a ferry to get to her. The memorial actually straddles the sunken battleship. It was quiet and serene, almost like a library or a church before a funeral. It was not as big as I thought it would be, at least not when compared to Kitty Hawk. The most visible feature of the ship is the barbette to gun turret number three—it pokes out above the water. I do remember looking down into the crystal clear water and thinking of all those men, more than eleven hundred of them still entombed. It was a very solemn time for all of us. The memorial was officially dedicated on Memorial Day 1962. As I got older, I've often thought back to that visit—these guys were our age and they had lost their lives thirty-four years earlier defending our country, their ship, and their fellow shipmates in an unprovoked attack.

We headed out of Hawaii on May 29 for a few days of training exercises. During flight ops that first day, an F-4 Phantom from the VF-114 squadron was conducting touch and go landings on the carrier. I was in my usual place on the foul line next to the crash tractor. We always kept our eyes on the planes coming and going, just in case we noticed something wrong and we could either run toward it to help out or run away from it to save our ass.

On one of the touch and gos, the horizontal stabilizer on the F-4 for some reason locked and the plane went nose up. You could see the pilot apply afterburners, but with a nose-up attitude and not much speed, the plane was obviously stalling. We watched as the pilot and RIO punched out about eight hundred feet up, ejecting safely into the sea. The plane was lost to Davy Jones with no chance of recovery, but fortunately the crewmen parachuted down into the ocean to our starboard side and the SH-3 plane guard helo was there within a couple of minutes. Both crewmen were recovered and neither were injured. We were not quite sure what went wrong, but it was explained to us later on that it was an "equipment malfunction" which is the Navy's way of saying, "it's none of your fuckin' business." That was OK with me—at least he didn't crash on the flight deck.

We got back to Hawaii on June 1 and had two more days of liberty. I got to see Kitty Wells in concert at the Enlisted Men's Club on the base. The Queen of Country Music, along with her husband Johnny Wright, played and sang for a couple of hours. I had met a WAVE earlier on the base bus and she and I had dinner together and then headed to the concert. This was one of those clubs with a nice dance floor, so we danced the night away. As the night wore on, she got more interesting as we danced closer. After the concert, we headed back to her place, but I did not stay too long. It seems her boyfriend was there and was quite perturbed that I had taken her out. I had no idea she had a boyfriend. So I left, *again*, empty handed.

We left Hawaii the second time on Wednesday, June 4. Our next stop was the Philippines, a trip that would take about two weeks. A little over a week out of Hawaii, Kitty Hawk experienced a major problem. One of the main engine rooms flooded around midnight: a steam line ruptured and then a sea valve malfunctioned causing flooding of the machine room space. No one was hurt and everybody down there got out. That was the *good* thing. The *bad* thing was the CO came over the 1MC and announced, "Anyone with scuba equipment please report to engine room #1 ... and bring your equipment." That was scary. I started thinking about abandoning ship, but those were just fleeting thoughts.

We did go to General Quarters though. We had to move crash equipment and aircraft to the port side on the flight deck since the flood caused the ship to list to the starboard side. *That* was a fun night.

One of the guys in Crash named "Big Willie" was a big black fellow. His real name was Shelby Williams, but he was big, so everybody called him Big Willie. He was a second class petty officer and a cool dude, always watching out for us peons, but he had his own agenda. He was a loan shark, so to speak. If anybody needed any money while in port, Big Willie was the man to see. Borrow $20 and pay back $40 on payday. No problem, money is always available. Besides loaning money to others, he was also one of the disc jockeys aboard Kitty Hawk.

Back in 1975, there was no satellite radio. Kitty Hawk had three radio stations: KROC, the rock station; KSOL, the soul station; and KRAL, the country station. Big Willie was a DJ for KSOL and had a two-hour spot in the late afternoon. I thought that was cool, so I asked if I might be able to do country. BW took me down to the station, introduced me to the station manager and a few days later, they put me on the air. I was known as Country Chet Adkins.

It took me a little while to get the hang of it, but because of my radio work in Guam (both flying and on the crash truck radios), I was a natural. The equipment was simple: two turntables to play LPs and two eight-track tape players to play commercials, not that we had that many. There were hundreds of LPs (Long Play records), all put together by the Armed Forces Radio Network (AFRN). We even had a phone for listeners to call in requests. Could I have possibly found another career?

I initially started out with an afternoon spot 1400-1600 (2:00 to 4:00), because I was on the night shift crew. Later, my spot was 0600-0800, just right since we did not need to be on the flight deck until 1000 for flight ops. I always started with a Chet Atkins guitar solo: *Yakety Axe*, an old Boots Randolph song (Boots Randolph played the saxophone and it was originally called *Yakety Sax*).

I would crank *Yakety Axe* up at 0600 and after a few seconds came over the radio: "Gooooood morning Kitty Hawk. It's six o'clock and time again for the Country Chet Adkins show." This was years before Robin Williams' *Good Morning Vietnam* movie. When I had a bad day on the flight deck, it was so relaxing to get down to the radio station and go on the air. We only operated the radio stations when we were at sea. I would keep this up the entire cruise and I had several fans on board; at least shipmates that would call me up to make requests.

During the cruise, I was also studying for my second class petty officer exam. While I had been a third class petty officer for only several months, I would be eligible to take the second class exam during the cruise. It was given twice a year and I could take it in early August if I was ready. I was not expecting to pass, but I figured I would take the exam anyway.

It you take the exam and pass it but do not get promoted, it is called a PNA, or Passed but Not Accepted. That was common for guys like me that had only been in rate for a few months. In the Navy at that time, certain things are given points to advance your rank. That included the amount of time in your current pay grade, any ribbons you may have been awarded, quarterly evaluation marks, and the number of times you have taken and passed the exam. I'm sure there were several other political BS points, but I was not aware of how that worked.

On the way to the Philippines, we established what was called the "Alert 5." This meant we had two F-4 Phantoms on the catapults ready to launch from a cold start within five minutes. This was kept up around the clock, mainly because the Russians did not work nine to five either. There would be a pilot and RIO in the cockpit waiting; nearby would be the starter equipment hooked up to the aircraft as well as a full plane crew, including maintenance and ordnance men. A yellow shirt would join them, all ready to go at a moment's notice.

We did this because there were Russian aircraft constantly flying reconnaissance missions over the carrier task force. We were still in the Cold War and we did not trust them any more than they trusted us. The two main Russian aircraft that buzzed us were Russian Bears which were four-engine jets and Russian Badgers which were four-engine turbo-props.

If they came anywhere near us, the Air Boss would come over the 5MC and announce, "Launch the Alert 5!" At that point, the plane captain and crew would start the F-4 Phantoms, spooling up the jet engines, checking the ordnance, and getting the catapult ready to launch. The yellow shirt would direct the plane up onto the catapult. Then, when all was ready, the Shooter would launch the aircraft. The goal was to have at least one aircraft in the air within five minutes and most of the time we made it with time to spare though sometimes there would be an equipment malfunction in which case we would launch the other one.

They would fly alongside the Russian planes taking photos, waving to the Russian crews, and smiling for the Russian cameras. One of the pilots told me that the usual scenario was that they would fly escort with the Russian Bear or Badger and smile and wave. Both the American pilots and the Russian pilots would take photos of each other. But, the pilot was always ready with his trigger finger, just in case. I was glad nothing ever happened; at least no one ever told us anything ever happened during those friendly exchanges.

On the backup, there was an Alert 15, meaning two more F-4s would be ready to launch within 15 minutes after the Alert 5. The crews were not in the cockpit for the Alert 15, but nearby enough to get ready quickly in case one of the Alert 5s could not get off. It was really quite a scene to watch these guys in action. Most of the time, everything went smoothly.

Several days out from the Philippines, we passed close to Guam. Glenn, Gary, and I went down to the communications office and we wanted to send a telegram to some of the guys we knew were still on Guam. We were trying to be smart asses in what we wanted to say, but when it came down to it, the Communications Officer pretty much put a limit on what we could say. We could not tell them we were passing by. We could not tell them we were on Kitty Hawk. We could not tell them that life on the ship was much better than life on Guam.

About all we could tell them was "Hi from Gary, Andy, and Glenn." It was disappointing, but I certainly understood the fact we could not reveal anything about who we were, our present position, and where we were heading. No telling who would be listening. Of course, we could easily write a letter to them and reveal everything since nobody ever checked letters like they did in Vietnam or World War II.

Our transit from Hawaii to the Philippines took about two weeks. During that time, the ship started what is commonly known as "water hours." This means the ship turns off the fresh water during certain hours and then it is turned on for only a couple of hours at a time. If you could not grab a shower during those times, you would have to "mudpack" it, meaning to hit the rack without a shower. That happened more times than you would think but we did not have it so bad. I felt sorry for the guys in the V-2 Division and the Snipes since they were probably caked in grease all day long. Talk about a slip and slide into the rack.

19 WESTPAC '75
Philippines, One Word: Hot!

Subic Bay Naval Station in the Philippines was our overseas home port, meaning we would head out to various places in the South China Sea conducting naval training exercises, but would come back to Subic Bay in between. This is also known as Forward Deployment. The Naval Station at Subic Bay was one of the nicer bases in the Navy. They say Guantanamo Bay (Gitmo Bay) Naval Station was the best. Since you can't go anywhere in Cuba, the Navy made it extra special. But the base in the Philippines was great— lots of activities on base to keep a sailor out of trouble. That is, if he stayed on the base.

The Philippine Islands, or PI as we called it, is a country of seven thousand islands that are peaks of a partly submerged mountain chain, only 6.5% of which are larger than one square mile, and about 750 miles east of Vietnam across the South China Sea. Coming into PI was also welcoming— after all, it was our new home port. Once the ship got within a hundred or so yards of the pier, several tugboats took over, gently nudging her toward the pier. You wanted to be careful with this maneuver since pushing 60,000 tons of metal too fast would be a bad day for everybody.

So how would I describe PI? Cheap hookers, San Miguel beer, Jeepneys, baluts, grilled monkey meat, Shit River, and martial law. Did I mention cheap beer? San Miguel beer was the local beer and I cannot tell you how many times I walked into a bar in Olongapo City right after work, ordered a San Miguel beer, and was handed one caked in a thick layer of ice—it was so cold and tasted so good, especially on those miserable hot and humid days. The only problem was that if you drank too many of them, you would get a bad case of the runs.

149

Baluts were, well, the most disgusting thing you could ever think of. Take a fertilized chicken egg and bury it in hot sand on the beach and leave it for about three months. Dig it up, remove the top of the egg, and eat it raw. It was considered a delicacy by Filipinos, but I can honestly tell you after seeing one of these up close and a Filipino girl eating it, I did not need to see anything more. Like the girl on Waikiki Beach—I was history.

Jeepneys were old World War II jeeps that had been refurbished by Filipinos. They still had the same engines, but had extended open rear end cabs, enough to carry six people comfortably or eight people cramped. They almost looked like the old Woody station wagons that were popular on the surf scene back in the sixties. They were all very flamboyantly decorated with different colors, flowers, and whatever else their owners could put on them. Jeepneys were all over the place and after a while you got to know who drove which one by the decorations and the music they played. They were the most common method for public transportation in Olongapo City.

Grilled monkey meat or dog meat? You think I'm kidding? There were usually a dozen or so BBQs of grilled meat between the main gate and Olongapo City and there was no telling what they were cooking. I thought it was chicken, like we had in Guam—doesn't everything taste like chicken? But several of the older salts told me that it could just as well be monkey meat or dog meat. Who knew? Most of the time it smelled great and tasted even better. Of course, when you're half-shitfaced, everything smells good and tastes great. There were also a couple of restaurants in Olongapo City that had glass cages in the windows which held live monkeys. I thought they were there for decoration, but if you said "such a cute monkey" on the way in, you might walk out and not see the same monkey in the cage.

We arrived in Subic Bay on June 19 and docked about 1000. Apparently right before entering port, every department head gave a lecture on V.D. and what to do to help protect yourself. Back then, there was no AIDS, so the only things we needed to worry about were standard venereal diseases like gonorrhea, syphilis, and NSU (Non-Specific Urethritis infection). Bos'n Robuck told us the best thing to do was to wear a prophylactic, otherwise known as a rubber hooey, which the ship provided for free. Failing that, after sex, take a leak. It was that simple. This would also be a learning experience for me, not only dealing with hookers, but also being in a foreign country. Prior to joining the Navy, the only other country I had been to was North Carolina.

Big Willie had been to PI before and clued me in on another thing. Don't have more than one girlfriend in the same bar at the same time. Apparently, there would be a riff between the girls which could easily escalate into something really nasty. These Filipino "social entertainers" could wield a butterfly knife like you've never seen and would not hesitate to cut you or your other girlfriend. I don't know if it was true or not, but several of the older salts said it happens, so I decided right then and there to *not* try to force the issue. There was no problem having a different girl in other bars, just not the same bar.

The Philippines currency was a piso. It was basically the same as the Spanish peso and pronounced the same, but it was spelled piso. Most of the time, the exchange rate was six pisos for one U.S. dollar. If you knew the right people, you might be able to find someone to exchange seven pisos for a dollar. Everything was cheap in the Philippines. San Miguel beer, made right there in the Philippines, was usually three pisos, a hotel room about thirty to forty pisos a night, and a decent meal was usually less than fifteen pisos. Don't ask how I know about the cost of the hotel room.

To get from the Naval base to Olongapo City you had to first cross what we called Shit River. It was about a hundred feet wide and as I understand, it was also used as a sewer where families that lived along the river dumped their waste. There was a wide, low concrete bridge that we crossed over the river to get to Olongapo City. Whenever we crossed the river, there was always a stench, but most of the time it wasn't too bad. There were usually several boats or canoes with a guy paddling and a cute kid, usually a girl standing on the bow, holding out a basket for you to throw money. In addition to the boats, young kids who could not afford a boat often swam in Shit River. It was a sad sight, but every now and then I would throw a piso or two.

One time, I saw a sailor who was taunting them. He would say, "Here's twenty pisos. Want it? Come and get it?" He would also taunt the girl to take off her shirt or something demeaning like that, and he kept it up for several minutes. Then, one kid swam over to the side. The sailor did not see him climb up on the river bank, run across the bridge toward him, and when the sailor was waving the twenty piso bill, he grabbed it and jumped into Shit River. You have to admit, that *was* funny.

My first time in the Philippines, I went with a couple of buddies into Olongapo City—they had been here before and I figured I would hang out with them to get an idea of what to expect and hopefully stay out of trouble. The streets looked pretty dingy and the sidewalks were lined with wall-to-wall bars and restaurants. Almost every bar had a live band and there were streets with rock bands, streets with soul bands, and streets with country bands. Years later I would tour Bourbon Street in New Orleans and memories of Olongapo City would come back to me.

Once you walked into a bar, you were instantly surrounded by three or four hookers (or as I described to my parents, social entertainers). Sailors called them Navy Relief, each vying for your attention and your wallet. The ratio of women in the bars to men was usually three to one; that is, three women to one man.

PI also had many massage parlors, some better than others. Gary told me about this one massage parlor and said I should check it out. "Ask for Pia," Gary said. I found my way down a dark alley to the place and walked upstairs. The lobby had dim lighting and I'm guessing it was to hide the uglier girls. I asked for Pia, but she was busy. "I'll wait," I said. A few minutes later, Pia came out and took me into a back room. Pia gave a nice relaxing massage, very much like in Guam, only much cheaper. Then when our time was about up, she introduced me to what was commonly referred to as a "Happy Ending." I'd be back.

My main hangouts were the bars that played country music. All of them had decent bands and I periodically got up on stage to belt out *The Auctioneer*. My favorite bar was the Country Caravan. They had a great band and a wonderful female lead singer named Susan King. She was Filipino and had a great voice. She took requests and knew just about every song I and others requested. I liked her so much that I asked for a photograph which I still have to this day. I did go to several other bars with country bands while in PI, but I always ended up going back to the Country Caravan.

Several of our guys in the division were Filipino. John Tabao was the division Yeoman and was Filipino. He had aunts and uncles who owned several bars and restaurants in the area and one day he made arrangements to get several of us out of Olongapo City to one of his family's establishments. LCDR Leone went with us on this trip. John managed to talk one of the Jeepney drivers down to a fairly reasonable rate.

This particular restaurant was about thirty minutes outside Olongapo City and was located on the beach. We caught a beautiful sunset, too. John had made arrangements for a complete meal with all kinds of fish, seafood, fried rice, chow mein, special salads, and a lot of beer. Everything was tasty but at this point in time and this particular place, I learned the most important lesson of eating in a foreign country—never, never (let me repeat, *never!*) ask what you are eating. If it tastes good, eat it. Never ask what it is, because in a foreign country, what you taste and what you eat are usually two different things.

Several times I stayed on the base in order to save some money. As I mentioned earlier, the Naval Base at Subic Bay was one of the Navy's best. Sometimes a group of us would hang out on the base playing pool (I was still good), head over to the archery range (I was still good), the go-cart track (I was still good), and miniature golf (I still sucked). During one of our outings we went to see a new movie that had just come out: *Jaws*. I don't think any of us went swimming in the ocean after that.

We were in and out of Subic Bay a total of seven times during the WESTPAC '75 cruise, usually for a week or ten days in port, and the same amount of time while underway. Kitty Hawk would be conducting exercises throughout the time at sea. Crash would be doing its thing both in port as well as at sea. Several times I would be on the night shift which wasn't so bad. There would be four of us on the night shift—I was the driver and we would have three other guys in the crash truck. We would not have to be in the truck on the flight deck at all times, only when we were called out. There were not any emergencies, but if there was a plane captain that needed to test his plane's jet engine, we would have to suit up and be on station. That happened fairly often, but then again, that's why we were there.

Flight ops usually ended at midnight. The night shift had to be on deck about an hour before just to see if there was anything we needed to prepare before the day crew was relieved. Most of the down time at night we spent playing cards, watching movies on TV, reading, or writing letters. I did not mind the night shift, but it was too boring for me. Gary Borne loved the night shift and tried to get it whenever he could, but Bos'n Robuck wanted us to rotate through. There were only two, third class petty officers in Crash: me and Gary Borne, and one of us had to be on deck at all times. Jeff Atteberry was a first class petty officer and the Crash LPO; Big Willie was a second class petty officer and assistant Crash LPO. Both of them worked the day shift. Rank has its privileges.

On one of the slower night shifts, I happened to pull out my guitar and was playing around like I often did. The guys were OK with me playing and singing even though it was country music. I think they were just being nice. I had been learning to play the lead for an old Johnny Cash tune, *Folsom Prison Blues*. I starting thinking about working on the flight deck and I rewrote the first verse, using the tune of *Folsom Prison Blues*:

I hear them planes a turning, they're roaring down the deck,
I ain't seen the sunshine, since I don't know heck,
I'm stuck on board this bird farm, with nothing else to do.
I've got them long, gone, lonesome, them old Kitty Hawk blues.

Yeah, I know, don't give up my day job.

When we were in port, at least in the Philippines, we had normal work hours from 0745-1130 and 1300-1530 (1:00 p.m. to 3:30 p.m.). We would clean our compartments and perform PMS on the flight deck equipment. We would often have training or book learning for different things, including keeping up our qualifications for the ABH rate. Glenn, Gary, I and several other third class petty officers in the division were also studying to take the second class petty officer exam. We would often study together.

There was always stuff to do, no problem in keeping busy, but it was not the most exciting time during the cruise. We knocked off at 1530 and sometimes I would head into Olongapo City, other times on the base, and other times I just stayed on the ship. I usually found myself on the ship when I did not have any money and had to wait until payday before I could go out.

The gates to the base were always guarded by Marines. Most of the time, these guys were cool, unless someone got out of hand, and then they would disappear into the guard shack with the sailor. One night I got out of hand coming back from a drinking night in Olongapo City. Coming through the gate, you always showed your military ID card and the Marine would wave you through. Keep in mind this was right at curfew and there were hundreds of sailors coming through the gates at the same time, much like cattle on their way to the slaughter house.

I was *slightly* drunk and when I came through the gate, I showed the grunt my ID card, but it was upside down. He asked nicely if I would turn it over. I said something stupid like, "Don't they teach you guys how to read upside down?" That was the wrong thing to say to a Marine. At that time the Corporal in charge ordered about four Marines to take me to the guard shack—oh shit! What now? It wasn't so bad though. They manhandled me, had me put my hands against a wall, spread my legs, and they performed a pat-down search. Fortunately, I wasn't carrying anything illegal. I lost a little dignity but they let me go back through the gate with my ID card held right side up. I would not make that mistake again.

On several outings at sea, we flew around the clock. That was hell on us because we had to have eleven crash crew on the flight deck during flight ops and there were only fourteen of us in Crash. At those times, we would take odd shifts, and one shift I worked thirty-one hours straight. We would find ways to sleep. You can get pretty cozy and grab some shuteye in the cab of the crash truck when you're dead tired. Not everyone would sleep at the same time. At least one of us would stay awake for any emergencies that crept up. Thank goodness it was usually quiet.

One day at sea during daylight flight ops, I was driving one of the crash trucks. We were parked just aft of the waist cats because planes were being launched off the bow cats. An A-7 Corsair was on Cat#2, ready to be launched. Everything looked normal and the plane was armed to the gills with both missiles and bombs. The JBD was up, the plane at full power, and the Shooter signaled to launch the plane. Everything went smoothly except for one thing—the A-7 dropped one of its 700-pound bombs on the flight deck on the way out. It skidded to a halt about a hundred feet short of the ship's bow.

Everybody in my truck saw it and there was one big collective, "Oh shit!" The catapult guys cleared the flight deck heading in all directions. We did not know how these bombs worked, whether it was armed and ready to explode or whether we should bend over and kiss our ass goodbye.

Bos'n Robuck was the first one to approach the bomb. He just walked up casually to it and looked it over. He then turned, looked at me, and signaled for me to drive up. I shook my head "no" and politely mumbled, "Hell no! That's a live bomb." About that time, a couple of the EOD guys came onto the flight deck, examined the bomb, and declared it safe—it was not armed. I didn't know it at the time, but it turns out Glenn Law was the yellow shirt directing the A-7. Years later, he told me he made record time hauling ass aft to the fantail after that bomb dropped.

What did we do? Gary drove the forklift over to the bomb, the ordnance guys helped move it onto the forklift and Gary was directed to dump it overboard. Everything was alright and we got back to regular flight ops. Just another fine day in the Navy.

On several occasions in port, I had the grand opportunity to serve Shore Patrol duty. This fun little exercise usually consisted of teams of two sailors dressed in their whites with an SP armband and a white web belt carrying a wooden baton.

Despite what you hear, SP does not stand for Stud Patrol. SP duty usually started after work hours at 1530 (3:30 p.m.). For some reason, my partner was usually Ed Boes and we got along fine. We would walk a beat, usually a mile or two in length, walking in every bar and restaurant on our beat, checking to see if there were any sailors out of hand, then move on to the next one. It wasn't bad, and I had the opportunity to visit all the bars and restaurants on the beat—sober.

One of the better things about Shore Patrol was that when chow time came, we would place an order at a restaurant, and then walk the beat and when we came back to that restaurant our chow would be ready for us—hot and tasty. My favorite was Shanghai Fried Rice and Lumpia which I've never been able to find anywhere in the US. I came close once in a Filipino restaurant at Pike Place Market in Seattle, but it was not quite the same. The food in Olongapo City was more than reasonable. One of my other favorites was fried shrimp. In 1975, the cost of a fried shrimp dinner, complete with fried rice, was about $1.50. In the states, it would have cost about $3.50.

They did not give us any radios while on Shore Patrol duty which was fine by me—less crap to carry around. There was a senior petty officer in charge of the Shore Patrol and we would report to him after each round and we had orders as to what to do if we encountered any problems, but thankfully for the three or four times I stood Shore Patrol in PI, there were no problems on my beat.

At the time I was in PI, there was martial law and the streets had to be cleared by midnight. The Philippines was under martial law from 1972 to

1981 under the authoritarian rule of the Philippines president, Ferdinand Marcos. We usually started letting everyone know about curfew around 2330 (11:30 p.m.) and most everyone either went back to the base or followed a hooker home or to a hotel. I had heard though, that the local Filipino police had orders to shoot on sight if they found anyone in violation of martial law, but I never heard of anyone getting shot. I did hear of some locals chasing a sailor or two back and since the base gates were closed at midnight, the sailor had to swim Shit River to escape. I tell you, the decision to make: Shit River or jail—not sure what I would do in that case, either.

One of my more memorable Shore Patrol duties was when we had to walk a beat on Grande Island, just off the shore of Subic Bay. It was a Saturday, so SP duty for us was 0800 to 1700. We took a twenty minute boat ride to get there. This was the first time in my life I had ever seen refugees.

"Operation Frequent Wind" was the final operation in Saigon at the end of the Vietnam War and it began April 29, 1975. The Marines loaded Vietnamese civilians onto helicopters and brought them to waiting aircraft carriers. They were then transported to the Philippines. Many of these refugees were on Grande Island when I took SP duty in September 1975. Normally, Grande Island was an island paradise frequented by Japanese tourists, but it was now being used to house Vietnamese refugees.

The people were quiet, reserved, and looked somewhat defeated. It was no surprise—they had to quickly leave their homes, many with just the clothes on their backs. We did not talk to any of them. We did not know any of the Vietnamese language and besides, there was a tall chain link fence separating them from us. There were several kids, however, who came up to the fence waving Vietnamese money. It was not worth anything to them, but I exchanged a few Philippine pisos for several Vietnamese dollars. It was a sad sight, but from what I've read and what I've seen, they were much better off here than in Vietnam.

On one of our Philippine port calls, I got to go to welding school. The division wanted to send several of us from Crash. We were taught by a local Filipino. He was a funny guy, too—short, dark-haired and dark complexion. This guy taught several of us how to weld, including my buddy, Gary Borne.

A couple of days into welding school, Gary and I started staying out late drinking and got back on base by midnight curfew. However, the welding school started at 0700, so we had to get up early, get chow, and head out, with about a mile to walk from the ship to the welding school, in order to get there by 0700. Have you ever tried to weld with a hangover? You've got a little steel rod in one heavily gloved hand and you wear a welder's helmet which has a very dark glass shield which no one can ever see out of.

But when you start to weld, which is actually just a process of electricity conducted between two different materials (the rod and the pieces you are welding), it produces a very bright white, intense, focused light. It's almost blinding, even if you're *not* hung over. On several mornings, we were hurting and usually got a tremendous headache. But, we learned how to weld and I was pretty good at it. This could be another career for me.

There was this one time, however, when we were at sea before flight ops. We had some down time, so a couple of us were practicing our welding skills on some scrap metal. I got a little carried away and put too much weld on the piece of metal. The other guy said, "No problem, I'll just chip if off." He pulled out the hammer and chisel and with one whack, a piece of metal came flying off and guess where it landed?

Once again, I headed down to Sickbay to have the corpsman remove a piece of metal, about a quarter inch in diameter, from my right arm near my wrist. I swear, as a kid growing up I probably made about a half dozen trips to the emergency room for one thing or another—the ER doctor and I were on a first name basis. I would probably pass that record here during the cruise.

July 10 marked an important day for me—two years even. I had joined the Navy two years earlier and only had two years left. That was 730 days, counting backwards. Not that I was looking forward to my eventual departure, it was just one of those things that sailors who were not lifers did.

Another spot we sometimes hit, not far from Olongapo City, was called Subic City. It was about a twenty-minute Jeepney ride. What set it apart? The hookers there were quite different. They tended to lean toward oral sex, whereas the hookers in Olongapo City would not have anything to do with that. Without going into a lot of details, there was a definite difference in women between the two cities.

One place we hung out in Subic City was called Marilyn's Club and Hotel. They even passed out business cards that read, "How would you like to be the KNOB of the NIGHT? Bring in 5 swinging dicks and you get yours for free." I still have that business card and when I meet shipmates who have been to the Philippines, we often talk about Subic City and Marilyn's Club almost always comes up. I have my card and they have theirs. While Subic City was different, it was an expensive ride, there were not as many bars, restaurants, or bands, and there was really only one reason to take the trip. I only went to Subic City twice—I found more fun things to do in Olongapo City.

It took a while for me to figure it out since I was a guy from the south, but apparently being a hooker was just a job—almost like a cook or a dishwasher or office worker. It *was* just a job to them. I know several sailors who fell in love while in PI and married their girlfriends. It took a lot of time and paperwork to get them to the states and most of them made it. The few that didn't, I guess the marriage was annulled and the girl stayed in PI. I often wondered if the girl really wanted to get married and live in the U.S. or if she was just trying to take the sailor for whatever she could.

I was getting paid about $130 every two weeks. I had a $100 per month allotment going to my Mom to keep in my savings, but back then, $130 was a lot of money. Of course, going into Olongapo City could eat up that wad up in a hurry, especially if you went out every night. I started to get smarter the more times we pulled into port.

For example, I learned that sometimes we pulled in a day or two before payday. That meant some guys did not have any money, but they had the need to go into town. So, I figured I would loan them twenty dollars and they would pay me back forty dollars a few days later on payday. Most guys paid me back without any problem. Only a few I had to ask more than once. It might not have been legal, but I knew several guys who did it and it really did not bother anyone. If anyone complained, you would just tell them to go see someone else, and maybe he would loan them the money, maybe he wouldn't.

Kitty Hawk headed out to sea again for a couple of weeks of exercises. This time out would be a deadly trip. As mentioned earlier, the first aircraft off the deck for flight ops was the plane guard helicopter from the HS-8 squadron. We had a crash tractor manned on the flight deck, as we always did, but did not have a crash truck manned which was normal operating procedures. Almost all the crash crew were either in the crash compartment or just outside shooting the breeze waiting for flight ops to start.

All of a sudden, the Air Boss came over the 5MC, "Crash to the flight deck! Crash to the flight deck!" We all hauled ass out onto the deck and all we could see was a helo trying to take off. It took a couple of seconds to realize what happened. The starboard main gear had collapsed and one of the helo ground crew was dangling from the wheel well. The main wheel tie-down chains were removed, but the helo was still tied down to the deck by the tail wheel tie-down chain. The pilot was hovering over the deck at about six inches. The plane captain directing the helo was trying to help the pilot keep steady, but it was tough since the helo was still tied down with one chain.

My pal Buddy Laney was riding on the back of the crash tractor and saw it all. He told me later that it was one of the most harrowing experiences in his life, being so close to a killer helo and not being able to do anything about it. He said his training kicked in and they were preparing for the worst—a crash on the flight deck. But, like the rest of us, there was little to do with the helo still tied down still trying to take off.

Several of us dunked down with a rescue stretcher and got close to the helo. About that time, the killer helo dropped the ground crew member and we grabbed his legs and pulled him out of range of those dangerous rotors. The flight deck medic was trying to put a compress on his head, but I knew this guy was long gone. His head was squished sideways about half its normal size—blood was everywhere as well as some brain matter. I had been through enough training to do what I did, as did everyone else. We put him into the stretcher and carried him over to the #2 elevator where he was lowered down and the guys rushed him to Sickbay. My pants and shirt were covered with blood and brains.

Meanwhile the helo was still hovering just a few inches off the ground. Our Crash LPO Jeff Atteberry was on his stomach crawling toward the helo. The only way this thing could end safely was to undo the last tie-down and Jeff was going to do just that. He reached the tie-down and when the plane captain saw what he was doing, helped the pilot keep steady while Jeff undid the tie-down. The pilot flew the helo off and everyone on the flight deck breathed a sigh of relief. That was a harrowing experience.

We weren't done yet—the second part of our name was "Salvage," so we had to figure out how to get the helo and its crew safely back on board. Fortunately, we had trained for such things and had a plan. Part of our crash arsenal included a crash dolly which is a heavy metal dolly about three feet wide and four feet long with four heavy rubber wheels. We had several mattresses brought up from below decks and tied these to the crash dolly. We then anchored the crash dolly to the flight deck in the recovery area using a half dozen tie down chains.

In order to get the helo back onto the flight deck, a helo plane captain served as the director which was standard operating procedure. We parked a tow tractor in front of him so that if something bad happened, he could at least dive and duck down behind the tractor, hopefully avoiding any flying helo parts. We moved all nearby aircraft to the aft part of the flight deck—no need destroying or damaging aircraft if it could be helped.

We also had the crash truck parked on the point on the starboard side with a full crew all suited up. The rescue guy fully suited up and standing on the back of the crash truck was Steve Deaver, a big strong Texan. He had joined us in the Philippines. The flight deck was cleared of all unnecessary personnel. All of the V-1 Division was up there though. We were in the catwalks standing by with fire hoses. I got out of the catwalk and went up to the crash truck and talked with Deaver. I told him to remember his training, do not do anything stupid, and watch his ass. I don't know what drove me to give him that pep talk, but maybe I was trying to tell *myself* that everything would be fine.

As the helo approached, the plane captain directed him slowly over the flight deck. The first thing the pilot did was hover over the flight deck and let the helo crew out. They had about a five foot jump down to the deck. The pilot knew what needed to be done, but it took three times for him to ease down before he was able to place the helo's crippled starboard wheel safely onto the crash dolly. We had placed enough mattress pads on it so that when he landed, the helo was almost level. Once he put the full weight of the helo down, he still kept the rotors going until the blue shirts and helo crew could tie him down to the flight deck. When that was done, he cut power to the engines. He was safe, we were safe, and there is a God.

The next step was to get the helo out of the recover area. We had an answer for that too, a little friend we called "Tilly," our crash crane. Gary Borne cranked her up and drove her over to the helo, but since I had not been checked out on how to hook up the crash slings for the SH-3 helo and he had, I climbed up into the cab to relieve him. He was pissed, because driving Tilly was easy compared to hooking up the helo. But, that's the way things go. After Gary hooked up the crash sling, I was able to lift the helo up enough for the crew to strap on a temporary wheel and then a tractor, so it was towed out of the recovery area. Once the helo was down on the flight deck safely, it took us about an hour to get it out of the way to resume flight ops.

I wish I could say that was a great experience—it was certainly a challenge—but we had lost a shipmate. AMS3 Andrew J. Wantulok lost his life. He was pronounced DOA when he got to Sickbay. From what we heard, he was removing the landing gear safety pins, something always done before a launch. The port side pin came out fine, but the starboard side would not budge. The squadron chief was all over his ass telling him to get the pin out so they could launch the helo. He started banging on it. It came out alright, but when it did the wheel collapsed. He was inside the wheel well when it collapsed, so he was caught by the weight of the helo. He left a wife and kid, too.

This was the first dead person I had ever seen. At the time, I did not feel any emotions, just adrenaline and my training kicking in. I think everyone felt the same I've often thought about that airman over the years. The flight deck was a dangerous and sometimes unforgiving place to work.

20 WESTPAC '75
Hong Kong, One Word: Tattoo!

We left Subic Bay on the seventh of August headed for Hong Kong. At that time, Hong Kong was still under British rule and we would be there for a week. China was closed to Americans, but I know several guys who found a way to cross the border for a day to explore.

When we left PI for Hong Kong, it rained for four days straight. I'm not talking a little Seattle-type drizzle. I'm talking a continuous, big frog-strangler torrential rain like the type we had in Florida. It was pretty miserable, even though we all had rain gear on. The worst problem was with our feet; they always seemed to stay wet and several of us got foot rot. It wasn't any big deal and the corpsmen gave us some cream, but it is hard to apply four times daily when you're working on the flight deck. My rash went away by the time we got to Hong Kong.

We were scheduled to have a white's inspection on the flight deck, too. That made a lot of standard Navy issue sense—forty-plus knot winds and rainstorms. The Old Man finally decided that instead of having a ship-wide white's inspection, each division would hold their own. Well, I guess that was better than getting drenched.

We got to Hong Kong on August 13. We did not have a pier to pull up alongside in Hong Kong like we did in PI or Hawaii. Instead, we anchored in the harbor near Green Island and had to take ferries into Hong Kong. We had what was called max liberty, meaning we only needed to be on the ship if we had duty. I had duty the first day in port, so I did not get to go into Hong Kong the first day.

I was one of the few guys in Crash who knew how to operate the Boat and Aircraft (B&A) Crane. It was a huge crane that swung out from the starboard side of the ship over the water and could raise and lower either aircraft or boats. The Admiral was on board Kitty Hawk and he wanted his boat in the water. No problem, I said. The Admiral's boat was kept aft on the hangar deck, so the V-3 Division yellow and blue shirts towed it to Elevator #3 which had been lowered to the hangar deck level. Bos'n Robuck was with me to make sure everything went smooth.

I lowered the hook on the B&A Crane so the guys on the elevator could hook up the boat to the massive 1,500 pound pulley. There were also three Boatswain's Mates in the boat making sure everything was hooked up properly. They used a heavy shackle to connect the four straps to the hook on the pulley. Nothing major, just standard operating procedures. There were four to five foot seas, but Kitty Hawk was so heavy and so big, it did not sway too much.

I operated the crane to slowly lift the boat and the three BMs off the elevator, then slowly swung the crane so that the boat was over the water. I then slowly lowered the boat until it was in the water. While it was not rough seas for the carrier, it was pretty rough for those guys in the Admiral's boat. They were trying to wrestle with a 1,500 pound pulley in four to five foot waves.

It was not easy. Every time they signaled me to lower the hook so they could undo the shackle, they got bounced around. Finally, one last time and they were able to undo the shackle, but at that particular point in time, the boat lunged backwards and the 1,500 pound pulley went right thought the windshield of the Admiral's boat. It was not a good day for them or me.

We all worked hard trying to prevent any mishaps, but with the rough seas, it was next to impossible. I was worried I might get written up for that incident, but I never heard anything more from it. In fact, Bos'n Robuck told me that I did a great job, despite the high seas. I guess if he was OK, I was OK. The Admiral had his boat, albeit a little wacked up, but I'm sure the BMs were able to fix the windshield.

The second day in port, I got to take liberty so I headed out with a couple of friends. The exchange rate was five Hong Kong dollars for one U.S. dollar. Steve Cummings, who had just been promoted to a third class petty officer and went from a blue shirt to a yellow shirt, Smitty, and I decided we would find a tour to see the sights. We knew we could always grab some beers later at the China Club, a popular hangout for sailors.

We found an all-day tour that took us up to Victoria Park, the highest mountain in Hong Kong, to have a great overlook of the Hong Kong harbor. Kitty Hawk was certainly the biggest thing in the harbor and she was just plain beautiful. I felt proud to be a part of her crew. We also got to Tiger Balm Garden which had a seven-story pagoda. It was built by Aw Boon Haw and his family in 1935 for a cost of $16 million Hong Kong dollars.

Part of the package included a boat tour through Aberdeen, the floating city in Hong Kong. Here, entire families lived on small boats called sampans, usually tied up parallel to a pier. That means if you wanted to get to the boat on the outside, you had to step onto the other boats between it and the pier. I've never seen such a crowded place on the water. I don't know how they did it.

We ended up at the Tai Pak Restaurant, a floating restaurant with exquisite decor. They served us a full six-course meal that was absolutely fantastic. I had learned earlier in the Philippines not to ask what I was eating, so I didn't ask. Because they were a floating restaurant, water cost three Hong Kong dollars which was equivalent to about sixty cents in U.S. dollars. Beer was free and we were able to drink all we wanted. I really enjoyed that place, too. Lots of good food spread out over a long time and all of us on the tour had a great time.

I wrote my parents and told them what a wonderful place Hong Kong was and that I was actually going on tours instead of hitting the bars. That was something I never did while in the Philippines (tours, that is; I certainly frequented the bars). I started comparing the cost of beer: $1.50 US a bottle in Guam, 40 pisos ($.45 US) in PI, and $4 HK ($.85 US) in Hong Kong. It was a crude currency comparison, but I think they got the picture. The same item in different countries cost different amounts. It is amazing how the world economy works—just compare the cost of beer and you'll have a good idea of the cost of living.

Mac's wife had flown out from Colorado to spend a week with him in Hong Kong. That must have cost a fortune, but she was working and could afford it. We got together one evening for dinner—she was a nice lady and Mac looked so happy to have her there with him. I know he enjoyed his max liberty. He came back to the ship right before we left and had a great big, shit-eating grin on his face for several days.

A few days into Hong Kong, Charlie Brown and I headed in together. He was going to get a tattoo of the Philippine national flag and wanted his girlfriend's name tattooed on top of the flag. That was cute, except Charlie Brown was married—and not to this girl. I did not know what was going on in his mind, but I figured I would go with him to watch out in case he did something stupid.

At the time, Hong Kong had dozens of tattoo parlors. It was also against Navy regulations to get tattoos in Hong Kong because you were never sure how clean the needles were. I guess being so young and so naive, we did not care. After all, we were Navy and we were invincible.

We checked out a few different tattoo parlors and finally Charlie found one he liked. Maybe it was because they offered free beer—I don't know. We wandered into Pinky's Tattoo Parlor and Charlie told the guy what he wanted and started getting prepped. I was looking around at all the tattoo designs they had and one of the other artists came up to me and asked if I wanted a tattoo. I do not know why, but I found an eagle that stood out among the hundreds of other designs. He asked "Which arm?" and I was hooked.

I sat down in the chair and watched this guy trace the eagle design on a piece of tracing paper. He then cleaned my upper right arm with soap and water and slapped the tracing paper on my arm, allowing the design to transfer to my skin. Meanwhile a sweet young thing brought me a beer. It tasted good. "Bring me another, please."

The artist then started inking the tattoo using a needle gun with a needle that had an in and out motion, much like my mom's old Singer sewing machine. He would dip the needle in a color ink and then started tracing the outline with the needle gun, periodically wiping the blood off my arm. It didn't hurt too much—more beer, please.

I was really fascinated by this artist's ability to first trace the outline of the eagle, then start coloring in the feathers. He told me in broken English that the first colors to go would be the whites, then the reds. The blues would be there until a couple of weeks after I died. He was not lying. As I write this today, 38 years later, the whites have all disappeared and the reds are almost totally faded. The greens and blues are still bright and crisp. When he finished, he wiped everything down with soap and water, then applied some Vaseline and put a gauze bandage on, telling me not to wash it for two days, then pull off the bandage and wash well with warm soapy water.

When we were almost done getting our tattoos, a sailor wandered into the tattoo parlor. He was really drunk, but staggered around and said proudly, "You guys ain't got *no* balls." At which point, he dropped his pants and skivvies and showed us his "barber pole." Apparently, a few days earlier he had someone tattoo a barber pole onto his tallywacker. We all roared. That was funny enough, but for years we've often wondered, "How did they do that? Did they have a 'special girl' who 'helped him' stay hard enough to get the tattoo?" To this day, it still boggles my mind.

I guess I had had about three or four beers, all free during the ordeal. It did not hurt much and it is the only tattoo I have. My tattoo at the time cost me forty Hong Kong dollars, or a little more than eight U.S. dollars. I do not know how they do it now, but I'm sure the technology has changed a little. I never got an infection and never wanted to have it removed. It had become part of my body and my soul and I was proud of it. Besides, my grandfather on my mom's side had been in the Navy and he had a tattoo, also. That was how I would break the news to my mom—start off by asking if Granddaddy had a tattoo. That should work.

We got back to Subic Bay September 4th for a much needed rest. We had almost two weeks in port though we had a normal 0730 to 1530 (7:30 to 3:30) work schedule while in port. That was not any problem for me since I did not need to go out drinking on the town every night. I also took duty for several different guys this time in, making a few more bucks.

# # #

On July 1, 1997, the British government turned Hong Kong over to the Chinese government. Although Hong Kong Island and Kowloon had been ceded to the United Kingdom in perpetuity, the control was for a 99-year lease. I did enjoy my six days in Hong Kong. I got to see some great sights and more than just the inside of bars and I got a great tattoo.

21 WESTPAC '75
Japan, One Word: Culture!

After Hong Kong, we started our longest time at sea without hitting a port—about five weeks. During this time, we had a few days of around-the-clock flight ops. That was pretty demanding and we had to split into two, twelve-hour shifts. Gary and I had to work longer shifts, as usual. I was on the day shift this go round which was fine by me. I got to do my morning radio show, so that made me happy.

We left PI and headed up to Japan. It turns out that we were on the edge of a typhoon and we experienced a lot of rough weather. All flight operations were cancelled. On the flight deck, we had to double all the tie-down chains on the planes. Instead of the usual six tie-down chains, each plane had twelve to fifteen tie-downs. All the equipment, including the crash trucks, all the tow tractors, and even Tilly had tie down chains.

During the day it got so bad that if we headed out onto the flight deck, we went in pairs with a life line tied between us. We even saw water coming over the bow. I thought they were waves breaking over the bow, but the waves broke lower, it was just the force that pushed the water over the bow. That was impressive though, especially since the flight deck was sixty feet above the water line. I can't imagine how the smaller ships managed these horrendous sea conditions.

We arrived in Japan on Friday, October 17 and we were in for a treat; we would have six days of max liberty in Yokosuka. As we pulled into the harbor, it was a bright clear day and we could see snow-capped Mt. Fuji off in the distance. The exchange rate at that time was three hundred Yen for one U.S. dollar. Japan was more expensive than PI and Hong Kong. A beer in Yokosuka cost 300 Yen ($1 US), compared to three pisos ($.45 US) in PI and $4 HK (Hong Kong dollars, about $.85 US).

On Sunday, Gary Borne, Bud Laney, Jim King, a couple of other guys from the V-1 Division, and I headed up to Tokyo. We took the bullet train and I'll tell you something, it was a bullet. Wow, I had never been on a train that fast before. It only took us thirty minutes to get there. The cost for the train ride from Yokosuka to Tokyo was only 300 Yen. The big problem was that it was Sunday and we had a hard time finding a place to exchange money. After an hour or so of wandering around Tokyo—and of course none of us spoke Japanese—we finally found a small store that gladly exchanged dollars for Yen.

The weather was overcast and cold, but because we were walking all over, we stayed warm. One of the first spots we stumbled upon was the Emperor's Palace, very old and very traditional Japanese. There was a huge moat surrounding the palace with lots of those humongous gold fish. We also spotted a Japanese McDonald's downtown. That was funny since we were not used to seeing American businesses in foreign countries. We recognized the golden arches, but the rest of the writing was gibberish to us.

Japan was a welcomed stop. We had been in PI for a while and had visited Hong Kong, but those seemed like third world countries compared to Japan. To me, it was more civilized, definitely cleaner, had more of a business and cultural feel to it. When I think about it, I never traveled or toured anywhere while in the Philippines which is a shame because I'm sure there were some wonderful places to visit. For some reason, I spent almost all my time either on the ship, the base, or Olongapo City. If I had to do it all over again, I would definitely find some other places to visit in the Philippines. That's what the lifers told me, too. You learn the ropes on your first cruise and you do more sightseeing and get more involved with the culture and the people on the second cruise.

Just outside the main gate of the Naval base at Yokosuka and across the street was Thieves Alley. They say "Many a sailor has lost his credentials here," whatever that means. But there was a group of us, so I wasn't too worried. By the way, does a sailor really ever have credentials?

Thieves Alley was loaded with bars and little gift shops and the owners liked to bargain. It was almost like Times Square in Manhattan or Bourbon Street in New Orleans. Here, you could bargain away and usually come up with some pretty good deals. You had to be careful though, because while a watch may say Rolex, it may not really be a Rolex on the inside, if you know what I mean.

The bars were something else. I could not drink the beer, it was so bad. We did find a wonderful place that served great corn dogs and ice cream, something that the crash crew craved. We frequented that cozy little spot several times—no beer though, at least not for me.

Once we left Japan, we headed north through the Sea of Japan and circumnavigated the main island. It was really cold and it did not help that we were flying around the clock. Since we did not have enough people in Crash to have two full shifts, several of us pulled double duty, working twenty-four to thirty-six hour shifts. We would catnap when we could, whether it was in the crash compartment or inside the crash truck.

Usually on the flight deck in the China Sea the weather was warm and all I wore on the flight deck was a pair of Army ODs, a red crash jersey, a red float coat, my boots and socks, and a cranial helmet. When we were in between flight ops, we would strip off our shirts which was fine in calm seas because there was not any danger of being blown off the deck. Besides, it was hot, the sun felt good, and we worked on our tans.

In the South China Sea, sometimes it rained and when it did, you would see a lot of guys take off their shirts and wash themselves out on the flight deck. There was not any soap, but it felt good and when we were at sea with water hours, this helped keep the sailor aroma down to a minimum.

There was this one time though when one of the Fly 1 yellow shirts actually brought a bar of soap up on the flight deck. We were also at water hours at the time. During one of these rain showers, he broke out his soap and lathered up. I think he was showing off, he was such a clown. The rain suddenly stopped. He was pretty soapy and no rain to rinse off and the fresh water on the ship had been turned off. He was pissed, but I think he went down to the head and rinsed off using the salt water out of the commodes.

It was quite a different story when we were in the Sea of Japan. I had my thermal long johns, my sweater, my Navy foul weather jacket, my rain gear, my aviator knit cap and even with all that on, it was still freezing cold. We were working long shifts too and there were many nights when we could not get down for chow. We would get box lunches, but the old horsecock sandwiches did not cut it.

Several times during this trip out, I called down to the galley and asked if we could get some hot soup. They said sure, come on down. So a couple of us made several trips down several ladders to bring up a huge 25-gallon container of hot soup. It tasted so good and all my guys got a break to come in and down some. It helped us choke down the cold sandwiches, too. We always kept the coffee brewing, too. That is something we never ran out of.

There were many times when I would come in off the flight deck to warm up and to get a cup of hot coffee. When I started drinking coffee in Guam, I would have it with cream and sugar; there was always plenty. But on the ship, I usually was the last one in to get coffee (I always let my guys come in first), there was never any cream or sugar, so I had to drink it black. I got used to that. There were also many times when I would tip the 100-cup coffee maker to get the last dregs of coffee, complete with grounds. But in that miserable weather, even *that* coffee tasted good.

We usually had several Russian visitors around us. Not only were there Bears and Badgers flying overhead ("Launch the Alert 5!"), but we also had Russian trawlers cruising alongside. I had never seen one of those before, but they looked like ordinary fishing boats to me. We waved, they waved. Hey, we're all friends here. This was during the Cold War and we did not trust them any more than they trusted us. There was not anything anyone of us could do other than carry on our regular duties during flight ops.

Heading back to the Philippines, we lost another helo, this one to the water. I was on night shift, so I was in my rack sleeping and heard the call over the 1MC, "Man overboard, port side." At the time, I did not know what it was, so I quickly got dressed and mustered up on the flight deck in Crash. My friend Jack Kuiphoff was driving a tow tractor that day and told me he drove over to the port side of the ship and looked down. The helo was on its side and the crew members were kicking out the windows and helping pull each other out—the helo was sinking fast.

In this case, apparently the helo was riding heavy and came in too fast and too low. Normally when a helo is going to land on the flight deck, the pilot brings the helo in off the port side *over* the water and *not* over the flight deck. The director then signals the pilot to fly sideways, bringing the helo slowly over the flight deck, ready to land. They do this for the exact reason why this helo went into the water. Had the helo been coming in over the flight deck, it would have been quite a mess. They say the worst part of a helo crash is not the fire, but the spinning rotors that hit the deck and fly into a million pieces of deadly shrapnel.

The helo apparently experienced engine failure and was forced to ditch alongside the carrier. There were five men aboard—all were unharmed and were rescued by the plane guard helo. After everyone was accounted for by the "Man overboard" call, I was able to get back to my rack for another snooze.

The very next day we had some surprise visitors. The USO had flown six beautiful women from the Miss America Pageant to Kitty Hawk for our entertainment. They had probably never landed on an aircraft carrier before, but they all looked great. I caught sight of them disembarking the COD from atop the crash truck. The only problem I had was that I had just come off the night shift working through the night and into the morning and was dead tired. While they were singing and dancing into the hearts of the Kitty Hawk crew, I was grabbing some much needed shut-eye. I did not get to see any of their performance which was done on a mock stage on the flight deck. But, I heard it was a wonderful show.

22 WESTPAC '75
Heading Home, One Word: Hallelujah!

We left PI on Thanksgiving Day, Thursday, November 26 heading back to the states. I was somewhat sad since I had gotten used to my favorite haunts in Olongapo City. The people were really nice and took care of us, and I'm not just talking about the hookers. I truly thought the Filipinos were a great people and felt like the U.S. presence helped them. But what did I know? I only saw the insides of the bars, the restaurants, and the hotels.

I know Olongapo City was not that well off, but then Manila was probably not much better either. The dictator, Ferdinand Marcos and his wife Imelda, ruled the country. It was rumored that Imelda had more than five thousand pairs of shoes. I could have told her that you can only wear one pair at a time. How can someone have so much, yet their country have so little? But then, there are so many other countries in the world with the same types of problems, including our own.

We would be stopping again in Pearl Harbor. The trip from PI to Hawaii was about two weeks. Once again, we established the Alert 5s and once again, we had to launch them several times to greet the Russians.

During these long cruises without flight ops, we would find things to do. For example, we were not the only ones on the flight deck. Most of the guys below decks could venture out and some of them were even jogging around the flight deck. Kitty Hawk did not have a gym and there was only one weight room. It was pretty funny to watch these guys on the flight deck too, because not everybody knew their way around and you would inevitably see someone trip over a tie-down chain and smack into the flight deck. It probably was not funny to them, but certainly to us. We had been blown down lots of times and tripped over so many tie-down chains at night, it was nice to finally see some other sailors get whacked.

170

I still had my radio show from 0600-0800. I started playing a Kitty Hawk theme song and played it every morning on the way home: *If We Make It Through December* by Merle Haggard. I did not write it, mind you, I just played it and we adapted it to the ship since we were heading home and hoped we would make it there in December.

When we got to Hawaii, I learned that the trip home from Hawaii to San Diego would be a Tiger Cruise. During this short cruise, Kitty Hawk sailors' sons, fathers, and brothers (no women) could come aboard and sail with us back to San Diego. What a great idea—see what dad does at work. The whole idea, of course, was to brainwash kids into joining the Navy when they got older. Actually, it was cool, seeing dads and sons together, especially those on the flight deck because that is where I worked.

One of the catapult officers was retiring from the Navy and his ten-year old son was on board. He took him around introducing his son to everyone and he was a cool little kid. Seemed very confident and cocky, just like his dad. One of the traditions on the carrier is that when the Shooter leaves, his flight deck boots are launched off the catapult. It was heartwarming to watch the Shooter and his son go through the routine of the launch, including the final salute to the boots, the hands in the air, swinging fingers, and then the launch of the boots. The kid had such a great time mimicking his dad and it brought back a lot of memories of me and my dad when I was that age.

On the way back from Hawaii we could also order up to a gallon of liquor, tax-free. We would be able to pick it up when we pulled into San Diego. I ordered only one bottle of bourbon. I guess I could have ordered more and sold it to someone who maxed out, but I didn't.

About 0500 the morning we were to pull into San Diego, the word was passed that we could pick up our liquor orders. I did not go get mine; I would get it later. However, most of the guys who did order went and got theirs. Of course, you were not supposed to drink aboard the ship, but several of the guys got really shitfaced before we pulled into port. It was funny watching them stagger off the After brow and down the stairs.

While we only visited the Philippines, Hong Kong, and Japan, there was so much scuttlebutt on the ship we heard about visiting other places. I guess the CO got his orders too, depending upon where the ship was needed and when. Scuttlebutt runs rampant on a WESTPAC cruise and one of the ports that we constantly heard we would visit was Christchurch, New Zealand. That would have been a treat, especially since we would cross the equator and would provide us the opportunity to experience one of the Navy's oldest traditions.

Crossing the equator on a Naval ship introduces a long-standing tradition. This rite of passage takes a first-time crosser, otherwise known as a Pollywog, and through the initiation process turns him into a Shellback. Back when I was in the Navy, the ceremony lasted a couple of days and included a lot of things some people would rather not know about.

The older and more experienced salts, at least those who were Shellbacks, took over the ship, including the officers. If the CO had not crossed the equator before, he was a Pollywog too, and would take part in the ceremony. Included in this ceremony was also the Royal Court: King Neptune, Davy Jones, and the Royal Baby, all shipmates, and all Shellbacks.

It would start early in the morning and even though the Pollywogs would be expecting something to happen, they did not know when or where. The Shellbacks in each division would be taking care of their own, getting them up out of their racks by various means, including using shaving cream, talc powder, eggs, salt water, or any combination of the above. Shellbacks would dress in different types of costumes and put on face paint, each to his own. Many dressed to look like pirates. Pollywogs would usually turn their uniforms inside out.

Then they were taken to either the hangar deck or the flight deck, depending upon the conditions of the ship's mission. There they would be subjected as a group to other various harassments, including swimming on the flight deck on their bellies, constantly being sprayed with salt water from a fire hose, or worse. There would often be a ritual of crawling through a sewage tube, made from old rotting vegetable material the galley had been brewing for a few days, and crawling up to the Royal Baby—the biggest, fattest, hairiest, and ugliest sailor on the ship—where you would have your face rubbed in his belly full of axle grease or he would have you eat hot mustard or some other disgusting thing.

All of this was in good fun, of course. When you passed the test, you received a certificate and a card for your wallet, signifying you had become a Shellback. This is something that sailors cherish their entire lives. You think you've gone through hazing when joining a fraternity or a sorority? This is hazing like you have never seen nor heard.

Nowadays, it is down to a day and you are not supposed to touch any sailor inappropriately though that may happen a bit in the wee hours of the morning. There are new rules now established by the United States Navy and while it is still considered a tradition, it is nothing like it used to be. For example, instead of crawling through the garbage tube, you might crawl or swim through a tank of dyed water. You can't touch 'em, you can't yell at 'em, you can't do nothin' to 'em. The Navy's traditions today aren't like they used to be.

We pulled into San Diego about 0800 on December 15, 1975, the day before my twenty-first birthday. It was a beautiful morning and coming through the bay, passing Point Loma on the port side and the Naval Air Station on the right, it felt like coming home. We had been on the WESTPAC cruise for what seemed like forever and other than Hawaii, this would be the first time in six months I had stepped foot on American soil.

When a ship comes back to home port from an overseas tour, we man the rails, another formal Navy tradition. That means that everyone participating dresses in the uniform of the day. In this case we wore winter blues. Sailors line up arm's length, called Dress Right, around the edge of the flight deck, facing out. If the ship was coming in, they're usually at parade rest unless there is a special memorial, such as the Arizona Memorial in Pearl Harbor, at which time they would come to attention at the appropriate time. But coming into San Diego, it was more relaxed. I felt a lot of pride and was happy to be coming back to the states. Unfortunately for me, I had duty that first day, but that was alright, because I did not have anyone meeting me on the pier.

As we approached the pier, we could see hundreds of Navy wives and children waving with signs of "Welcome Home, We Love You." The signalmen on deck were signaling to their wives. We did not have cell phones back then, so everyone with anyone was desperately looking over the crowd until they spotted a familiar face. Then you could see the joy in their eyes and the frantic waving, "I'm here, I'm here." It was very touching and emotional.

The new fathers got off first and the moms and their babies were greeted with open arms and tears—lots of joyful tears. Even some of the older guys staying on the ship were tearing up. It was such a wholesome sight and even though I was still only twenty years old without a wife or girlfriend, it was a touching scene. The reunions are very heart warming. While a few of the wives had flown to the Philippines, Hong Kong, or Japan for a brief visit with their husbands, this was the first time many of them had seen each other in six months. It was truly wonderful to see so much love and affection in one place.

So now that I was a worldly man, what wonderful things did I come away with from the cruise? I had faced several close calls on the flight deck. I had seen death and it was not pretty. But all of that time on the flight deck during flight ops, I gained a higher respect for life. Sure you can grab ass every now and then, but you also have to realize that your life can be yanked away from you in a second. It is hard to explain the confidence I had gained during the cruise. It is almost like each new duty station in my Naval career was a building block, one on top of the other.

Besides Guam which is really a U.S. territory, this was the first time I had been outside the United States. We went to three different countries: the Philippines, Hong Kong, and Japan. Each had their own cultures, their own foods, and their own traditions. While I did not really tour PI that much, I definitely took advantage of touring Hong Kong and Japan. I think all in all, I came away with a greater appreciation for the United States. Even at twenty years old, I still had my own opinions about our country, what I liked and what I did not like, but as my dad often told me, "There is no better place in the world to live than the United States." You know what? He was right.

# # #

There were several unique aspects to the WESTPAC '75 cruise. This was the first time that Kitty Hawk transited the Sea of Japan and encountered this colder climate. This gave the fleet admiral as well as all crews in the Carrier Task Force an opportunity to freeze their gonads off. Of course, I never did see the Admiral down on the flight deck, but I guess rank has its privileges. The air wing got to wave to more Russians than ever before. This would also be the last deployment of the S-2 Tracker aircraft, the gasoline powered, twin engine, anti-submarine planes. They had been around a long time and it was time to retire them. They would be replaced with the newer S-3 Vikings.

During 1975, including the WESTPAC cruise, Kitty Hawk was at sea for 186 days and in port 179 days. Of her port calls overseas not including Hawaii, she saw 82 days at anchor or alongside. These included 68 days in Subic Bay during seven visits, seven days in Hong Kong, and seven days in Yokosuka. The ship's records also kept statistics of reenlistments during the year. Of the 496 first term eligible, 109 sailors reenlisted, a little over 20%. Of the 76 career lifers, 72 reenlisted, almost 95%.

The U.S. Naval Base in Subic Bay was the largest U.S. Navy installation in the Pacific. In 1991, Mount Pinatubo vented, sending tons of ash and smoke throughout Clark Air Force Base and Subic Bay Naval Base. Both were immediately evacuated—Clark would never open again and the Subic Bay facility would only open for a brief period. Despite heavy negotiations between the United States government and the Philippine government, President Corazon Aquino, who favored keeping the U.S. presence in PI, issued a formal notice for the United States to leave by the end of 1992.

On November 24, 1992, the American flag was lowered in Subic Bay for the last time. This withdrawal marked the first time since the sixteenth century that no foreign military forces were present in the Philippines.

23 WESTPAC '75
San Diego

The first day we got back to San Diego, I had duty which I did not mind. I did not really have anywhere to go or anyone to see. I had made arrangements to fly home for the Christmas holidays, but would not be leaving until December 20. I would have three weeks leave, too. My friend, Gary Borne had ordered a new car while in the Philippines; it was waiting for him at his home in Hagerstown, Maryland. It was a brown, four-door Ford Granada, not really the type of car I thought Gary would drive, but then everybody has his own taste in style; and besides, the only thing I've seen Gary drive was a crash truck. That was pretty cool—order a car while overseas and have it waiting for you for Christmas.

Prior to leaving for home, I made arrangements with Brack Barker and John Sideris, a couple of friends from the Operations Division, to meet a few days after New Year's in Pensacola, Florida where John lived. We would drive back together to San Diego in John's Gran Tornio. We were planning a straight drive through, with no stops except for gas and food, so we figured it would take about two to three days.

I flew back to Florida on December 20. My sister picked me up at the Jacksonville airport and we drove back to Gainesville together. She had her 1972 orange VW convertible and it was a great drive. It was good to see Anne; she had not changed much since I had last seen her nine months earlier. I didn't really realize how much I had missed her. We had a good visit on the drive back.

I stayed home for two weeks through the Christmas holidays and then took a Greyhound bus up to Pensacola to meet Brack and John. We started out in the afternoon heading west on I-10 and got through New Orleans with no problems. I thought we might stop for a short visit since I had never been to New Orleans, but Brack and John were itching to get back to the ship. I did not argue. After all, I was just hitching a ride.

Do you know how long a drive it is across the state of Texas? It is long, it's *really* long, and not that exciting for most of the drive. We took turns driving, changing every few hours, stopping to eat when we got hungry, and stopping for gas when the car got hungry. I was driving through the night while the other guys were sleeping. Around 0400, I got tired and woke John and he took over.

About 0600 we were going through some podunk town in west Texas and something happened to the car; the radiator temperature started going up— it was not going to be a good day. We pulled into the only gas station and since it was so early, the station had not yet opened up. The sign said it would open at 0730. We popped the hood and saw the radiator was leaking where it was not supposed to. We figured we hit something on the road and for some reason it popped up and busted the radiator, causing the leak.

Across the street was a twenty-four hour restaurant, so we headed over there to get some chow to eat and to wait until the gas station opened up. The food was not bad, but we were more concerned about fixing the car. When the station opened up, the mechanic looked things over and said the radiator had a leak. Well, I could tell we had a real sharp mechanic here; must have been at the top of his class. He ended up pulling the radiator. They did not have the tools there to seal the radiator leak, but they could take it over to the next town, about thirty miles away. However, this was a Sunday and the radiator repair shop was closed, so we would have to stay overnight.

This little podunk town had three businesses: a gas station, a restaurant, and a hotel. I think they were probably all in cahoots, but who was to say. We checked into the hotel, got a couple of six packs of beer and chilled out. It was not the most exciting part of the journey. The next day, I rode with the mechanic who was taking the radiator to be fixed. It did not take too long to fix the radiator.

A couple of hours later, we were back on the road again, thank God. We were in that town a little too long, but as I told Brack and John, it could've been worse. We could have had the radiator go in that long hundred-mile stretch of road with no gas stations. Coming through New Mexico and Arizona was kind of boring, but when we got to the Arizona-California border, the scenery started picking up. The mountains were fantastic and since dawn was just starting to break, it was a beautiful sight.

We got back to the ship on Tuesday, January 6, 1976. It was good to be back aboard. It's funny, when we had been at sea for the six-month cruise, I could not wait to get off and get back home to see my folks. But getting back aboard, it almost felt as good as when I got back home in Gainesville. I've heard many sailors say the exact same thing.

Since Gary Borne had bought his car, I was itching to buy something and I was partial to trucks. I had seen Mac's truck. He had a bitchin' Dodge RAM four-wheel drive truck. I was leaning towards a truck, but since I had never owned a car before, I was not sure how to shop for one. I looked around at a few places in San Diego. The Dodge trucks I was looking at were about $5,000 to $6,000 at the time. Some of the guys had told me that I could probably get a better deal in Washington, so I decided I would wait until we got up to the shipyards. Besides, it would give me some time to save some money between now and then.

I got the nerve up to go and visit Bonnie. We had exchanged a few letters and a few phone calls over the last nine months. She had been transferred to San Diego and I had called and talked with her several times. I decided that I needed to go and see her. If for nothing else, to try and explain to her what I think happened and how I felt now as opposed to how I felt back in Guam. It was not going to be an easy conversation, but one that needed to be had.

We had a good visit, some good laughs, and we both shed some tears. I think we both felt a little awkward since it had been almost a year since we had last seen each other. We had both grown in different directions, but I'm sure we still had feelings for each other. I don't think you ever get that close to someone and not feel like they have been a part of your life, no matter how short or how long the relationship lasted. She told me that no matter what happens, she would always have a place in her heart for me. I think I felt the same way and I told her so.

Bonnie returned my silver dollar and we parted as friends. She knew how much it meant to me and she did not need it anymore. I guess we were just two lonely people that had found solace with each other while on Guam. I never regretted spending time with her. She was a good kid from Oregon. I wished her happiness and moved on.

You would not think we would do much training at sea since we were planning on heading up to the shipyards in Bremerton, Washington and literally be out of commission for a year, but we did. I was told that I would be training as a yellow shirt director during this short at sea period. I had made the entire WESTPAC cruise as a firefighter in Crash, so I was ready to work the other side of the ABH rate. I was stoked.

Well, so much for the yellow shirt duty. When we headed out to sea in early February, the division had lost its Yeoman, John Tabao. He had completed his sentence and had been honorably discharged from the Navy. Apparently someone found out I could type, so the division officer and Chief Breig decided to pull me into the V-1 Division office. That sucked big time. I was not a happy camper. I wanted to be out on the flight deck again, and this time as a yellow shirt.

They said it did not make sense to train me as a yellow shirt director if we were going to be in the shipyards for a year. The lieutenant also told me that not only could I type, but I was probably the only guy in the division that was organized enough to handle the workload. I was flattered, but then later I figured he was blowing smoke up my ass. I asked them to put me back into Crash, but they said this was the way it was—deal with it! This was about the time in my Naval career when I started the mantra, "I love the fucking Navy and the Navy loves fucking me!"

I decided it was not worth fighting for and I would do as I was told, like it or not. Besides, it was only for ten days. Better yet, most of those ten days at sea were wet and cold, so *not* being on the flight deck during flight ops in that nasty weather was OK by me. I did get to do my radio show though and that made life a little easier.

During this short cruise, I took the opportunity to write my mom and dad another one of those serious, philosophical letters. "You know, I've matured one hell of a lot since I've joined the Navy. Even though there are a lot of bad times, you remember them as 'experiences' and they help out in the future. I've learned a lot about life and about people, especially myself. I know that I can do anything I want, as long as I work at it with all I've got.

"I realize now that the Navy does not hold my future. I have to do something else. I'm not sure what I want to do, but I want to do something useful. My mind is mature enough to know that once I set my mind to do something, I can do it." Yes sir, I had come a long way from that 18-year old bright-eyed and bushy-tailed kid that worked in the dive shop after flunking out of FSU. My confidence level and self-esteem were high and I was still young. I thought the world was mine to conquer.

When a ship prepares to change home ports, sometimes there are sailors who do not want to leave with her for one reason or another. It could be they like the place they're in; it could be that their wives are pregnant and soon to deliver; it could be that their families are settled and kids in school. Any number of reasons.

The Navy understands this and sometimes allows sailors to swap duty stations to another ship, meaning that if they can find someone in the same billet who wants to swap, then the Navy usually allows it. In our case, if a shipmate wanted to stay on a carrier instead of heading to the dry docks, then the Navy would probably let them as long as they found someone of equal rank to swap with. It is not really that difficult and it is a more common occurrence than you would think.

I was not one of those, because I wanted to experience the shipyards and the Pacific Northwest. I would not be disappointed.

24 BREMERTON
Shipyards

Kitty Hawk was scheduled to leave San Diego in early March to head up to Bremerton, Washington. We knew we would be in the shipyards for about a year. There would be some major work done on the ship including renovations to accommodate the new, heavier F-14 "Tomcat" fighter jet and the S-3 "Viking" anti-submarine jet aircraft Kitty Hawk would take on. We would also be in the dry docks and that was something I wanted to see—a 60,000 ton aircraft carrier up on concrete blocks. The only vehicles I had ever seen on blocks were some old Chevy and Ford pickup trucks back home in Gainesville.

This would be a complete move, including moving entire families. During this short cruise, there would only be ship's company—no air wing personnel would be aboard. The families traveling on Kitty Hawk, women and children included, would be assigned to their own staterooms. We were told to be on our best behavior—there would be more than three hundred dependents traveling with us. We also were going to be taking aboard cars and boats. The transit to Bremerton became known as "Operation Ark."

Of course, since cars would be on both the flight deck and the hangar deck, the V-1 Division and V-3 Division were to handle the movement and placement of all vehicles. No, the Handler did not use the Quiji board for this spot. However, I did get to take part in this fun little exercise. I can't tell you how many cars they were loading, but the dock workers put a ramp between the pier and elevator #3 so that the cars could be driven aboard.

We were very well organized in my opinion. Once the cars came up the ramp from the pier on elevator #3, they drove straight across to elevator #4 on the port side. We could bring a load of eight cars up to the flight deck, so we would do that first. While the elevator was being raised, we had the next set of drivers park their cars on the hangar deck starting as far forward as possible. When the elevator came back down, we would direct another eight cars onto it and start over again. Once on the flight deck, we directed the drivers to park their cars starting on the bow and worked our way aft. It was, as my friend Tony Davis put it, controlled chaos.

It was quite an interesting day to say the least. Once the owners parked their cars and got their bags out, most of them put a thick coat of car wax all over their cars. The ride up to Bremerton in the early spring would probably be a little wet. The wax would protect the finish from the salt water spray.

Several of the guys and their families decided they would drive up and those that chose to drive were given four days leave to get from San Diego to Bremerton. I did not really want to drive up, so I stayed aboard the ship. Besides, my last ride with Brack and John was still fresh in my mind and John had driven his car on board. He was not going to drive up to Bremerton, either.

Kitty Hawk departed San Diego on March 8, 1976, and on Friday, March 12 we entered the dry dock at Puget Sound Naval Shipyard in Bremerton, Washington to commence a one hundred million dollar complex overhaul, scheduled to last just more than twelve months. Besides renovations for the F-14 and S-3, including additional storage and maintenance space, the ship was also scheduled to replace the Terrier Surface-to-Air missile system with the newer NATO Sea Sparrow system, and added elevators and modified weapons magazines to provide an increased capability for handling and stowing the newer, larger air-launched weapons.

I had never seen snow before in my life except in pictures and movies. Coming in through Puget Sound on a bright sunny morning was beautiful, to say the least. And when we rounded the corner and spotted Mt. Rainier in the background, all 14,000 snow-covered feet, it was nothing short of spectacular. I was thinking that I would really like it here. While we first entered Puget Sound in the morning, it took us another few hours to maneuver through the sound and into the dry docks. They were going to start pumping out water from the dry dock that day.

We started off-loading the cars and as expected, it was a slow process. I felt like a traffic cop, trying to help people maneuver out of tight spots and without bumping into each other. Most everyone was patient. I think everyone expected it would take some time. About 1800 (6:00 p.m.), Gary Borne, Ed Boes, and I headed out—we had decided we would try to find an apartment and move in together. We had been stationed in Guam together as well as Kitty Hawk and we got along fairly well.

We found a great place: a three bedroom, one bath apartment about ten miles from the shipyards on the outskirts of Bremerton. These were brand new apartments and we were the first tenants in the apartment we rented.

Rent at that time was $215 per month. We split it three ways. There was no furniture, so we found a furniture rental place and had furniture delivered the next day. The furniture rental (beds, chairs, couch) was an additional $40 per month. There was not any grass around, but the apartment manager had painted the dirt with green spray paint. I had never seen that before, but what the hell, nobody asked my opinion.

It took two days for the shipyard workers to pump out the water in the dry dock. We had heard there were scuba divers in the water making sure Kitty Hawk settled down on the concrete blocks just right, but that was not the type of diving I would want to do. When all the water was pumped out, we started the major overhaul, most of which would not affect us much in the V-1 Division.

There was still one active aircraft assigned to Kitty Hawk—the twin-engine, gasoline powered C-1 COD. Because of that, we needed to maintain an around-the-clock crash crew at the Kitsap County Airport which is where the COD aircraft was stationed. Thank God, I was not assigned that duty. There were two shifts of three-man crews, Port and Starboard, that worked one day on and one day off. They drove the Kitty Hawk's Oshkosh MB-5. These guys were bored out of their gourd since the plane only flew a few times a week, but they had to be on duty whether the plane flew or not. I went out there a few times to visit my friend Jack Kuiphoff and to let them know they weren't alone. Not a bad place, not a bad duty, but a little too boring for me.

After a few months in the shipyards, Gary Borne was assigned to the crash crew at Kitsap County Airport relieving Jack. While it was boring, Gary told me that it was skate duty. Besides, he said several times a month, the C-1 crew would fly down to San Diego for training and almost every time would fly back with twenty to thirty cases of Coors beer.

Our normal workday was to be 0730 to 1700 (5:00 p.m.). The first week or so in the shipyards, we were getting used to the new work hours and even though we might have finished our workday early, we couldn't leave. The XO even put the word out that no one would leave the ship in civilian clothes before 1700.

We found out that we were going to renovate all of the V-1 Division spaces including our berthing compartment, each of the Fly compartments, and the Crash compartment. In addition, we would have to renovate the areas around those spaces including the catwalks. By renovate, I mean we had to strip the paint down to bare metal and repaint. We would also strip our berthing compartment floors of the old vinyl tile and put in new tile. That was going to be a big chore. But what the hell, we had a whole year.

The shipyards provided several barges called APLs (Auxiliary Personnel Lighter) that were outfitted to be two-story berthing compartments to hold the ship's crews while their spaces were being renovated. They were floating barges, tied up at the pier and located a couple of hundred yards away from Kitty Hawk. Another APL served as the mess hall. You could not stay in your berthing compartment on Kitty Hawk while the floors were being redone with new tiles and the walls all being stripped down and repainted. It was quite a mess and was going to take some time, so that was why everyone was moved to the barge. Not every division aboard ship was being renovated at the same time, so berthing aboard the APL was more on a rotation schedule.

I soon realized that my new job as division Yeoman was not a bad thing. All the other petty officers were put in charge of work crews and every day they worked in filthy conditions. We were able to provide all our guys with heavy-duty coveralls so their utility uniforms wouldn't get too dirty. Everyone was issued ear plugs and hard hats. We were using pneumatic needle guns to chip the paint off the metal and that took a long time. Once the paint was chipped off, we used electric disc sanders to take it down to the bare metal. We probably had a dozen of these crews going at one time. Most of this was done by the blue shirts with the yellow shirts pitching in when needed, but in more of a supervisory role. As they say in the Navy, Shit Rolls Down Hill, so it was a good time to be a petty officer.

About two months into this overhaul, our division officer decided it might be better for us to purchase our own sand blaster and help make the job go quicker. It took a lot of time to get the paint off the ship using needle guns and just as long for the guys to sand down to the bare metal using electric sanders. Once that was done, we had to put on an initial coat of primer paint, then three coats of my favorite color—battleship gray. So, a sand blaster would definitely help speed things up.

Work aboard the carrier in the shipyards was boring for me. But we weren't working sixteen or eighteen hour days or around the clock so that was good. Most of the time, I would be working in the office doing whatever a Yeoman was supposed to do which was a lot of paperwork and a lot of typing. We had a new division officer, Lt. Richard Lockram, who had been an F-4 Phantom RIO. He was a good guy and we got along well.

Every now and then, something just comes along that blows your socks off. I had been known as one of the division scavengers, finding things we needed to help do our job better. I wasn't the only one though I was one of the few who confessed. I was looking for some special metal containers for Crash and could not find them anywhere on the ship and none of the yard birds I had been dealing with could find any either.

I did locate some at Naval Air Station Whidbey Island. It was a bit far to drive, but I made arrangements to hitch a ride in a CH-46 helicopter which was heading up that way the following day. I got to the flight early enough and was expecting a flight of about thirty minutes, but I was in for the ride of my life. It seems we had an Admiral on board and the helo pilot decided to take a little side excursion over the Olympic Mountains.

The day was one of those bright, blue, clear, and crisp days—you know the kind. My mom used to call them Champagne Days. The pilot took off on time and headed northwest to fly over the Olympics. I swear there were some times when I felt like I could reach out and touch one of the glaciers I thought we were flying so low. It was breathtaking to say the least. The flight up took about two hours and I didn't mind at all. Glad to have the Admiral onboard.

When I was in Guam, I was impressed with our division training officer, ABH-2 Tom Cullen. In May 1976, I was assigned training officer duties for the V-1 Division. Another yokel was assigned Yeoman duties. Besides, it was still a lot better than chipping paint and sand blasting. They even gave me my own office, away from everyone else, so I had no one to bother me all day long. I had prescribed things to do as a training officer so I started organizing how I would get these guys trained and what types of qualifications we needed to keep up with.

I had the guys one afternoon a week for training. Most of the time, I showed films of various activities regarding ABs. These included flight deck firefighting as well as directing aircraft. The firefighting ones were always gruesome, especially where there was a crash on the flight deck. We showed the Forrestal fire several times since it was one of the worst aircraft carrier fires ever and a great teaching tool.

We also showed films about liquid oxygen and how to properly handle LOX. It was one of the most dangerous liquids we could ever encounter. One of the training films showed a man on a gurney in an emergency room that had been burnt over 100% of his body. He was still alive, but they had given him morphine for pain though it didn't look like it helped much. The thing I remember about this particular training film though was not the gory skinless man, but the fear in his eyes. He knew he was going to die and his eyes revealed that. Apparently he died about a minute after that film was taken. I still remember those haunting eyes—not something easy to forget.

I also taught classes in basic First Aid; after all, I had passed First Aid at FSU. Other classes included basic seamanship, where several other petty officers made asses out of themselves trying to teach the guys how to tie basic knots. It was funny watching this three-ring circus, but the funniest thing was listening to the various styles of colorful Navy language when they couldn't get it right. I thought I cussed like a sailor, but I was an amateur compared to some of these guys.

There wasn't that much to being a training officer—mostly making sure all of the guys in the division were meeting their PQSs (Personal Qualification Standards), tracking their training, both what I taught as well as other training, and mostly staying organized. It was kind of boring, but I got to wander about the ship anywhere and anytime, visiting with my guys. It was, no doubt, a pure skate job and I was good at it.

Also in May, the ship's Public Affairs Officer arranged for a tour to the bottom of the dry dock. I wasn't going to miss this. We climbed down a lot of stairs to get to the bottom. Kitty Hawk was sitting on hundreds of blocks each about four foot by four foot square and anywhere from three to six feet tall, depending on where they were placed under this ship. It was quite an awesome sight to see this humongous ship up on blocks.

The ship's two anchors were lying on the ground up toward the bow, along with hundreds of links of chain. Only one of the four propellers was down there on a huge platform. It must have been about twenty feet in diameter and was nice shiny brass. The others were being refurbished. There were four long propeller shafts each about three feet in diameter that would hold the propellers. We were also able to walk under the ship's two rudders each about fifteen feet long and about twenty five feet tall.

The bottom of the dry dock was muddy, but that was to be expected since this was up in the Pacific Northwest and it often rained. Besides, I'm sure that there was some water runoff from the ship from time to time. All in all, I think we spent about three hours down there.

My good friend, Glenn Law, reenlisted that day at the bottom of the dry docks. It was a proud occasion for Glenn—this was his first reenlistment. Neither of us realized it at the time, but Glenn would make the Navy a career for 22 years.

Around the first week in August, I decided that I wanted to move back aboard the ship or at least the APL. I wasn't really having any problems or issues with Gary or Ed, but since I had recently bought a truck, I was *always* short of money. I figured moving back aboard would help me save that $100 a month payment. Besides, Gary was being transferred to the crash crew at the Kitsap County Airport and he would probably live out there full time.

That was an easy move for me, too. On this particular APL, the racks were stacked two high instead of three as on the ship. Lots more room and these racks had the coffin type storage lockers under the racks—more storage, too. I felt right at home moving back in. While I did accumulate a few more civilian clothes, I didn't have that many. Back then, the look was bell bottoms pants and polyester shirts. I had a few of these types of shirts and they were quite comfortable.

Toward the end of September, the shipyard workers had finished scraping, priming, and painting the ship's hull. I can't tell you how much paint they used, but it must have been at least a million gallons. It was now time to take the ship out of the dry dock, so they started flooding the dry dock, slowly at first to be sure nothing shifted too fast. I was on board for this part and it was neat watching the entire process. The great flood took a full day and best of all, no leaks. The tug boats pulled us out of the dry dock which was now flooded to equalize the water in the dry dock with the water in Puget Sound, and parked us alongside pier #6. That was where we would remain until we left the shipyards.

In January, the yard birds started applying non-skid onto the flight deck. That was fun. We had already stripped it down to bare metal, applied a primer coat of paint as well as some deck gray paint, and now the task was to spray on the non-skid. There were two yard workers working at the same time so we had to furnish a couple of guys up there to help them out.

The only thing our guys had to do was to cover the pad eyes so they wouldn't get sprayed with the non-skid coating. They used a four-foot pole with a five-inch round metal plate attached to the end. "Don't wear your good shoes" I told them since this stuff would splatter all over the place. It was kind of neat to see the flight deck getting back into shape. I guess it was also a sign that we were getting close to finishing the overhaul in Bremerton.

Just to let you know how ridiculous the Navy can be sometimes, at least in our division during our stay in the shipyards, our berthing compartment on Kitty Hawk was stripped and painted four times and we retiled the floor twice. It seems there was friction between the two V-1 Division chiefs—one would say one thing and we would do it, then the other would complain and we would do it again. I think that is the main reason I didn't stay in the Navy. I found myself being caught between chiefs one too many times. I think a lot of the guys felt that way, too.

I had taken the E-5 second class petty officer exam in August while on the cruise. As I thought, I was a PNA, Passed but Not Accepted. I figured I didn't have enough time in rate. But then again, neither Gary, Glenn, nor the other guys who took the E-5 exam with me on the cruise were promoted. It was to be given again in early February so I started studying again—nothing else to do on the ship, so why not. Besides, I *was* the Division Training Officer.

In late April I found out that I had passed the E-5 exam and I would be promoted to a second class petty officer, ABH-2, on June 16, 1976. I couldn't believe it. Gary, Ed, and Glenn passed too, but they wouldn't be promoted until a couple of months after me. That was a hoot, because they made third class months before I did and now I would be senior to them. This could get interesting.

I actually got a waiver because you are supposed to have three years of service before being advanced to E-5 and I was one month short, but because I had come into the service as an E-2 (Airman Apprentice), they gave me the waiver. I guess that year in FSU was worth it even though I had been asked to leave.

25 BREMERTON
Life Outside the Shipyards

During our time in Bremerton, I also started looking around for a new truck. I wasn't quite sure what I wanted, but I figured I would be able to find something with one of the big three: Ford, Dodge, or Chevy. Seattle seemed to be a good place to go and I had to ask someone to take me around. My friend Jack Kuiphoff was happy to go into town with me. He had his own clunker and I pitched in for gas. The first few times in, we didn't find anything. Prices were still around $5,500 to $6,000 and I was hoping to find something a little cheaper. I had $1,300 saved up between the time on the cruise and with the monthly allotment I had been sending to my mom to put away in savings for me.

One Sunday morning I was reading the local Seattle paper that someone had left in the division office and came across an ad for a brand new Chevrolet truck. The dealership was not in Seattle, but in a small town called Gig Harbor, just north of the Tacoma Narrows bridge, about a half hour drive south. I had no clue where that was, but Jack drove me down and I looked over what they had. I did not see anything I wanted. All the models on the lot were automatic transmissions and I wanted a manual. Then the salesman told me I could order whatever I wanted and it would be custom built, just for me. He seemed like a nice enough man (they are always nice when they take your money).

He worked up the numbers and I ordered exactly what I wanted: a two-wheel drive, short-bed Chevy Custom Deluxe, Catalina blue, 3-speed manual transmission on the column ("three on a tree"), and a 350 cubic-inch, eight cylinder engine with about 300 horsepower. The total cost without tax and license was $4447.47. I would pay $1,300 down and make $100 monthly payments. Sweet!

186

The salesman told me my truck would take between four and six weeks; I should've known better. It took a little more than eight weeks, but it finally came in. Jack gave me a ride to Gig Harbor to pick her up and it was love at first sight. I gave her a test drive and she felt right. I had grown up driving a 1954 3-speed Willys Jeep and loved to shift gears. This was awesome. I signed all the papers and drove her off the lot, knowing she was now mine—well, mine and the bank's.

We had found a couple of bars around Bremerton, close to the main gate. What a surprise—between sailors and shipyard workers, they probably made a lot of money off us. I was not going to get into debt though, because I had just bought a truck and was making those dastardly $100 monthly payments. I did go every now and then with some good friends. Most of the bars had a wooden shuffle board game which was always a challenge. I got pretty good at it though and it did seem to pass the time. I still liked to play pool, but I was by no means a pool shark. I did not get into betting on my games, either. While I was good, I wasn't *that* good.

There were all kinds of women hanging out in the bars. Some were good-looking, some were *not* so good-looking. I guess most of us men that came to these bars were either sailors or shipyard workers and that probably did not bring in the most attractive women. There were, however, a lot of "Bremerloes." Those were the husky women who hung out in the Bremerton bars. I knew a few and while most were very nice, none were all that attractive. But as the old Mickey Gilley song says, *The Girls All Get Prettier at Closing Time.*

While there were several bars around the shipyards, some were better than others. But I found *my* bar, Bill's Inn, located several miles outside of Bremerton. This would be my major hangout for the rest of my time in Bremerton. The bands there played country music and they also had a huge dance floor. The first time in and after a couple of beers, I went up to the band and asked them if they knew *The Auctioneer.* They said they did and I told them I knew the words so they invited me up to sing.

I felt like I was at home. I had been on stage several times over the past couple of years, sometimes a little less sober than others, but this time I was very comfortable on stage—no stage fright whatsoever and I wasn't half lit, either. The crowd seemed to really like it too so I figured I had found *my* hangout.

Sunday nights at Bill's Inn was jam night. That meant anyone could get on stage with the band and jam with or without an instrument. I was a regular there on Sunday nights, as were a couple of other people that I noticed. We started to hang out together, too.

One night while jamming, I was in for a big surprise. I got my first guitar when I was twelve years old. My sister had given me a record called *Play Guitar with the Ventures.* The Ventures was an instrumental group with lots of hits in the sixties such as *Wipeout, Pipeline, Hawaii Five-O*, and *Walk, Don't Run*. The four songs on the record which taught you how to play rhythm, bass, and lead guitar were *Memphis, Tequila, Honky Tonk*, and *Walk, Don't Run*. I learned them all and that is how I learned how to play guitar.

During one night at Bill's Inn, I was on stage doing my thing jamming with the house band when a tall guy joined us and took over the lead guitar. I was jamming with my guitar and playing rhythm while this guy was playing lead guitar behind me while I was singing. This was Nokie Edwards, the lead guitarist for the *Ventures*. I was beside myself. Here I am singing some of my favorite country songs and the guy playing lead guitar for me was the same guy who taught me how to play though he didn't know. It was almost like a dream. We got to talk a little bit, but he was swamped by fans; he was from the Tacoma area. That was a night I would never forget the rest of my life.

It was not unusual for us to stay at Bill's Inn until the early morning hours. I usually had a friend or two with me. We would close the bar down at 0200 and head back to the ship. But for some reason, we were always hungry and some of us were a little drunk. I don't know why because we had been drinking since 2100 (9:00 p.m.). We would stop by one of those 24-hour breakfast restaurants and we began to get picky and only stopped at the ones that had pictures on the menus. That way, all we had to do was point at what looked good.

After a few months in Bremerton, I decided that instead of hitting the bars every night, it might be better for me to find a part-time job. I looked around and found a gas station right down the road from our apartment. It was an Amoco station and since I had spent several years working at my Uncle Walter's station in Gainesville, I figured I could do the same here.

"Good afternoon. My name is Chet Adkins and I would like to work for you. I'm in the United States Navy, currently aboard the USS Kitty Hawk which is in dry dock and we'll be stationed here for another nine months. I've got several years of experience and can do oil changes, tune ups, and tire work. I'm a reliable employee and can work nights and weekends."

All that in one breath. I had practiced this routine and figured that the worst that he would say was no. As a matter of fact, Hal Ambaum hired me on the spot; it was in May. He had an opening and I could start working that Friday night. I was pretty impressed with myself, being able to walk up to the owner, tell him I would like a job (as opposed to asking him) and telling him what I could do. This is something that I would remember and use again many times in my life—confidence, that what's it all about. I would be making two dollars an hour and that was good money back then. I only made ninety cents an hour while working at my uncle's gas station in the early 70s.

June 16, 1976 marked a big day for me; I was able to sew my second class crow on. That's Navy lingo for being promoted to a second class petty officer. I was so proud of myself; I made second class in less than three years, something that is almost unheard of in the Navy. I would be getting a fifty dollar pay raise which meant I would be getting paid $516 every two weeks. I was making the big bucks now.

I thought back to that phone call from my mom and dad when they first found out I had flunked out of FSU. In my own way, I had been trying since that time to make my parents proud of me and even though they never, ever showed disappointment, I always felt I needed to prove something to them. This was one of those moments that I thought was an auspicious occasion. Several of us headed out to Bill's Inn; we were going to party.

Bremerton is only a couple of hours away from Mt. Rainier. I had met a girl, Regina, and she took me up to Mt. Rainier on January 1, 1977. This was the first time in my life I had ever been in snow. I *was* the kid in the candy store. I threw snow balls, I made snow angels, I slipped and slided every which way and busted my ass several times. I had the time of my life. And to think it took twenty-two years for that to happen. That was one of the best days in my life, too. Regina was a good kid and also had an eight-year old son, but she had a few too many problems and I did not really want to get involved. We had a few dates, but then I moved on.

During my time in Bremerton, I tried to take advantage of all the Navy had to offer. It was slim pickins in a place like Bremerton as opposed to a large Naval station like San Diego. But, I did what I could. One counselor that worked for the Navy Campus for Achievement told me I could take an assessment test, one that would provide me with some ideas about what other people with similar likes and dislikes did for a living.

In other words, I had to answer some random type questions and he would run it through his computer, get the results, and I would learn what type of career that might interest me. It turns out that other men with my same interests were Maritime Navigators, whatever that was. I really did not see myself working on the ocean for the rest of my life, so I told him thanks, that's good to know, but don't leave the lights on. Who knows, I might have been happy being a maritime navigator. But, I do know this as I write this book, I've been very happy and very blessed with the different roads I have traveled.

One of the other things I wanted to do while in Bremerton was to take a course or two at the local community college. I enrolled in Olympic Community College and took a class in electronics. Since I knew I would be getting out of the Navy in July, I was trying to figure out what I wanted to do with my future. My thought process was that electronics had been around a while and everyone needed to use electricity, so why not give that a shot. Before this class, about the only thing I could do electrical was turn the light switch on and off, and even then only when I was sober.

At that time, this particular college course cost $83. The class was four days a week; class time was one hour, followed by a three hour lab. It counted for ten credit hours (OCC was on the quarterly system). The Navy picked up 75% of the tuition, so I only had to lay out about twenty bucks. Pretty good deal if I say so myself. I was learning how to work the Navy system.

The course instructor knew his stuff. I learned a lot about electronics, how things work, and all that other electrical crap. But the thing that stuck out in my mind about this guy was his philosophical musings. One that stands out which I've used for years since then: "If you can't dazzle them with brilliance, baffle them with bull shit."

It took a while to get used to working all day from 0730 to 1700, then going to school four days a week from 1800 to 2200. But I was on a roll and while it was keeping me busy, it also kept me out of the bars and off the streets. I had to quit my job at the gas station. I talked with Hal about it and he agreed that I was doing the right thing. I liked him and he was always a great boss and looked after his employees. I told him that I would help out on the weekends if he got into a bind.

One of my good friends in Crash, Jim Riley, got married at his family's place in Port Townsend, Washington which is out on the Olympic peninsula. It was a beautiful wedding and his bride Cassie was adorable. I had brought my guitar along and after the ceremony and the reception, Jim and Cassie asked that I play a few songs. I started out with the romantic *A Time for Us* from the movie *Romeo and Juliet*, one of the top love songs at the time. I must have done a pretty good job, because not only were Jim and Cassie teary-eyed, but several other couples were holding each other tight and gazing into each other's eyes. I know it wasn't country, but it seemed like the right song and the right time. Besides, I would get to Merle, Johnny, George, Tammy, and Patsy later in the night.

Jim came from a family of fishermen and fished the Alaskan waters for king crab. If you've watched the reality TV show *Deadliest Catch* about crab fishermen, you get the idea. Jim was a good guy to know, too, and while I tried not to take advantage of his friendship, I never turned down a dinner of king crab and beer—"I'll bring the beer."

After the wedding, a couple of us stopped by Jim and Cassie's apartment in Bremerton. We short-sheeted his bed and loaded it with sugar and corn flakes, one of those mindless things we did in the old days when people got married. They never found out who did it, either.

I also got up to Vancouver, British Columbia a couple of times. It was a beautiful drive, about three and a half hours from Bremerton, and I took a friend of mine, Mike Binette. Mike and I were hanging out a lot, especially when I was jamming or playing my guitar and singing in a bar. I called Mike my business manager; he was a good kid from Boston. We ended up staying in a cheap hotel outside of town, but headed down to the gaslight district for some fish and chips and cheap Canadian beer. We were looking for chicks, too.

The funny thing about Canada, at least from a southerner's point of view, is that they use funny money—Canadian money. Plus they are on the metric system. How many liters to a gallon of gas? If a liter of gas costs nineteen Canadian cents, how many American dollars is twenty gallons?

The other thing was the temperature. The outside bank thermometer signs were reading seven degrees, but we were riding around with the windows down. It just did not feel that cold outside. It took us a couple of hours to realize that it was seven degrees *Celsius*. I was having a tough time, but I managed. Then I got to thinking, if they were on the metric system, then three American days of vacation would equal about seven days of Canadian vacation, wouldn't it?

I also took a three-week vacation in August and headed home to Gainesville. I was able to catch a military transport flight from McChord AFB Washington to Macon AFB Georgia, then a commercial flight to Jacksonville, where Anne picked me up. I had never flown a MAC (Military Airlift Command) flight before and this was a C-141 four-engine cargo jet. There were no windows and only a couple of seats in the cargo bay. Everything else was a cot. They gave us box lunches and no surprise— horsecock sandwiches. But I did not complain; I was getting a free ride to Macon, Georgia.

It was good to be home for a while, visit with the folks, and spend some much needed down time at Kingsley Lake. I had picked up a bad head cold and just sat out on the dock baking it out.

I dated several girls while in Bremerton. Most of them I met in bars. Actually, *all* of them I met in bars. We drank a little, ate a little, danced a little, and a few other things a little. Nothing serious and I think we parted ways as friends. That's the way to do it. I was not ready to settle down yet. Too much life left to live.

One of the girls I dated I had met at Bill's Inn on Sunday jam night. Her name was Brenda and she had a wonderful voice. I really enjoyed listening to her, especially when she sang Patsy Cline songs. After she finished her set, I went over and introduced myself and we sat and talked for an hour or so. She liked listening to me sing too which really flattered me since I thought I had an OK voice. She gave me her number and told me to call her.

The next day, Monday, I gave her a call. Why wait? She invited me over to dinner later in the week and I took her up on her offer. She lived with her mom and her grandmother—three generations of women in one household. What was I getting myself into? Her grandmother was a neat lady too, as well as her mom. Granny made me what she called a poor man's apple pie. She had a device that looked like long tongs with a double metal spatula on the end. She buttered up two pieces of bread, sliced some apples onto one piece, added a little sugar and cinnamon, put the other piece on top and buttoned down the hatches, so to speak. She then held it over the stove burner and cooked both sides. It was delicious.

I had brought my guitar with me and after dinner, Brenda and I sang a couple of songs that we both knew. This was the first time we had sung together and without sounding too pretentious, it was a match made in heaven. Our voices blended so well and we nailed the songs. I don't think either of us expected that. We were pretty excited about the possibilities.

Brenda was five years older than me and my mom always warned me about older women. But I would find out soon enough on my own. Brenda had breasts just the way I liked them: one on the port side and one on the starboard side—both in front. We dated for a couple of months during my stay in Bremerton. While we continued to practice our duets, she was ready to find a job as a singer. She had been in a jazz band for a while, but she and the band leader did not get along that well so they parted ways. I was still on the ship and could not practice as much as she could, so after a couple of months *we* parted ways. I did go hear her several more times, but the initial spark wasn't there anymore.

26 BREMERTON
Winding Down in the Shipyards

After January 1, 1977, every letter I wrote home I began with the "188 days and a wake up" or however many days I had left in the Navy. I was getting short and I could feel it. I tried not to let it get to me, but I couldn't help it. I knew the Navy was not for me, but I was determined to complete my four year commitment.

I had to leave my Chevy truck in a parking lot which was about a half mile from the ship. That wasn't so bad. I definitely needed the walking exercise, but there were many times the weather was not so good. After all, this *was* the Pacific Northwest. Besides, the ship was also being painted so I did not want my brand new blue truck to get splattered with battleship gray paint.

The base had a bus that ran to and from the parking lot so I often rode that, along with a bunch of other shipyard workers and sailors. There weren't too many women that worked in the shipyards, but those that worked there, well, let's just say that sometimes it was hard to tell if they were a woman or a man.

One day after work, we were heading to the parking lot in the bus and there was a woman yard worker walking along the side of the road. She saw all these guys on the bus and started shaking her thang, so to speak. The guys on the bus were hooting and hollering and the more they hooted and hollered, the more she strutted. She started to tease the guys with a little more leg and while she was walking along teasing us, she walked straight into a telephone pole. She fell with a bang. She got back up, but that was one of the funniest things I had ever seen. We were all laughing.

A couple of months before we were to leave the shipyards, I was appointed Crash LPO. I was a second class petty officer and since I had experience in Crash and had been on the ship for a couple of years, the division officer decided he would put me in charge. I knew the real reason though. I was a short timer and while we would get out to sea a few times before I was discharged, they were not quite sure where to put me. I didn't mind though, Crash was a tight group. I also knew that we would be getting a new first class petty officer in the division soon and he would take over Crash. That suited me fine.

We were getting close to finishing up in the shipyards. The V-2 division had replaced the catapults so they would be able to take on the heavier F-14 Tomcats. We were still tied to the pier, but the shipyard harbor police barricaded off the water in front of the ship so they could test the catapults. It would not be good to put a plane up there to test, so instead they used small barges on wheels and hooked them up just like a jet plane to the launch shuttle on the catapults. They were about the size of two Cadillacs side by side. It was funny to see them shoot these "no loads" off the ship. They would fly out a couple of hundred feet and land with a big splash.

It was then and there when I came up with one of my most famous quotes in the Navy. Back in the mid-70s there was a series of quotes about retirement: "Old truckers never die; they just get a new Peterbuilt." "Old lawyers never die, they just lose their briefs." You've heard these before. I came up with one for ABs: "Old ABs never die, they just keep shooting 'no loads.' " Yeah, I've heard it before—don't give up my day job.

We had one set of sea trials before we left Bremerton. In late March, we headed out to sea for four days, flying a few aircraft onboard, trapping them, and then watching them shoot off the catapults. Everything on the flight deck looked OK, but from what I heard, some of the snipes were having problems down in the engine rooms. I was in charge of Crash, although it would be only a short time, but we did our job and did it well. We had a bunch of new guys—about half the total crew—and it was my job to break them in right. We still only had ten guys in Crash though.

The weather in Bremerton, as in most of the Puget Sound area, had been absolutely beautiful at times, but most of the time it was dreary, wet, and drizzly. But, I'll tell you this; on those cloudless, crisp, blue, Champagne days, there is no prettier place on God's green earth. A few years later, when I graduated from college, my wife and I moved back out to the Seattle area and spent a great year there.

So what did I take away from Bremerton? I started to realize my normal pattern of a new duty station: get acclimated to the new surroundings, learn where the best bars are located, drink a lot and find good, cheap places to eat, find where the women were then find the right women to hang out with, then start to wind down by staying onboard more. That happened in Guam and again in the Philippines. In both places I hit the bars early in my tour, and then settled down to duty. Hong Kong and Japan were short visits, so there really wasn't a routine. I followed the same pattern up in Bremerton. I don't know if that is the norm for other sailors, but it seemed so for me.

I did not have any problem finding women or dating. I had several good relationships while in Bremerton, but none as close as I thought I had been with Bonnie. I did not have the same feelings and that was probably good. I did not need to get into another heavy relationship; I enjoyed playing the field too much.

I saw snow for the first time in my life. I was singing on stage more and more and people seemed to appreciate it. I was seriously thinking about becoming an entertainer—could this be another possible career? After all, during my entire year in Bremerton, I had made a total of seventy dollars singing in bars as a paid entertainer; maybe I needed a little more work. But, I had also found a new love: electronics. I made an "A" in the electronics course I took at Olympic Community College. Maybe that could be a potential career. Who knows, only time would tell.

27 USS KITTY HAWK
Shakedown and Adios

Kitty Hawk completed her major overhaul in March and departed the Bremerton shipyards April 1, 1977 to return to San Diego. For those of us who wanted to drive, the CO gave us four days to get from Bremerton to San Diego and since I had my new truck, I took advantage of that drive.

I drove alone, no riders except for an occasional hitchhiker. Hitchhiking was a lot safer back in the mid-seventies than it is now. I drove down the coast once I got to Oregon. It was some of the most beautiful scenery I had ever seen and I took my time. There was very little development and only small seaside towns along most of the way. I had bought a camper top for my truck a couple of months earlier and had built some storage boxes and lined the truck bed with thick foam and carpet I had scavenged from the shipyard. I also had some curtains that a girl friend of mine had sewn. It was quite comfortable to sleep in. I did all my cooking on my Coleman stove and, with my guitar, serenaded some of the other campers in campgrounds along the way.

I took the full four days to drive to San Diego. It did not make much sense to hasten the trip since I did not have anywhere to stay if I arrived early. I got to the ship about four hours after she docked at the pier. I also needed to get a parking sticker from the main base and that took a little time. But even though I had a great trip down and the scenery was spectacular, it felt good to be back aboard Kitty Hawk.

The first few days on board were little more than muster, keep yourself busy, and turn to which was the Navy's way of saying, "Clean up." There were several hundred dependents that came back down with the ship and it took a while to get them off the ship—I helped offload the last few groups.

They also needed to find housing on the base so that is why the ship had a short stand-down.

Once we were back in San Diego, the V-1 Division Officer, Lt. Lockram, reassigned me to become a yellow shirt and I ended up in Fly 3. It was to be one the best experiences in my life. I also carried several other collateral duties, including the Division Yeoman, the Division Training Petty Officer, the Division Career Counselor, and the Division First Aid Petty Officer. I did not mind though, I was a short timer and I was a yellow shirt—what could be better than that?

Every yellow shirt used the same basic hand signals on the flight deck to direct aircraft, but every yellow shirt sooner or later developed his own style. We learned all these in A School in Lakehurst, New Jersey and while I tried to be standard, I know I slipped into the Adkins style of directing. When I first went onto the flight deck, I was in training, but since I had been around for a while, it did not take me too long to learn the ropes. Smitty was helping me out, especially in the tough spots.

It was a lot easier to either tow or taxi a plane going forward than backing it up. The tow tractors were also a challenge. While I had backed up a lot of fishing boats over the years, these were completely different. Backing up a fishing boat on a trailer goes the opposite way of the steering wheel since there is only one point of contact, the trailer hitch. Since aircraft tow tractors have two points of contact: the trailer hitch on the back of the tow tractor *and* the nose wheel of the aircraft where the tow bar is connected, the plane goes the way the tractor is turned. It sounds confusing, and it is, but you get used to it.

I had been in Crash for a long time and when I drove the crash trucks, I seemed to always be in somebody's way. The yellow shirts were always telling me to move out of the way. Now it was my turn, but since I had been in Crash's shoes, I asked a little nicer. That is, until the driver either did not pay attention or did not move fast enough. Then I would be all over them.

After a major overhaul like the one we had in Bremerton, the ship had to go through all types of training and qualifications, not only to make sure everything worked, but also to train the crew and the air wing. This is what keeps the Navy in top operating condition—training, more training, and additional training on top of that training.

Our first time out at sea was almost a homecoming. It wasn't just me; it was the whole crew, at least those of us who worked on the flight deck. I may have sounded like a lifer, but it felt really good to get back out to sea and get into the routine of flight operations.

We got the Navy's newest fighter, the F-14 "Tomcat." They were bigger than the F-4 Phantoms, but did not look as mean. Instead of a fixed wing that folded for parking, the F-14 had wings that retracted back toward the rear of the plane, almost like a bird tucking its wings. The wings would be fully extended for takeoff, but during flight for speed, they would retract in the swept wing position, providing less wind resistance and letting the F-14 quickly reach supersonic speeds.

The F-14, also known as a "Turkey," could reach speeds of 1,500 mph or mach two-plus at altitude. It could break the sound barrier at sea level. It carried a crew of two: a pilot and a RIO, similar to the F-4 Phantom. The F-4 Phantom was originally designed in 1958 and after almost twenty years of service was replaced by the F-14. We trained with the same squadrons and many of the same pilots—they had learned to fly the new F-14s.

We also got the newer S-3 "Viking" anti-submarine warfare aircraft, also called "Hoovers" because it sounded like a vacuum cleaner when they applied full power. These guys replaced the older gasoline-powered S-2s and carried a crew of four. Similar to the S-2s, their mission was to drop sonobuoys and helped track enemy submarines. These planes had a huge cockpit window, similar to the old AMC Pacer automobile. When the movie *Wayne's World* came out, the scene in Garth's AMC Pacer of everyone singing Queen's *Bohemian Rhapsody* and bobbing their heads in time to the music reminded me of the S-3.

On our first at sea period, one of the ship's crew jumped overboard. I'm not sure if he was on the flight deck or the hangar deck, but he jumped and started swimming back toward San Diego. The CO announced over the 1MC, "Man Overboard! Man Overboard! Starboard side," which meant the guy was on the right side of the ship and the ship turned into that side so that hopefully he would not get sucked under the ship into the massive propellers.

I was not sure of the whole story, but rumor was that this kid had received a letter from home and his mom had been in a bad automobile accident and lost both legs. I guess he thought he needed to get home to be by her side, I don't know. I also heard that when the rescue helo crewman jumped in to get him, he was fighting him all the way back. He did not want to come back aboard.

Between the time Kitty Hawk got back to San Diego and the time I was discharged, we were at sea six times. I was a yellow shirt in Fly 3, Flight Deck Director #36. The third time out I asked to be the Gear Puller, the yellow shirt that stood on the angle of the flight deck directing aircraft out of the recovery area after they've trapped. It only took a couple of cycles with Smitty for me to get trained.

You stand in the crotch, between the angle and #2 catapult, just forward of the #2 JBD, just starboard of the foul line. You could be in deep shit if anything happened so, as Smitty put it, "think about where you are and where you want to jump." The job was simple: wait until the plane traps safely, run out to meet the plane and make sure the pilot sees you (you're about twenty feet away), give him the hook up signal, and if the hook raises, start taxiing him out of the recovery area, turning him to the starboard side, give him the signal to fold wings, and pass him along to another yellow shirt in Fly 2. Then thirty seconds later, do it all over again.

This was my favorite job on the flight deck. I don't know why, but I enjoyed this post more than any other. There was, however, one harrowing experience that almost changed my mind.

We were running flight ops as we always did and I was in the crotch directing aircraft out of the recovery area. During this particular flight op, we were launching at the same time as recovering. We had recovered the first batch of F-14s and A-6s and were bringing aboard the A-7s. At the same time, we were launching F-14s on cat #2, right next to me. It was really loud when you are that close to an F-14 in afterburner, even though I was in no danger of getting blown over.

After the third A-7 Corsair landed and I taxied him out of the recovery area, I was watching the next one approach. He was flying a little awkward so I figured he was a new pilot still working on his quals and not used to landing on a flight deck. Meanwhile, an F-14 was preparing for launch right next to me and my attention was bouncing back between the F-14 in full afterburner preparing to launch and the A-7 landing. I was stooping down ready to spring into action when the A-7 landed. As it hit the deck, it grabbed a wire with its hook and the pilot applied full power as they always did. The only problem was that this A-7 pilot not only applied full power, but also pulled back on his elevator at the same time. He had the cable in his tail hook, yet he was also about ten feet off the ground fixing to make a big splat.

Let me pause here at this particular moment in time and relay to you what was going on. For one, the A-7 Corsair was in the air about ten feet above the deck with an arresting cable in his tail hook, soon to splatter on the flight deck. I was less than fifty feet away. To my left, about twenty feet away was an F-14 Tomcat in full afterburner ready to launch. To my right, about five feet away was a sixty foot drop down to Davy Jones' locker. It was not looking like a good day. I basically had two choices to make: one, become instant toast or two, find out if Davy Jones really does have a locker.

At that moment, I think every flight deck crash training film I had ever seen flashed through my mind and none of them were good thoughts. I had heard of an A-7 Corsair earlier on the Constellation that had done the exact same thing, but when he slammed down onto the flight deck, the nose gear slammed up and pierced the cockpit, right between the pilot's legs. The pilot was OK, but the A-7 was not. No fire, thank God, but it took a while to clear the recovery area. That was the thought I had in my mind.

I jumped up very quickly. The Shooter on cat #2 had seen what was happening and immediately went into an abort mode, shutting down the F-

14. The A-7 slammed into the deck, but the nose gear held and did not go through the cockpit. The pilot was a little shaken, as was I, but we both managed to get the A-7 out of the recovery area without having to change skivvies. I was fine after that, but it did shake me up a little bit. Smitty came over and asked if I needed a break; I took him up on his offer. As my dad would say later on when I relayed this particular story, "Builds character, doesn't it?"

During one of our sea times, one of the yellow shirts found a listing of what was commonly known as Falcon Codes. I do not know who created these, but the idea of the Falcon Codes was to provide a short cut of "thoughts" that you could not say over radio frequencies. Most of them were vulgar and since you would get your ass chewed out if you muttered "Beats the shit out of me" or "You must have shit for brains," you would instead say Falcon 103 or Falcon 173.

We had fun with these on the flight deck and most of the time, you would say it quickly and no one could tell who was saying it. As I got closer to my discharge date, my favorite was Falcon 116 which meant, "Short! Fuck it!"

I had my Chevy truck which I aptly named the Chet Mobile and I parked it in the lot adjacent to Kitty Hawk. I had also gotten used to doing my own laundry, even though you could still get your Navy uniforms cleaned on the ship. I did not bother looking for an apartment. Why waste money when you have free room and board? I spent some time off the ship as usual but the ship would not wash civilian clothes so we had to do our own. These days, carriers not only have their own laundry service, but they also provide debit-card-operated washers and dryers where you can wash your own clothes.

Just outside the gate of the North Island Naval Station was the city of Coronado, a small bedroom community with several streets of shops and diners. Steve Cummings and I would often take our dirty clothes into town, walking since it was only about a half mile, and do our own laundry. We had a system down: we would drop the loads in to be washed, then walk next door to a small diner and order a hamburger and fries. When we were done with that, we would go back and throw the clothes into the dryer, then back to the diner for apple pie and ice cream. When we finished eating, the clothes were done. It helped to pass the time. Every now and then, we would walk across the street and catch a movie, leaving our clean clothes in a mesh bag behind the concession stand. The theater folks were quite nice to us military guys.

Steve was a really smart kid from Peoria, Illinois. He and I had been on the tour together in Hong Kong and had begun to hang out together. Steve was an exceptional ABH and an outstanding yellow shirt. In fact, in February 1977 when we were in the shipyards, Steve had been selected the Kitty Hawk Sailor of the Month.

I had also checked into the flying club at the Naval Air Station. I figured I would be here for another few months and should fly a few more times before I left. I did not fly at all in Bremerton—the only reason was that I was paying for a truck and did not have much extra cash. I wished I had though, because that was some beautiful country. I got checked out in both the Cessna 150 and the 172 and since I had my pilot's license, I could take passengers up. Several of my friends got the benefits of my flying experience and the area around San Diego, especially up north toward Oceanside and Laguna Hills, was spectacular. South of San Diego toward Mexico, it always seemed to be smoggy.

Gary Borne, Ed Boes, and I took a trip one day down to Tijuana, Mexico. It wasn't far from the base and we took a bus to the border crossing which took less than an hour. Once at the border, we had to go through the Border Patrol which was nothing more than showing them our military ID cards and telling them we would be back by midnight. Sort of like the time when you went on your first date in high school—your parents wanted to know who, what, where, when, and if you were a guy, how.

We walked into Tijuana which took about another thirty minutes. Even though there were taxis all over the place, we were saving our money. We hit a few bars, tried to bargain with a few Mexicans that were selling some worthless crap from booths on the street, then ended up in a bar to grab some food and a couple of drinks. We were immediately surrounded by three young Mexican girls that sat down really close to us. Who knows where this is going: it could be interesting.

I ordered a beer for me and a drink for my new friend. I paid for it with a twenty dollar bill—they took US dollars—and put the ten back in my pocket. We were drinking and shooting the bull and the girls were rubbing themselves all over us. My new friend was rubbing my crotch and I was naturally reacting. I asked her if she wanted to find a room, but she kept talking and kept rubbing. I ordered another beer and was feeling pretty good. Soon thereafter, I guess the girls got bored or whatever, so they decided to leave. Besides, we hadn't bought them more than one drink.

It was getting late, so we decided to head back across the border and back to the ship. Along the way we were talking about the hot women and Ed made a comment about faking his girl out by *not* putting any money in his front pocket. She was rubbing him anyway. It took a minute to sink in, then I checked my front pants pocket. The ten dollar bill I had put in there after ordering the drink was gone. The girl had rubbed it out. I laughed out loud and Gary and Ed both asked what was so funny. I told them the story and we all had a good laugh on me. I was not going to be able to live this one down.

Dave Sharp was also another good friend. He was from Texarkana and was one of the blue shirt tractor drivers in the division. He had found a decent bar at a bowling alley called "The Alamo" and talked several of us into going there. It had a tight band, playing great country and oldies music, as well as having a large dance floor. Another place I would soon call home.

In fact, I was at The Alamo almost every Friday and Saturday night. It was far enough from the Naval base in San Diego that it attracted some nice looking women. I took advantage of that, especially since they had a large dance floor. I met several young ladies there and on several occasions, we went out on a date or two. I made the mistake though that I should have learned from Big Willie in the Philippines. Never, *never* date two girls who frequent the same bar. It only took once and I lost both of them, so to speak, but I guess I deserved it.

The house band at The Alamo was a really tight four-piece band and knew almost every country song in the book. Their lead guitar player was the best I had ever heard and also played a mean pedal-steel guitar. There was always a crowd and the dance floor was always packed. This was the type of place where everyone on the dance floor would sing along to the dance tunes—you know the type. Back then, there were some of the older songs that required hand movements, like the "mash potato," the "swim," the "bump," the "hand jive," and the ever popular "twist." We all had such a good time there.

On one of these occasions, I had found a good dance partner and spent most of the night dancing with her. During one dance she kept staring at me and I asked her what she was thinking. I should point out here that you should *never* ask a girl what she's thinking—it might shock you. "I'm undressing you with my eyes." Well, this could be interesting.

We danced a few more dances, then got a table and ordered drinks. I was obviously interested and when she got that wistful look again, I again asked, "What are you thinking about?" I should point out *again* that you should never, *never* ask a girl what she's thinking. "I'm dying of cancer and only have three months to live." Well, goodbye is all she wrote. Like the beach babe on Waikiki Beach, I was history. No sense getting involved with this nut case. Good call, too, because I saw her several more times at The Alamo several months after that using the same line with different guys.

After the third or fourth time at The Alamo, I asked the band if they knew *The Auctioneer*. Of course they knew the song, but could not sing it. I climbed up on stage and sang *The Auctioneer* which was always a crowd pleaser. I also sang a couple of other songs too, then took my bows and got off to dance some more.

This was a popular place and one of San Diego's leading country radio stations, KZON, held a talent contest in May. Since I had been singing there for a while, everybody, including the band, said I should enter the contest. Well, the only problem was that Kitty Hawk was supposed to be at sea the day of the contest. Lt. Lockram gave me a few errands to do so I would stay at the Naval Station through the day of the contest, then fly out with the COD to Kitty Hawk the following day. I liked Lt. Lockram, "old buddy, old pal, great friend of mine!"

There were five of us that had entered the talent contest: two women and three guys. A couple of the contestants played their own guitar and sang; they were outstanding. The rest of us used the house band which I thought added much more to the performance. I was the last one up; they obviously did not follow the alphabetical order rule. I didn't mind, it gave me the opportunity to have a few drinks of courage before I was to go on. The guy before me, whom I thought was fantastic, belted out an old Jim Reeves tune, *Make the World Go Away*, a song I had sung many times. He got a thunderous round of applause which he so deserved.

My turn—no doubt I was going to sing *The Auctioneer*, my favorite song. The band was up for it and I think I sang it this time better than ever before. I was under a little pressure from being in the contest and it showed because I forgot the words to the last verse. It didn't matter though. I just sang the first verse over again. By the time I got up on stage, the crowd was half-drunk anyway, so what did they care. But I did get a great applause, one that lasted for a long time.

When it came down to it, the band judged the contest based on the crowd applause for each contestant. We were all lined up and everyone got a great hand; when they got to me, the last one, it was out of sight—I think everyone was on their feet hooting and hollering. I was having a great time. I won the talent show and was presented with $150 check and a gift certificate to a local restaurant. I tell you, this could be another career for me.

In June 1977, a new high tech science fiction movie was out and a few of us wanted to see it since everyone was talking about it. We must have gone to three or four movie theaters around San Diego, but there was no way we were going to stand in line for three hours waiting for tickets. The Internet World Wide Web did not exist back then and you could not order tickets online through Fandango. It would be a few more months before I was able to see *Star Wars*. This reminded me of the long lines of cars during the oil embargo when I was in Guam.

My last couple of days aboard Kitty Hawk were full of mixed feelings. These emotions were different than when I had been in Guam. I wasn't leaving a girlfriend—I was leaving a home. I wasn't being transferred to another duty station—I was leaving *for* home. Kitty Hawk had been a great ship and most of the crew that I worked with I considered family.

My sister Anne had flown out to San Diego—we were going to drive back to Florida together and see the country. I took her on board the ship for a grand tour. I told her not to wear a dress since the ladders were very steep and anyone at the bottom of the ladder could see well up the ladder, if you know what I mean. I showed her the ship's forecastle, our berthing compartment, the mess hall, the Crash compartment, and all over the flight deck. We did not have any planes onboard, but it was still a grand tour for her.

I sang my last song at The Alamo when Anne came out. I wanted her to hear her little brother belt out a tune or two. I think she enjoyed it and I had set her up on a blind date with one of my friends, "Stretch" Andrews. He was one of the guys who labeled his shower shoes Port and Starboard. A nice guy and great Fly 2 yellow shirt.

I had to fill out a lot of paperwork which I really did not mind. I knew the main reason was because I was getting discharged. The last paper to sign was my discharge papers, the infamous DD-214. No problem—"press hard, the third copy's yours."

And with that, I was no longer a member of Uncle Sam's Sailing Club. I was once again a civilian. Of course, at the time it did not really feel any different, and it would take some time before I realized I was truly out of the Navy.

While I was technically out of the Navy, I was still considered "Inactive Reserve," meaning the Navy could call me up out of the blue if they needed me. I would be Inactive Reserve for two more years. My dad suggested that I stay in the active Navy Reserve which meant I would have to meet one weekend a month and two weeks in the summer, but I said "No, I had had enough."

It is also a Navy tradition to have someone carry your seabag off the ship for you that one last time. I thought about it, but I did not ask anyone, mainly because I was ready to boogie and I did not want to say goodbye to anyone else. I closed up my lockers in both Crash (I secretly kept one there without anyone really asking) and the V-1 Division berthing compartment. I packed my seabag with all my Navy uniforms as well as my civvies. The Navy lets you keep all of your uniforms—like I might wear them again.

I had dressed in civvies—blue jeans and a pull over shirt—to make my last walk across the After brow. As usual, I saluted the petty officer of the watch and asked one more time, "Permission to go ashore, sir." He bid me farewell and good luck. I saluted the flag one more time, even in civilian clothes—it was an old habit. I thought about leaving a souvenir behind, something for my buddies to remember ol' Chet Adkins, but I didn't. Like I said, I was ready to leave. It was me, my seabag, and my 12-string guitar.

There was no fanfare, no band, no one on the pier waiting for me. There were no tears or sorrowful looks. Anne was back at the hotel I had put her up in, so I headed to my truck, threw my seabag in the back, and headed out through the gate one last time. It had been an interesting career—all *three years, eleven months, and 29 days: but who's counting?*

28 USS KITTY HAWK
Decommission

After forty-eight years of faithful service, USS Kitty Hawk was decommissioned in Bremerton, Washington on January 31, 2009. Her active duty covered the Vietnam War, the Gulf War, and the Global War on Terrorism. Throughout her lifetime, Kitty Hawk had 407,511 arrested carrier landings and 448,301 launches (who keeps these statistics?). On August 6, 2008, the final trap and catapult launch was made, and the ship pulled into San Diego the next morning for the turnover to the USS George Washington.

She had been to the shipyards many times for retrofits, including the $100 million overhaul in Bremerton, Washington in 1976, in which I participated. The carrier completed the overhaul in March 1977 and departed the shipyard April 1 of that year to return to San Diego. I was aboard Kitty Hawk during that entire time.

Kitty Hawk left San Diego for the last time on Thursday, August 28, 2008 bound for its next stop: Bremerton Naval Ship Yards. The Kitty Hawk Veterans Association had been working diligently with Kitty Hawk and the Navy to get former shipmates on board for this last cruise and had been successful. Unfortunately for me, I was stuck in Arkansas attending a trial in which I was supposed to testify as an expert witness, but never did. So I missed the chance of a lifetime to make one last cruise on her. However, sixty-five former crew members made the cruise, including thirty-eight crew members who had been onboard when Kitty Hawk was originally commissioned in 1961; these guys are affectionately called "Plank Owners."

More than two thousand former shipmates, crew members, guests, and distinguished visitors attended the January 31, 2009 decommissioning ceremony in Bremerton. I made this special trip. This was the first time I had seen Kitty Hawk in more than thirty years.

When I first got to Bremerton, I walked up and down the pier several times, admiring her and remembering my time aboard. Since the ship was docked on the starboard side as always, the bow was closest to the parking lot. I thought of the many times I stuck my head out the mooring lines porthole, looking down at the huge keel piercing the water like a hot knife through butter. I looked up at the bow and caught sight of the safety nets and thought of the times I had stood on the bow at sea with my foul weather jacket unzipped, holding it with my outstretched hands and leaning over so far it felt as if I might take off and fly.

I thought of the hundreds of times I had climbed the steps and made the trip across the After brow saluting the colors and the watch, coming aboard and leaving the ship. The elevators were as big as I remembered them— enough to hold two F-14 Tomcats with crews ready to man them for flight operations.

Unfortunately, because there were so many civilians and guests aboard, the crew would not allow us to tour any of the ship nor go up onto the flight deck. We were restricted to the hangar deck which is where the ceremonies would be held. That was OK though. Just seeing her and being able to board her one last time was enough.

As I climbed aboard her for the ceremonies, I experienced a wide range of emotions. In July 1977, all I wanted to do was get off the carrier and get out of the Navy. Thirty-two years later, I was happy to be aboard her one last time. The ship's CO, Captain Todd A. Zecchin, served as the master of ceremonies and gave an eloquent presentation of Kitty Hawk's rich history. Admiral Timothy Keating, Commander, U.S. Pacific Command, also gave a wonderful, heartfelt speech since he had also served aboard Kitty Hawk.

It is not certain what the next step will be for Kitty Hawk. There is a lot of scuttlebutt floating around including selling her to India. But what most people are hoping, old shipmates as well as the new shipmates, is that Kitty Hawk's final resting place will be in North Carolina, home to her namesake.

Currently, the United States maintains ten aircraft carriers in service. The newer Nimitz-class nuclear powered carriers cost about $4.5 billion to construct compared to the $265 million price tag for Kitty Hawk in 1961. Of the twelve carriers, eight of them are considered Nimitz-class carriers which means they are CVN-68 or higher. Since the Nimitz was first commissioned in 1975, the Nimitz-class carriers have been around for more than thirty years. The following is a list of active (as of 2013) United States aircraft carriers:

Designation	Name	Commissioned	Home port
CVN-68	Chester W. Nimitz	May 3, 1975	San Diego, CA
CVN-69	Dwight D. Eisenhower	Oct 18, 1977	Norfolk, VA
CVN-70	Carl Vinson	Mar 13, 1982	Newport News, VA
CVN-71	Theodore Roosevelt	Oct 25, 1986	Norfolk, VA
CVN-72	Abraham Lincoln	Nov 11, 1989	Everett, WA
CVN-73	George Washington	Jul 4, 1992	Yokosuka, Japan
CVN-74	John C. Stennis	Dec 9, 1995	Bremerton, WA
CVN-75	Harry S. Truman	Jul 25, 1998	Norfolk, VA
CVN-76	Ronald Reagan	Jul 12, 2003	San Diego, CA
CVN-77	George H.W. Bush	Jan 10, 2009	Norfolk, VA

Under Construction:

CVN-78	Gerald R. Ford	2015	(Gerald R. Ford class)
CVN-79	John F. Kennedy	2020	(Gerald R. Ford class)
CVN-80	Enterprise	2025	(Gerald R. Ford class)

GLOSSARY

O'dark hundred: Pronounced "oh dark." Refers to some point really early in the morning, like 0200, which would be pronounced, "oh-two-hundred."

O'dark thirty: One half hour after "O'dark hundred."

1MC: One of many communication circuits aboard a ship, this is probably the most widely recognized. When used, it is heard on every external speaker by everyone aboard the ship.

A-Farts: A slang term for Armed Forces Radio & Television Service. A-Farts is received via satellite all over the world and offers a variety of shows. Some of the most entertaining offerings are the propaganda commercials it frequently airs since regular advertising is not permitted.

Affirmative: A "yes" response.

A-Gang: A term used to describe the Auxiliaries Division of the Engineering Department. Members are commonly known as "A-Gangers."

Air Boss: Air Officer. A term used to describe the head of the Air Department. His assistant is the "Mini Boss."

Airedale: A term used to describe a sailor who works on or around aircraft, whether shore duty or at sea.

Air Wing: The aviation detachment on board the ship usually comprised of several different air squadrons.

A.J. Squared Away: A term used to describe a sailor who is always "squared away," meaning always having a perfect shave, perfectly ironed uniform, spit-shined shoes, haircut with less than 1mm of hair, spotless uniform, etc. Anyone who has been designated with this nickname is most likely a lifer who has no life outside the Navy. Compare to "dirtbag" below.

Another Fine Navy Day!: An expression voiced (in a very cheery manner) on occasions when, in fact, it's not that much of a Fine Navy Day at all.

Assholes and Elbows: A term usually used by a superior enlisted man, such as a CPO and used to describe a deck hand on his hands and knees holystoning a wooden deck. As in "All I want to see is assholes and elbows," as spoken by a Boatswains Mate.

AWOL: An acronym for "Absent without Leave."

Aye: Another word for "Yes" (I understand).

Aye, aye: Another term for "Yes" (I heard the order, I understand the order, and I intend to obey the order). Similar to the Army's "HUA"—Heard, Understood, Acknowledged.

Bag of Dicks: A term used to receive or pass on to a fellow sailor a complete bone job, usually one of which that is given to you at 1500 and will require at least 3 hours to complete. Also called "getting bagged."

Balls to The Wall: An expression that originally referred to the balls on top of the throttles in an aircraft. If one needed full throttle, the balls were, quite literally, pushed forward to the firewall—hence, "balls to the wall."

Bandit: A term used to describe aircraft positively identified as hostile.

Barney Clark: A term used to describe a slider topped with a fried egg. Also known as a "One-Eyed Jack."

Barricade: Also called the barrier, a huge nylon net strung across the landing area of an aircraft carrier's flight deck to arrest the landing of an aircraft with damaged gear or a damaged tail hook.

Batphone: A dedicated outside telephone line (not for personal use) typically for shore power or security purposes, and usually only from one station to another.

Battle Group (BG): A term used to describe a group of warships and supply ships centered around a large aircraft carrier and its airwing. Usually consists of one cruiser, one supply ship, and one or two destroyers, frigates, and submarines. The term has been sanitized and is now referred to as the Carrier Strike Group (CSG).

BCG's: An acronym for "Birth Control Glasses." Nearly indestructible Standard Navy-issue corrective eye wear worn by new recruits. They are so named because they are so thick and hideous that you are guaranteed never to have sex while you are wearing them. The term has become obsolete due to more normal looking frame choices offered nowadays (outside of recruit training, at least).

Beer Day: On many Navy ships, even in the present day, all hands are given two beers if they are underway without a port call for a given period of time—generally 45 days. Both beers are opened when they are given to the crew member to prevent them from being hoarded. Considering what you have to go through to "earn" a beer day, they are definitely not the best deal.

Bells: The Navy way of announcing the time of day aboard ship, usually over the 1MC. One bell corresponds to 30 minutes past the hour. Bells will only be rung as a single strike, or a closely spaced double strike, with a maximum of eight bells (4 sets of 2). Bells repeat themselves every 4 hours. For example 2 sets of 2 bells, followed by a single bell could be 0230, 0630, 1030, 1430, 1830, or 2230.

Benny, bennie: Another term for a treat or a reward, derived from "Benefit."

Bent Shitcan: A term used to describe someone somewhat below Navy standards.

Bilge: The lowest part of a ship, below the engines where fluids like used oil and sea water gather. Also, another term for a very nasty location.

Bilge Rat: A term used to describe someone who works in the engineering spaces.

Bilge Turd: A derogatory term for a "Boiler Technician," typically from Machinist Mates who attend the identical "A" School.

Billet: An assigned position within a command. Usually, a permanent job assignment.

BINGO: A term used to describe the minimum fuel needed to return to base (RTB).

Birdfarm: Another term for an aircraft carrier.

Bitchbox: The intercom or an amplified circuit used to communicate between spaces of a ship.

Bitching Betty: The computer generated female voice heard in an aviator's earpiece when something is not as it should be. Usually caused by unsafe flight conditions or an enemy threat.

Black Shoe: A term used to describe any "surface Navy" personnel. See also "Brown Shoe."

Bluejacket: A term used to describe an enlisted sailor below the rank of E-7 (Chief Petty Officer).

Bluejacket's Manual: The handbook of seamanship issued to new Navy recruits.

Bluenose: A term used to describe an individual in the Navy who has crossed the Arctic Circle.

Boat: Water craft small enough to be carried on a ship, unless a submarine, which is *always* called a boat. A ship may be called a boat but *only* by members of its crew, and only those who have actually completed a deployment aboard a "boat."

Boats: A shortened nickname used to describe a sailor in the Boatswain's Mate rating.

Bogey: A term used to describe unknown aircraft which could be friendly, hostile, or neutral.

Bolter: A failed attempt at an arrested landing on a carrier by a fixed-wing aircraft. Usually caused by a poor approach or a hook bounce on the deck, this embarrassing event leads to a go-around and another attempt to "board."

Boondockers: The medium cut combat boots issued in boot camp to new recruits.

Boondoggle: A term used to describe any unorganized, inefficient evolution. It is similar to a "goatrope."

B.O.S.N.I.A.: An acronym for "Big Ol' Standard Navy-Issue Ass," from the apparent widening of the hips due in part to the cut of the working uniforms.

Bosun's Punch: New sailors on ship are sometimes assigned to find this mythical tool in the office of one of the ship's Bosuns (Boatswain). The sailor is then typically punched very hard in the shoulder by the Bosun in question.

Bounce Pattern: A term used when several aircraft are practicing touch and go landings at the same airfield.

Brain Fart: A term used to describe a condition when, under stress, one cannot recall or perform something that would normally be easy or second nature.

Branch: The lowest organizational level in most Navy commands, below department and division.

Bravo Zulu: A term used to describe a job well done.

Bremerloes: A term used to describe a female of husky build. It originated at Bremerton, Washington in the shipyards where they are rather common.

Brig: Another term for jail.

Brigchaser: A term used to describe a Sailor escorting a prisoner to the brig.

Broke-dick: A technical term describing malfunctioning or inoperable equipment. Example: "The fuckin' aux drain pump is a fuckin' broke-dick."

Brown bagger: A term used to describe a married sailor who brings his lunch from home in a paper bag.

Brown Nose: A term used to describe a sailor trying a "little too hard" to make rate by sucking up to superiors. Can also refer to those who wear khakis (Chiefs, Officers) since it is assumed that most have "brown-nosed" to obtain their present position.

Brown Shoe: Any "Naval Aviation" officer or CPO. It is a reference to the brown shoes that were exclusive to the aviation community. It has since become outdated as all naval officers and Chief Petty Officers (Chiefs) wear brown shoes. However, because of cultural bias among "lifers" (career personnel), this term remains active. Note: Aviators still wear brown shoes with their khaki uniforms. Being called a brown-shoe is considered a term of endearment. "Black-shoe" is a derogatory term used by aviators in reference to ship drivers, much like carrier aviators refer to the carrier as "the boat" just to piss off the black shoes.

B.T.S.O.O.M.: An acronym for "Beats the Shit Out of Me." A usual response from a sailor who hasn't a clue.

Bug Juice: A term used to describe the Kool-Aid-like beverage in dispensers on the mess deck. They are usually side-by-side—Orange or Red. Before the turn of the century, bug juice was also used as a replacement for cleaning agents used to clean decks.

Bug Juice Sunrise: A term used to describe orange bug juice with a splash of red bug juice.

Bulkhead: Another term for wall.

Bulkhead remover: An in-joke shared by veteran sailors and often delegated as a task to new sailors, as in, "Go get me a can of bulkhead remover."

Bullet Sponge: Another term sailors use to describe a U.S. Marine.

Bun: A term used to describe a sexually active female sailor.

Burn a copy: A term meaning make a Xerox copy of a document or sheet of paper.

Butt Kit: Another term for an ash tray. Aboard ship, it is a can with a hole in the lid, usually hung from the bulkhead near watch stations.

CF (pronounced Charlie Foxtrot): An acronym for "Cluster fuck."

CAG: A title used when addressing the airwing commander. It is a holdover from the days when airwings were called air groups and stands for Commander Air Group. It can also refer to the airwing itself, as in CAG-14.

Cake Eater: A term used to describe a sailor who reenlists. This is derived from the fact that upon re-enlistment, most commands present you with a cake at your ceremony.

Canoe Club: Another term for the United States Navy.

Canoe U: Another term for the United States Naval Academy.

Captain's Mast: A Navy term for non-judicial punishment under Article 15 of the Uniform Code of Military Justice. Depending on the rank or position involved, the name of the procedure may change, i.e. Admiral's Mast, OIC's Mast.

Carrier Strike Group (CSG): See "Battle Group."

Carry on: An officer's reply to a junior person's call to "attention on deck," meaning all present rise and come to attention as a sign of respect. "Carry on" allows personnel to continue whatever they were doing.

CDO: An acronym for "Command Duty Officer."

Chain of Command: The strict order or hierarchy from the least ranking individual up to the highest ranking individual within a particular command. It is also known as the "pecking order."

Chest Candy: The ribbons, insignia, and awards worn on a uniform.

Chit: The name given to the document a sailor fills out to make various types of special requests (i.e. emergency leave, move off base to civilian housing, etc.).

My Wife Chit: A special request that uses the wife as the excuse or justification for needing to be absent.

Chit Chipper: Another term for a paper shredder. So named because you can't do anything with a chit, especially one that is "lost in routing."

Chow: Another term for food.

Chow Boss: Another term for the Food Service Officer.

Chow down: Another term meaning to eat.

Chow Hall: Another term for the dining room.

Chowdale: A term given to airwing personnel that spend all their time in line for chow, holding up those that actually have things to do.

Chub Club: Another term for sailors assigned mandatory physical training due to being overweight.

C.I.C.: An acronym for "Combat Information Center."

Cinderella Liberty: Another term for liberty that expires at midnight.

Civvies: Another term for civilian clothing.

Cleaning Stations: An hour-long field day evolution where everyone drops what they're doing and cleans their spaces.

COB (Submarine Service): An acronym for the "Chief of the Boat," usually the senior chief aboard.

COD: An acronym for the "Carrier Onboard Delivery," the mighty C-2 Greyhound, which ferries people and supplies to and from the carrier on a regular basis.

Coffin Locker: Another term for a personal storage area located underneath a sailor's rack.

Cold Shot: Another term for a catapult launch from a carrier in which insufficient speed is attained to generate lift. It is often fatal for the aircrew if they do not eject in time.

Colors: Another term for the American flag. Also, it can mean the raising, lowering, or presentation of the American flag.

Comp Time: A shortened term for Compensation Time, time/days off during the week for shore-based sailors who had weekend assignments, above and beyond mere watch-standing.

Corpsman Candy: Another term for the sore-throat lozenges handed out at Sickbay in lieu of any substantive treatment. Sometimes, they are accompanied by two aspirin.

Cover: Another term for a hat.

Cracker Jacks: A slang term for the dress blue uniforms worn by sailors below the rank of E-7.

Crash & Smash: A term used to describe the permanently assigned flight deck firefighting personnel in the V-1 Division. Also, a game played by aviation personnel involving several long tables and a great deal of beer, wherein the aviators attempt to replicate with their bodies the arrested landings their aircraft make.

Creamed foreskins: Another term for creamed chipped beef. See also "SOS."

Crow: Another term for the eagle insignia for petty officer rank used on a white uniform.

DD214: A sailor's dream: the official discharge papers.

Davy Jones' locker: A term used to describe the bottom of the ocean.

Dear John Letter: A letter (or nowadays, e-mail) that a sailor receives in which his significant other breaks up with/leaves him while he is underway.

Deck: Another term for floor.

Deck Ape: A term used to describe non-designated enlisted person serving on the deck force, often as result of washing out of "A" school or being stripped of another rating.

Deep Six: An obsolete term for throwing something overboard; refers to the "deep six," the lowest fathom (six feet) before the ocean floor.

Department: The highest organizational level in most naval commands. Common departments are admin, deck, air, engineering, operations, and maintenance. Departments are further broken up into Divisions.

Detailer: The Bureau of Navy Personnel (BUPERS) person responsible for personnel assignments for sailors and officers.

Dickbag: A term used in place of "Douche bag," but also can be used in place of "dirt bag."

Dick Skinners: Another term for hands. For example, "get your dick skinners off my white hat."

Dicksmith: Yet another derogatory term for hospital corpsmen.

D.I.L.L.I.G.A.F: An acronym for "Do I Look Like I Give A Fuck?" A term indicating supreme indifference; "Gaffer."

Dirtbag: A term often used by an annoying lifer who has no life outside the Navy to insult a sailor for having a few wrinkles in his uniform, having missed a spot while shaving, having a small spot on his uniform, or having hair barely touching his ears. Compare to "A.J. Squared Away" above.

Dirty-shirt wardroom: Another term for the forward wardroom for pilots on an aircraft carrier wearing (sweaty) flight gear. As opposed to formal ship's wardroom.

Ditch: To intentionally crash land an aircraft as "gently" as possible—usually into the water. This is generally done when fuel is almost all used up with no hope of making it to a safe landing area, or when a slowly developing but potentially fatal emergency occurs.

Division: Middle organizational level in most naval commands, below Department and above Branch. Divisions are usually headed by a junior officer (JO).

DIVO: An acronym for "DIVision Officer."

Ditty bag: Any mesh bag, but so named because usually used to contain soiled laundry.

Dixie Cup: The white visorless canvas hat sailors wear with their dress uniforms.

Donkey-Dick: A term used for many nozzle shaped implements.

Douche Kit: A container (usually zipper closed) for toilet articles such as shaving cream, deodorant, after shave lotion, etc.

Down: A term used to describe something that is not working, out of commission, broken, or a "broke-dick." In aviation, a non-flyable aircraft, usually for maintenance reasons. When applied to an aviator, it means he or she is not allowed to fly. This can be for a variety of reasons: medical, personal, disciplinary, etc.

Drifty: A term used to describe a sailor lacking the ability to stay focused while attempting to perform a given task. (Petty Officer to sailor, "Is there something the matter with you? You are acting drifty today!"

Drifter: A term used to describe a sailor who at all times lacks the ability to stay focused. Also called drift-pack, or in the very extreme case "COMNAVDRIFTPAC," a parody of COMNAVSURFPAC.

Drop a Chit: The act of filling out a chit.

Drop your cocks and grab your socks: A saying that the petty officer of the watch yells in the sleeping quarters when it's time for everyone to get up. Often first heard in boot camp.

Dynamited Chicken: Another term for Chicken a la King or Chicken Cacciatore.

EOD: An acronym for "Explosive Ordnance Disposal."

Fart sack: Another term for a canvas mattress cover.

Fart Suit: A dry suit worn by aviators when flying over extremely cold water. So called because of the rubber seals at the neck and wrists which keep water out in the event of water entry. These seals also keep all flatulence inside the suit, where it remains hot and mixes with ball sweat, pitstink, and various other foulness. This foul air is released by removing the suit, or more amusingly by pulling one of the wrist seals open while squatting and pointing at an unsuspecting individual, thus forcing all the stench in his direction.

Field Day: A term used to describe when all hands clean-up and usually lasts on a good day about 3-4 hours. (30 min of cleaning and 2-4 hours of fucking off.)

Field Survey: To discard a worn-out item ("in the field," often off the end of the pier) instead of submitting for formal "survey" to determine redistribution or disposal. Sometimes items are passed down to a needier local unit.

F.I.I.G.M.O.: An acronym for "Fuck It, I Got My Orders." It refers to a sailor's refusal of a long or tough assignment near the end of a duty rotation. Also seen as a name badge at this time, so officers/petty officers will forget your real name.

Fighting gear: Another term for eating utensils.

Five and Dimes: A watch rotation where the sailor or watch team stand five hours of watch, then have ten hours off (to clean, perform maintenance, train, get qualified, conduct drills, take care of divisional business or their collateral duty, eat, shower, and occasionally sleep). This follows from a three-section watch rotation and results in the sailor standing watch at a different time every day and night, repeating every three days.

Flag Deck: The command level on large ships for Admirals (called a flag rank, because they are entitled to show a flag with appropriate number of stars on a car, ship, etc. if they are present).

Flattop: Another term for an aircraft carrier. Also, the haircut worn by truly motivated sailors.

Fleet Up: A term used to describe when a second in command takes his senior's place upon that senior's transfer, retirement, or other re-assignment.

Flight Deck Buzzard: Another term for chicken (food).

Flight Line: The area on a ship or station where aircraft are made ready for flight. Also used as a prank on gullible new sailors, as in "Go get me 100 feet of flight line from the crash shack."

Float Check (also Flotation Testing): An expression used to describe the act of deliberately throwing something overboard.

Floating Bellhop: A derisive Army term for sailor.

FNG: An acronym for "Fuckin' New Guy"—self-explanatory. Also referred to as a new "boot."

FOD: An acronym for "Foreign Object Damage." Caused by foreign object debris, such as nuts, bolts, or anything that could be sucked into a jet engine, therefore damaging it.

FOD Walk Down: A periodic, organized search on an aircraft carrier flight deck or hangar deck looking for debris that a jet engine might ingest.

Four (4) by Eight (8) Watch: The worst watch section to be in because your first watch is 0400 to 0800, then you work your duty station until 1600, followed by your second watch 1600 to 2000, every day.

Fried Horsecock: Another term for fried baloney.

FTN: An acronym for "Fuck the Navy," a common epithet used when complaining about naval policies or regulations and is often scrawled on the walls of toilet stalls by sailors who have been assigned to clean it for a reason.

FTN Striker: Another term for a sailor whose stated goal/desire is get discharged.

F.U.B.A.R.: An acronym for "Fouled up beyond all repair" or "Fucked up beyond all recognition."

F.U.B.I.J.A.R.: An acronym for "Fuck You Buddy, I'm Just a Reservist."

Fuck You, "strong message follows.": Seen on a numerical list of epithet substitutions (the unauthorized "Falcon Code").

GAF: An acronym for "Give a Fuck." Often heard as, "I have a GAF attitude."

Gaff Off: A term used to describe when a junior person ignores or purposely fails to show proper respect to a senior person. Examples may include blowing off an assigned task, not saluting, or using improper forms of address.

Galley: Another term for the crews' mess, or dining area. A place where food is prepared for consumption.

Gedunk: Another term for candy, or a place that sells candy in a short form of Gedunk bar.

General Quarters: (GQ) Every sailor has an assigned duty station to man during an emergency.

Ghetto: Another term for pen-bay barracks, usually reserved for single sailors who are in transit or otherwise temporarily assigned there.

Gig line: A term used to describe the visual line formed by uniform zipper, belt buckle, and buttoned shirt seam. It is also used as another in-joke to send new sailors on a wild goose chase. See "Bulkhead Remover."

GITMO: A nickname for Guantanamo Bay Naval Station on Cuba.

Goat locker: A term used to describe a lounge or galley for the exclusive use of Chiefs.

Goatrope or goatfuck: A term used to describe any situation that is "FUBAR."

Golden Shellback: A term used to describe a sailor who has crossed the equator at the 180th Meridian.

Good Humor Man: A term used to reference to the Summer White uniform. This is an all-white short sleeve uniform that makes the wearer look suspiciously like the ice cream man.

Grape (Aviation Service): A term used to describe a sailor in an aviation fuels rating. So named because of the purple flight deck jersey he wears.

Great Mistakes: A common epithet used when complaining about RTC/NTC Great Lakes, Illinois.

Grinder: The exterior paved area of any military compound used for formations.

Grog: Initially, this referred to the watered down rum ration given daily to sailors in the Royal Navy. Presently in the USN, it refers to the alcoholic brew offered at social events like "dining-ins" and "dining-outs." Depending on the wardroom and in particular on the person preparing the grog, it may be pleasant and delicious or one of the most foul and disgusting beverages ever conceived.

Ground-Pounder: A Navy term used to describe Marines, specifically those in the infantry.

Grunts: Another derogatory term for Marines.

222

G.U.A.M.: An acronym for "Give Up and Masturbate." A common sailor's complaint about being stationed on the remote island of Guam.

Gundeck: A term used to juryrig something; falsifying or misrepresenting records and reports.

Gun Boss: Another term for the Weapons Department head.

Guns: Another term for a sailor in the Gunner's Mate rating.

Gunwale (pronounced "gunnel"): A term used to describe the top of the hull portion of a ship that runs down the port and starboard sides.

Gyrene: A derogatory Navy term for a U.S. Marine. Also called "Jarheads."

Hatch: Another term for a door.

Head: Another term for the bathroom (The term comes from the days of sail, because wind would blow from the rear of the ship forward and the bathroom would be located at the front "Head" of the ship to carry the foul smell of excrement away from the crew).

Helo (pron. hee-low): A term applied to all naval helicopters (from the standard message abbreviation HELO).

Here today, GUAM tomorrow: A term used to describe when a sailor receives orders from one island to another island, as in ADAK to GUAM.

Hockey pucks: Another term for Swedish meatballs (also, trail markers, porcupines, road apples).

Hollywood Shower: A termed used to describe a long shower that wastes water. See "Navy Shower."

Hoover: A slang term for the S-3B Viking, mostly due to its unique engine noises.

Horse Cock: A term used to describe a large log of baloney usually put out for lunch or mid rats. A Horse Cock sandwich is one of the least favorite boxed lunches.

Hot Dog: A term used to describe a sexually active male sailor.

Hot Racking: A term used to describe sharing racks. In the submarine service, there are usually more men than racks, so while one sailor is on duty, the other is in the shared rack.

Hummer: A slang term for the E-2C Hawkeye, mostly because of the sound of its props.

Ice Cream Social: A term used to describe when ice cream is typically served at 2100 on the mess decks on Sundays when underway.

IFBM: An acronym for "Instant Fucking Boatswains Mate." An "A" school washout assigned to the ship's deck force.

ID10T: An acronym for "Idiot," pronounced "Eye-Dee-Ten-Tango." Similar to "bulkhead remover," an inexpensive way to derive enjoyment from inexperienced personnel. "Recruit, go get me an ID10T form, and step on it!"

Irish Pennant: Another term for a loose thread on uniform.

INT WTF: Letters Pronounced Individually. INTerrogative What The Fuck. See "WTFO." Usually used in a text/teletype medium where WTFO is over voice communications.

IYAOYAS: An unofficial acronym commonly found on the uniforms of airedales who specialize in ordnance handling. Read as "If you ain't ordnance, you ain't shit" Pronounced "Yay-OHS" and yelled out during ceremonies.

Jarhead: Another term for a U. S. Marine.

JARTGO: An acronym for "Just Another Reason To Get Out."

Joe Navy: Another term for a lifer with no life outside the Navy.

Knee-knockers: A passageway opening through a bulkhead. The lower lip of the opening sits at shin height.

Knuckle Buster: A pneumatic tool for removing perfectly good paint from steel.

Ladderwell: Another term for stairs. (This is a holdover from when all climbing was done by ladders.)

LDO: An acronym for Limited Duty Officer—generally a senior and highly qualified enlisted person who is given a commission and continues to work in his or her field.

LDO Security Blanket: Another term for a Good conduct ribbon. Even though an LDO can choose to wear only his/her top three ribbons, they never do. Because they always have at least three higher than Good Conduct and they need to have that one on display lest they be mistaken for a real junior officer. LDOs need their Good Conduct ribbons every bit as much as Linus needs his security blanket.

Leave: Another term for vacation time.

Liberty: A term used to describe free time away from work or the ship, usually after working hours or in port. Differs from "Leave" (see above) in that you must stay close to your home station and it is generally much shorter.

Liberty Boat: A boat assigned to transfer sailors to and from their ship when in a port that requires the ship to drop anchor instead of pulling pierside. Trips to the beach are generally low key. Trips back to the ship in the wee hours of the night are usually very entertaining.

Liberty Hound: A term used to describe a sailor who loves liberty more than anything else.

Liberty Risk: A sailor who loves liberty a little too much. So much so that he puts himself in danger by drinking too much, getting into fights, or pissing off the locals.

Lieu-fucking-tenant: illustrates Navy practice of including a swear word INSIDE another word.

Lifer: a name given to both officers and enlisted men who love the Navy and make it clear they want to be in for 20 or more years. Lifers will try to convince others to re-enlist. Also lifers say things like "there is nothing a sailor needs that is not in his seabag" this usually is a comment implying a sailor does not need to see his spouse or children.

Lifer: An acronym associated with people coasting through their Navy career, stands for "Lazy, Incompetent, F***, Expecting Retirement," or "Lowly Indignant F*** Evading Reality."

Lifer Dog: (See "Lifer" above) "Call me an asshole, call me a cocksucker, call me a son-of-a-bitch; just don't call me a Lifer Dog."

Living the Dream: A sarcastic term used when someone is asked how they are, they reply with this which sounds upbeat and a positive term, and they are actually miserable. "How are you doing today PO Jones?" "Living the dream, Captain."

Loop: An officer, usually a LT or LCDR, who is an admiral's aide. So called because of the gold braided loop that they wear around their arm.

LOST: Line Of Sight Tasking—when a senior officer, usually the XO, tasks the first poor bastard JO who walks across his path with some time-consuming, inane project that he knows absolutely nothing about.

Love Boat: Term referring to a subtender comprised primarily of female sailors. Also, a nickname for CVN-69.

LSO: Landing Safety Officer or Landing Signal Officer. On a carrier, this officer stands just to the port side of the landing area and talks to each pilot as he makes his approach for an arrested landing.

LST: Tank landing ship, or "Large Slow Target," a now removed type of amphibious warfare ship.

L.T.D.B: "Living the Dream Baby." Often used sarcastically in reference to Naval lifestyle.

Mail Buoy: A fictitious buoy that mail for a ship is left on. Usually new sailors are given a mail buoy watch for the entertainment of the more seasoned sailors.

MARINE: acronym for Marines Always Ride in Navy Equipment...or Muscles are Required Intelligence Not Essential... or My Ass Really Is Navy Equipment., or My Ass Rides In Navy Equipment.

Marine candy bars: urinal cakes.

Mast: Preceded by Captain's or Admiral's, but these are generally not spoken. A form of non-judicial punishment in which a sailor finds himself standing tall in front of the old man when he really screws the pooch.

Meat Gazer: Unlucky individual designated to make sure the urine in a "Whiz Quiz" actually comes from the urinator's body. This is accomplished by spending all day meat gazing, or looking at dicks while guys are pissing.

Meat Identifier: A side dish during chow that helps in identifying usually nondescriptive looking main dishes. i.e. Applesauce: indicative of pork chops, Horseradish: Prime Rib Beef...etc.

Meatball: Fresnel Lens Optical Landing System, a visual landing aid used by naval aviators landing on a carrier.

Mess Crank or Mess Bitch: A sailor who works on the mess deck, not rated as a cook.

Mess Decks: Chow Hall or Eating Establishment on board ship.

Mess Deck Intelligence: Rumors (mostly false) that spread throughout the ship like wildfire. Often concern radical changes to the ships schedule. See "Rumor Control" or "Scuttlebutt."

Midnight Requisition: To "borrow" (with varying degrees of consent) a needed item from another unit. Often condoned when essential to get underway.

Mid-Rats: Short for MIDnight RATions. Leftover lunch and dinner plus PB and J.

Mid-Watch: Watch from 0000-0400, usually results in no sleep before or after this watch. Also referred to as "dog watch."

Mustang: An officer who came from the Enlisted ranks.

Muster: to gather or meet with the intention of determining assets. For example, morning muster report indicates who is present and accounted for.

NAVCIVLANT/NAVCIVPAC: described as where a soon to be departing sailor from active duty's next station will be.

NFO: Naval Flight Officer—flies alongside the pilot as weapons officer.

NAVY: acronym used by disgruntled sailors for "Never Again Volunteer Yourself."

Naval Infantry: A derogatory term for the U.S. Marines.

Navy Shower: While underway, fresh water must be manufactured from sea water. A common-sense way of saving it is to first wet down while taking a shower and then TURN OFF THE WATER. Lather up and wash. Finally, TURN ON THE WATER to rinse off. A continual disregard WILL attract a punishment shower with scrub brushes.

No Balls: A term used to suggest that a person does not have the testicular fortitude to perform the action that he claims he can/will do. This is often spoken to female sailors out of sheer habit.

No Load: Another term for a useless sailor, or one who does not pull his share of the load. Named for the maintenance catapult shots where only the shuttle is moved down the track with no aircraft attached.

Non-skid: A rough epoxy coating used for grip on weather decks. Also, another term for toilet paper.

Nonskid Wax: A fictitious substance used for waxing non-skid decks. Usually something junior sailors are sent looking for.

Noted: A term that is usually passed down from an officer, when the sailor tells the officer of something that will have little or no positive effect on the officer, but may have a great effect on the Blue shirt. For example, "Sir, if we do this thing now, I can go home as soon as it's done." Officer: "Noted."

No-Shitter: A sea story which is mostly (never completely) fictional, unverifiable as well. Examples: "Hey, this is no shit, but I once blah blah blah..." or "Hey this is a no-shitter, I got a buddy who once blah blah blah..."

Nuke: Another term for an Engineering Department crew member responsible for turning main shaft via atom-splitting. It also refers to ordnance type that is neither confirmed nor denied, which may or may not be handled by a different Department.

Nuke it out (or simply "nuke it"): A term used to describe a sailor who over thinks a simple task. Alternately, it is often used by nukes to suggest someone ought to put forth at least a little thought before giving up on a problem.

Nuclear Waste: A pejorative term for sailors who exit the Nuclear Power training program without successful completion.

Nut to butt: A term used to describe standing in line, close quarters, body to body, each man's chest pressed to the back of the man ahead, or "nut to butt."

Occifer: Pronounced "ossifur," it is a derogatory reference towards officers in general, particularly junior officers.

Officer's Candy: Another name for urinal cakes.

Old Man: A term used for the Commanding Officer or Admiral in command, regardless of gender. The term is usually used when the CO has gained the respect of subordinates.

Old Salt: Another term for a Navy veteran. See "Salty," below.

On my six: A Naval aviation expression referring to having someone or something at my back, on my tail, directly behind me, relative to the hours of a clock; 12-dead ahead, 3-starboard or to the right, 6-aft or behind and 9-port or to the left.

One-eyed Jack (See also "Barney Clark"): A tasty treat served at mid-rats consisting of a slider topped with a fried egg.

OOD: An acronym for the Officer of the Deck (Officer of the Day); the officer in charge of the ship or the command at that time.

Operation GOLDENFLOW: Another term for a command-wide urinalysis test.

Oscar: A term for the buoyant dummy used during man-overboard drills. Named for the Oscar flag that is flown during a man overboard evolution. Being "Nominated for an Oscar" can refer to a sailor being thrown overboard.

Ouija Board: Another term for the flat board used by the Air Handler in Flight Deck Control with small airplanes, bolts, etc. that can be moved around to indicate aircraft position and status on an aircraft carrier.

Overhead: Another term for a ceiling.

Paddles: Another term for the LSO (see above).

Paper Assholes: Another term for gummed reinforcements (office supplies).

P.A.P.E.R.C.L.I.P.: An acronym for People Against People Ever Reenlisting Civilian Life Is Preferable. A term used to show dissatisfaction with enlistment or unity amongst a brotherhood of bitter and disaffected sailors, specifically submariners. Often symbolized by the wearing of a paperclip on the uniform in varying levels of prominence to indicate the sailor's level of disgruntlement. May also be burned into the skin. C.L.I.P. also used as Civilian Life Incentive Program.

Passageway: Another term for a hallway.

P.C.O.D.: An acronym for "Pussy Cut Off Day," which is slang for the last day of a long deployment that sailors could get laid and still obtain Venereal Disease cures from the Hospital Corpsman and have it be effective in time to return to a wife or girlfriend waiting at home.

Pecker-Checker: A derogatory term for Hospital Corpsman.

PFM: An acronym for "Pure Fucking Magic," a term applied to when things work, but you don't know how, but they work.

Piece: Another term for a rifle, as used in manual-of-arms (rifle drill).

Pier-Queer: An Air Force derogatory term for a Sailor (as opposed to the Navy term for Air Force personnel which is simply "queer").

Pit: Another term for a sailor's rack or bunk. Usually used among those who aren't particularly pleased with shipboard life.

Pineapple Fleet: Another term for the Pacific Fleet which usually refers to the Seventh Fleet (in the western Pacific) and specifically to ships stationed in Pearl Harbor.

POD: An acronym for the Plan of the Day. An official document issued by a command that states all activities going on that day, from 0000 to 2359. It also contains the Uniform of the Day.

POG: An acronym for "Person other than a Grunt." A term often used by Marine Infantry (Grunts) to refer to anyone who is not them.

Polish a Turd: A term used to describe how to make the most of a bad situation.

Pollywog: A term for an individual who has not crossed the Equator, who must go through rituals that sometimes cross the line to be hazing to become a Shellback. This practice can be traced back hundreds of years and is conducted in many Navies across the globe.

The Pond: Another term for the Deep Blue Sea. Where deep-water sailors ply their craft, "The Pond" may be Atlantic, Pacific, Indian, or other. Used in slang expressions such as "Talk to me when you've got some Time on the Pond."

PQS: An acronym for Personal Qualification Standard. A card carrying various qualifications for a warfare badge or similar which must be signed off by a superior or expert.

Port: The Left side of the boat or ship (when facing the bow). Also, the left side of an aircraft when facing the nose from inside. Also a term for place of arrival for ships.

Port and Starboard: Terms used to describe a rotation of two duty sections or watch teams, one designated port, and the other starboard. This is generally not considered to be a good situation.

Port and Re-port: A term used to describe a watch stood without relief. One designated Port, and the other... wait, there is no other... only Port once again, hence the term re-Port.

Powder Monkey: A term referring to a sailor sent back and forth for an item, usually tasked to retrieve something from below-decks. It derives from young boys who served on wooden ships that retrieved powder for broadside firing.

PT: An acronym for "Physical Training." Also, a required exercise regimen.

Pucker Factor: A term used to describe the tension caused by high stress during a difficult or dangerous evolution. So named because your sphincter tends to tighten up or "pucker" involuntarily during such times. For example: The Pucker Factor was high when he landed that Turkey single engine with complete AC power failure at night.

Puddle Pirate: A derogatory term for members of the US Coast Guard.

Pushbutton: A term applied to a six-year enlistee with advanced schooling. The Enlistee is immediately granted E-3 rank upon completion of basic training and E-4 rank upon completion of "A" school. Frequently, the Enlistee also has an opportunity to extend to eight years, and immediately gain E-5 rank within 2-3 years total service, like "pushing a magic button to gain rank."

Quarters: A term used to describe the gathering of all the people in the organization. Quarters can be for the entire command or just the department, division, or branch. Quarters is used to present awards, pass information, and make every sailor squeeze into their ill-fitting, rarely-worn uniforms at least once a year.

Queer: A nickname for the EA-6B Prowler. It is also a derogatory term for Air Force Personnel.

Rack: Another term for a bed.

Rack Burns: A term used to describe the reddish marks seen on the face of a sailor who has just emerged from sleeping in his/her rack. It is scorned upon if he/she was not supposed to be there.

Rack Hound: A derogatory term, but usually spoken with a hint of envy. A term used to describe a sailor that spends more than his/her fair share of time in the "Rack." Usually spoken when seeing somebody with Rack Burns; "You are such a Rack Hound!"

Rain Locker: Another term for a shower.

Raisin: A term used to describe a new recruit or junior sailor, predominantly heard at Naval Training Commands, usually used by seasoned "A" School students to refer to sailors with one or more weeks less time in the service. The Fleet equivalent is "Nub," "Newbie," or "Hey, Shitbird."

Ramp Strike: A term used to describe when an aircraft gets drastically low while attempting to land on a carrier and strikes the "round down," or stern of the ship, usually with devastating results.

Rate Grabber: A term used to describe an enlisted member with the goal of (and succeeding in) making rate (promotion) quickly.

Rats: A shortened term for "mid-rats."

Ready Room: A large space aboard a carrier that is the focal point for each of the squadrons in the airwing. Each squadron has one on the O-3 level, and each pilot has his own seat. The Ready Room is used for a variety of reasons such as training, "AOM's," "Roll-ems," etc.

Red-Roper: A slang term for a Recruit Division Commander (RDC), in reference to the red rope worn around the left shoulder. They used to be called "Company Commander."

Reefer: A term used to describe a refrigeration ship carrying frozen foods.

Rent-A-Crow: A term for a sailor advanced to E-4 because they graduated at the top of their "A" school class. The Navy 'rents' them for an extra year in return for being promoted.

R.H.I.P.: An acronym for "Rank Has Its Privileges." See also "SRDH."

R.O.A.D. Program: An acronym for "Retired on Active Duty," which refers to someone who is approaching retirement so they don't care about getting any real work accomplished.

Roast Beast: Another term for Roast Beef or any meat served aboard the ship that even the cooks who prepared it don't know what it is.

Roger That: A term of understanding and acceptance when given an order or other information. It can be used with varying inflection and tone without consequence to signify enthusiasm or disgruntledness without stepping outside the bounds of professionalism.

Roll-em's: A term used to describe movie night which is usually shown in the Ready Room or the Wardroom.

Rollers: Another term for Hot dogs.

Rotor Head: A term used to describe a sailor who flies or maintains rotary-winged aircraft (helicopters).

Rubber Hooeys: Another term for condoms.

Rumor Control: The often wildly inaccurate rumors that concern fictitious changes to the ship's schedule. Usually takes the form of "Hey, did you hear <insert ship name here> had a fire in their main machinery room and can't get underway so our cruise got extended by a month?" See also "Mess Deck Intelligence."

Saltpeter: A chemical supposedly added to "bug juice" or scrambled eggs aboard ship to stifle a sailor's libido.

Salty: A term used to describe an old and experienced (or simply old and sea-worn, as in "my salty hat") sailor. It can also refer to the traditionally profanity-laced language patterns of sailors.

Scrambled Eggs: A term used to describe the gold embroidered decoration on a Commander's/Captain's cover. Admirals have Double Eggs. The similar silver clouds and lightning bolts addition to an Air Force Major's hat is called "Farts and Darts."

Screw: Another term for a propeller.

Scullery: Another term for the washroom for eating implements such as knives, forks, trays, and cups.

Scuttlebutt: Another term for a drinking fountain or rumor (originated from the rumors that would be spread on board ship while gathered about the water barrel).

Sea and Anchor Detail: Every sailor has an assigned duty station to be manned when the ship is either pulling into or out of port. On submarines it's called the Maneuvering Watch. (Coast Guard: Special Sea Detail.)

Sea chest: A trunk or storage container used for a sailor's personal property.

Sea Daddy: A term used to describe a senior, more experienced sailor who unofficially takes a new member of the crew under his wing and mentors him.

Sea Lawyer: A term used to describe an argumentative, cantankerous or know-it-all sailor. A sea lawyer is adept at using technicalities, half truths, and administrative crap to get out of doing work or anything else he doesn't want to do, and/or to justify his laziness.

Sea Stories: A term used to describe often exaggerated or embellished tales from previous deployments or commands told by seniors to juniors. Sea Stories almost always involve alcohol. Good sea stories should involve creative embellishment, in as much as you should tell it better than the guy you heard it from, with yourself (or an un-named "buddy") as the new star. Add some contemporary details and those youngsters are memorized, as they should be.

Secure: In general, a term used to prepare something for stormy travel—to secure a window is to shut it. However, it's often used as a stronger form of "cut it out," as in "talking is secured" or "I'm going to secure your mouth if you don't shut the hell up" or "your fruity ways are secured, Fireman Smitty."

Senile Chief: A slang term for Senior Chief.

Shark shit: A term used to describe a sailor who has fallen overboard and is lost forever.

Shellback: A term used to describe an individual who has crossed the Equator. See also "Pollywog."

Shinbuster: Another term for a "knee-knocker."

Ship over: Another term for re-enlist.

Shipmate: A term used to describe any fellow Sailor. Also, used as a derogatory term against all junior enlisted personnel i.e. E-5 and below. An Officer, Chief, or First Class will use this to show they think so little of you, they haven't bothered to take the time out of their day to learn your name. Used in the Junior Enlisted Community to parody this.

Shipwreck: A term used to describe any fellow sailor. It is often used as a derogatory term.

Shit in a Seabag: Another term for stuffed green peppers.

Shitbag (also Shitweed, shitstick, shithead, shit stain, or shitbrick): A term used to describe any fellow sailor. It is often used as a derogatory term and a term of endearment. Also, a derogatory term for a sailor who has been awarded punishment at mast, or any less-than-par sailor. Also known as "Shitbird."

Shitbomb: A term used to describe an extremely unpopular topic brought up at the end of a (usually long and boring) meeting that requires a lot of work from everyone present. The worst ones are "drive-by shitbombs," where someone pokes their head in, "throws the shitbomb," and leaves.

Shit Can: Another term for a trash can, or the act of throwing something into the trash. As in "Shit can that chit, you're not getting any liberty."

Shit-on-a-shingle: A term used to describe the traditional Navy breakfast: creamed chipped beef on toast.

Shitty Kitty: A slang term for the USS Kitty Hawk which was the worst ship in the United States Navy, and also the oldest. It has been designated this name due to the fact it that it looks like shit, smells like shit, and the chain of command will work you round the clock and not give a shit.

Short Seabag or Without a Full Seabag: A term used to describe a sailor who reports aboard without a full uniform; deficient in aptitude or intelligence.

Short Timer: A term used to describe sailor with less than 90 days until discharge or transfer who has an attitude to match.

Short Timer's Chain: A chain that hangs from the belt of a "short timer" for all to see, with one link representing a day, (signifying too short to care) and usually starts with 30 links. Verbal equivalent is "__ days and a wake-up."

Shutterbug: Another term for a Photographer's Mate (PH).

Sick in Quarters (SIQ): When a sailor is too ill or incapacitated to perform his duties, he is thus required to report to his rack (quarters), where he will remain until healthy again. For personnel aboard ship, this means to remain in bed, while onshore this may simply mean to stay home for the day. Only qualified medical personnel can recommend SIQ, and only the command can authorize it.

Skate: A term used to describe a sailor who avoids work in general while not being detected. For example, the ability to "skate" out of work undetected while being assigned to a 14-man working party.

Skate Golden: The ability to "skate" out of work while being assigned to a 7-man working party undetected.

Skater: A term used to describe a sailor who gets away with doing no work.

Skipper: A term used in reference to the Commanding officer of any Ship, Unit, Platoon, or Detachment regardless of rank. Generally, it is only applied to someone who has earned the speaker's respect.

Skittles: A term used to describe sailors who work on the flight deck of a carrier. So named due to the different colored jerseys they wear.

Skivvies: Another term for underwear.

Skivvy waver: Another term for a Signalman (because of signal flags).

Skylarking: A term used to describe messing around or not doing assigned work. It is derived from the physical activities done by sailors to dislodge an aground sailing ship from the bottom: "All hands lay aft (forward) for dancing and skylarking."

Sliders: Another term for hamburgers and cheeseburgers.

Smoke Pit: Another term for the designated smoking area. This is almost always used when ashore.

Smoking Lamp: A term used to describe when smoking is permitted. "The smoking lamp is out" or "lit in specified spaces or throughout the ship." A 1MC announcement specifying where smoking is permitted or prohibited during certain hours or operations.

Smoking Sponson: A designated smoking area aboard aircraft carriers, usually right below the flight deck on the exterior of the ship's hull. Also, a great place to catch up on scuttlebutt and unwind after a long day.

Smurf: Another term for a recruit who is in his first few days of boot camp who hasn't been issued uniforms yet, and thus wears a "Smurf Suit" (see below).

Smurf Suit: A term used to describe a set of blue sweat pants and sweatshirt issued on arrival at boot camp which is worn for the first several days and thereafter used mostly for PT.

S.N.A.F.U. An acronym for "Situation Normal All Fucked Up."

Snake Eaters: Another term to describe Special Forces personnel such as Navy SEALs, Green Berets, etc.

Snipes: A term used to describe sailors assigned to the Engineering rates, i.e. Machinists Mates, Boilermen, Enginemen, and Pipefitters.

Snivel: To request time off or to not be scheduled, usually for personal reasons. Most schedule writers will have a "snivel log" for such requests, which may or may not be granted based on the needs of the unit and the sniveler's standing with the schedules officer ("Skeds-O").

SPLIB: An acronym for "Special Liberty," or Comp-Time.

Socked-in: A term used to describe when the ceiling and visibility at an airfield or over an air-capable ship are below minimums for takeoff and landing.

S.O.P.: An acronym for "Standard Operating Procedure."

S.O.S.: An acronym for "Shit-on-a-shingle."

Sparky: Another term for a Radioman.

Split Tails: Another term for female sailors. It was used more often in the early days of surface ship integration.

Spook: Another term for a CT, IS or some kind of intelligence type.

Spudlocker: The area below the ramp of an aircraft carrier. Landing in the spudlocker results in a broken aircraft and is often fatal. Also used for a potato (spud) storage room.

Spunk: Another term for Cool Whip or anything like it.

Squid: A term used to describe a surface warfare sailor, as opposed to one of the other warfare communities. It is increasingly becoming more common to represent ALL sailors, however.

S.R.D.H.: An acronym for "Shit Rolls Down Hill." See also "RHIP."

Starboard: The right side of the boat or ship (when facing the bow). It is also the right side of an aircraft when facing the nose.

Steel Beach Picnic: A term used to describe a celebration on the weather decks of a ship and usually involves near beer and barbecue.

Striker: Another term for a sailor receiving on-the-job training for a designated field (or rate).

Swab: Another term for a mop.

TAD or TDY: An acronym for "Temporary Additional Duty" or "Temporary Duty."

Tape Zebra: A term used to describe the maddening condition aboard ship, especially aircraft carriers, where passageways are "taped off" so that they may be waxed, dried, and buffed in the middle of the night. It seems that the passageways are purposely chosen to maximize delay and frustration when a pilot has to do an oh-dark-thirty preflight or some other duty. Junior enlisted sailors take special delight in denying officers access to these passageways and relish in their disgruntled detours. Likewise, junior officers thoroughly enjoy when a man overboard or general quarters is called in the middle of the night, and they rush to get to the head of the line so as to crash through tape zebra and trample through the wet wax.

T.A.R.F.U.: An acronym for "Things Are Really Fucked Up."

Target: A submariner's term for the Navy surface fleet.

The Boat: An airdale term for the ship their airwing is attached to. "We're going to 'The Boat' for a few weeks."

Tin can: Another term for a Destroyer.

Topsider: A term used to describe anyone who is not a nuke.

Trap: A fixed-wing arrested landing on an aircraft carrier.

Trice Up: A term for making up your rack (bed). The old racks had a trice or hook to hook it to the bulkhead or wall. Hence the term "All hands heave out and trice up." Or, to jump out of your rack and make it. It originally referred to hammocks, in days of yore before berthing spaces.

Tube steak: Another term for hot dogs (also, called "dangling sirloin").

Turkey: A slang term for the F-14 Tomcat.

Turn-to: Another term for "Get to work."

Two-Digit Midget: A term used to describe a sailor with 99 or less days until his/her "End of Active Obligated Service," or EAOS.

Turn 'n Burn: A casual term for "Get busy!" From formal daily announcement, "Turn to ship's work," often given as direct order "Turn to!"

UA: An acronym for "Unauthorized absence." The Navy's term for AWOL.

Uncle Sam's Confused Group (USCG): A derogatory term for the US Coast Guard, an organization that is the 5th armed service, yet falls under the Department of Homeland Security.

UNREP: An acronym for "UNderway REPlenishment." Taking supplies from the supply ship by maneuvering alongside and passing lines between the two vessels. Differs from "VERTREP."

USS Backyard: Another term for a sailor's home of record, to which he or she happily returns upon discharge.

USS LASTSHIP: Another term for a sailor trying to tell a story, or give an example of how business was handled at their last command.

USS Neverdock: Another term for a ship that seems to stay out at sea for unusually long periods of time. For sailors, this is usually their own ship.

USS Neversail: A term for the mock-up ship found in boot camp, also called USS Recruit. It can also refer to real ships that seldom leave port, such as Sub-tenders.

USS Nottagain (DD 214): A term used by sailors separating from the Navy when asked which command they are going to. Also can be used by former sailors when visiting old friends and asked by new personnel which ship they are on. DD 214 is the form that must be filled out for a military member to get discharged. DD was also the type designation for pre-missile destroyers.

Vampire Liberty: A term used to describe when a sailor gets the day off for donating a pint of blood.

VERTREP: An acronym for "VERTical REPlenishment." Taking supplies from the supply ship via helo pick up and drop off. Back in the day this was most often accomplished by the mighty CH-46 Sea Knight ("Phrog"), although any aircraft with a cargo hook installed can do it. Differs from "UNREP" (see above).

Very well: An acknowledgement from a Senior to a subordinate.

Vitamin M: Similar to "Corpsman Candy" above, but in this context relating to Motrin which is occasionally used to combat the various aches/pains/headaches associated with military service.

Vultures Row: The place where people can watch flight operations without being in the way, typically the O-7 to O-9 level on an aircraft carrier's island.

Wardroom: Another term for the Officer's mess, or dining room. It is also used to collectively refer to all the officers at a command.

Warrant: A term used to describe a warrant officer. In the Navy, warrants are generally older and more experienced in a particular area of expertise than a commissioned line officer, much like an "LDO." Warrants almost always come from the senior (E7-E9) enlisted ranks.

Watch: A term used to describe a period of duty, usually of four-hour duration, six-hours on submarines. The day at sea has long been divided into watches which are called: midwatch (0000 to 0400); rev watch (reveille) (0400 to 0800); forenoon watch (0800 to 1200); afternoon watch (1200 to 1600); and the first watch (2000 to 2400).

WEFT: An acronym for "Wings, Exhaust (or Engine, for prop aircraft), Fuselage, Tail" and is a method by which ship's lookout stations can visually identify aircraft within the vicinity. However, since training for this tends to be spotty at best, identification of aircraft is often incorrect, leading to the second definition: "Wrong Every Fucking Time."

WESTPAC/WESPAC: An acronym used to refer to the western Pacific area of operations; it can also refer to a type of deployment in which a unit heads to multiple locations throughout said area. Often used in, "Damn, we just did a six-month WESTPAC, barely got home for a week, and now we're heading out again?"

Whidbey Whale: A term used to describe a dependent wife that is Orca fat even though her husband has maintained the same basic size during their marriage.

Whiz Quiz: Another term for a "Piss Test" or urinalysis.

Widow/Widower: A term used to describes wives (and now husbands) with spouses on deployment. Single, for all intents and purposes, until the day their spouse returns from deployment. Prefaced by the type or theater of service the deployed spouse is in, e.g. "WESTPAC widow" or "Boomer Widow."

Wings: A term used to describe the Naval Aviator or Naval Flight Officer breast insignia. It can also refer to the Enlisted Aviation Warfare Specialist breast insignia.

Wog: A short term for "pollywog," as in "wog ceremony," or "wog day."

Wolf Ticket: A term used to describe highly suspect information. It can refer to malicious "scuttlebutt," exaggerated "no-shitters," or blatantly phony sea stories.

Working party: When there is a load of supplies, the Quarterdeck will call for a "working party" to be manned by each division of the ship.

Workups: One- to 6-week periods preceding a deployment during which the ship and/or its airwing practice and prepare. Widely known workups involving the carrier and the airwing are TSTA, COMPTUEX, and RIMPAC.

WTF: An acronym for "What the Fuck" (pronounced "Whiskey Tango Foxtrot" using the phonetic alphabet). A colorful way of asking what just happened, i.e., "What the Fuck?"

XO: Another term for the Executive Officer.

XOI: An acronym for "Executive Officer's Inquiry." A step in the non-judicial punishment process in which the wayward sailor appears before the executive officer (XO). After hearing the details of the case, the XO may recommend dismissal or refer it to the Commanding Officer (CO) for "Mast."

Yardbird: Another term for a shipyard worker.

FALCON CODES

100 Congratulations, You Fucked Up.
101 You've Got To Be Shitting Me.
102 Get Off My Fucking Back.
103 Beats the Shit Out Of Me.
104 What the Fuck, Over?
105 It's So Fucking Bad, I Can't Believe It.
106 I Hate This Fucking Place.
107 This Place Really Sucks.
108 Fuck You Very Much.
109 Beautiful, Just Fucking Beautiful.
110 That Goddamned O'club.
111 You Piss Me Off.
112 Let Me Talk To That Sonofabitch.
113 Big Fucking Deal.
114 Get Your Shit Straight.
115 You Bet Your Sweet Ass.
116 S H O R T. Fuck It.
117 That's a Fucking No-No.
118 A Hell of a Good Deal.
119 Shit Hot.
120 If CAG Saw That, He'd Shit.
121 That Pussy Is Really Sweet.
122 And Then the Shit Hit the Fan.
123 You Obviously Have Me Confused With Someone Who Gives A Shit.
124 I Hate This Fucking Place So Much I Could Shit.
125 I Think I'm Going to Puke.
126 Give a Shit, Just Give a Shit.

127 I've Got an Old Rusty Load.
128 I Could Just Shit.
129 Roger That.
130 I Can't Help You - I Wasn't There.
131 What CAG Means Is ......
132 Here Comes Another Fucking CAG Ops Brainstorm.
133 (WETSU) We Eat This Shit Up.
134 Those Shit Heads Fucked Up Again.
135 I Just Blew It.
136 I'll Be Right Back, You Lucky Bastard.
137 The Fucking Maid Woke Me Up.
138 The Fucking Maid Didn't Wake Me Up.
139 Your Shit is Weak.
140 You Horny Fucker.
141 You Piece of Shit.
142 Fuck You—A Strong Letter Follows.
143 There's No Goddamn Mail Again Today.
144 Adios, Motherfucker.
145 You Ask For One More Low Pass; You Won't Get Launched For a Fucking Week.
146 You May Not Have Any Fucking Fuel.
147 My Fucking Bladder Hurts.
148 I Have a Fucking Bladder Over-Pressure Light On.
149 Everybody Needs a Fucking Hobby.
150 Happiness Is a Warm Pussy.
151 You Eat Shit, Chase Rabbits, and Bark At The Moon.
152 Balls of Fire.
153 Get Your Ass in Gear.
154 That Motherfucker in CIC is Dreaming Again.
155 The Fucking Helos are All Fucked Up Again.
156 While You Were Gone, the Whole World Turned to Shit.
157 You May Not Like the Fucking Staff, But the Fucking Staff Likes You.
158 Fly the Fucking Ball.
159 Get Your Head Out of Your Ass.
160 Get Fucked.
161 Snake Shit.
162 Don't Rock the Fucking Boat.
163 Everything I Touch Turns to Shit.
164 You Just Stepped on Your Dick.
165 Fuck It - Just Fuck It.
166 If You Say "I Don't Know" One More Time, I'm Going to Cram a Sonobuoy Up Your Ass.

167 Hang It in Your Fucking Ear.
168 I Love You So Fucking Much, I Could Shit.
169 I Love the Fucking Navy and the Navy Loves Fucking Me.
170 Shit House Mouse.
171 Show Us Your Tits.
172 Fuck You and the Horse You Rode in On.
173 You Must Have Shit For Brains.
174 Would You Like a Kick in the Ass to Get You Airborne?
175 What Does It Take to Get a Clearance Out of This Fucking Place?
176 Just Fly the Bus and Leave the ASW to Us.
177 You Are So Fucking Stupid, You're a Menace to Society.
178 This Bastard Has More Downing Gripes on It Than the USS Arizona.
179 Comments and Recommendations, My Ass.
180 Just Out of Curiosity NAV, Where The Fuck Are We?
181 Those Fucking CVA Pukes.
182 If I Hear the Fucking Words "CV Concept" Again, I'm Going to Shit.
183 That Fucker Runs Like a Well Oiled Machine.
184 Those Fucking ASW Pukes.
185 If I Called For Shit, You Would Come Sliding in on a Shovel.
186 There's Hate in My Heart and Bile in My Blood.
187 Either Shit or Get off the Pot.
188 Cool It, The Chaplain is Here.
189 Isn't This Shit Ever Going to End.
190 I Think I've Fallen in Love With My Hand.
191 How About Getting This Fucking Shit Straightened Out.
192 Bite My Ass.
193 Why Don't You Tell It to Someone Who Gives a Shit.
194 If You Think I'm Shitting You, Try It.
195 You've Got a Lot of Fucking Balls.
196 Who's the Fucking Cunt at The End of the Bar.
197 Same to You, Fella.
198 I Just Got Fucked.
199 Merry Fucking Christmas.
200 Happy Fucking New Year.
201 If You Can't Take a Fucking Joke, You Shouldn't Oughta Suited Up.

ABOUT THE AUTHOR

Andrew Z. ("Chet") Adkins III is currently the Chief Information Officer at a large law firm in West Virginia. After spending three years, eleven months, and 29 days in the United States Navy, he worked as a firefighter with the City of Gainesville, Florida while attending college. He completed bachelor's and master's degrees in electronics engineering from the University of Florida.

After working several years as a design engineer, he became an independent legal technology consultant. He established the Legal Technology Institute at the University of Florida Levin College of Law where he was director and primary consultant for thirteen years. He retired in 2010 and began pursuing a career as a nature photographer.

Retirement lasted about a year when an old friend called him back into active duty to join the law firm of Steptoe & Johnson PLLC. He continues his hobbies in photography and writing.

He and Becky, his wife of 33 years, currently live in West Virginia. His two children, Evelyn and Jared, are also pursuing their life's dreams.

Made in the USA
Las Vegas, NV
25 November 2022

60297488R00144